E.J. PRATT ON HIS LIFE AND POETRY

E.J. Pratt (1882–1964) is one of Canada's best-known poets. This volume collects for the first time his own comments on his life and work, from the mid-1920s to the 1950s. From it comes a greater knowledge of the man who wrote the poetry and a better understanding of his creative process, from the conception of an idea to its ultimate publication.

Pratt's good humour, sincerity, and extraordinary capacity for friendship emerge in these pages, as does the great significance of his formative years in Newfoundland, accounting for his life-long orientation towards the sea and his deep respect for the human spirit. His view of human nature unfolds along with his concept of heroism, focusing on the forces of faith and fate that combine to create the enigma of human existence.

Some of the commentaries are of a general nature, describing his background, his publishing career, his view of the relationship between source material and poetry, and other aspects of his poetic theory and practice. Others interpret and set the stage for specific poems. Included are the texts of two interviews Pratt gave on the CBC in the 1950s. Fragments of his comments on shorter poems help us to understand the works; at the same time, the complete texts of several addresses and longer introductory pieces, written in Pratt's witty and exuberant style, make fascinating reading in and of themselves.

Both general readers and scholars interested in the poet, his work, and the cultural currents in Canada during the first half of the twentieth century will find value in this book.

Susan Gingell's introduction explores the nature of the commentaries and suggests their value in understanding Pratt's work and its literary and social context.

SUSAN GINGELL is a member of the Department of English at the University of Saskatchewan.

THE COLLECTED WORKS OF E.J. PRATT

GENERAL EDITORS: SANDRA DJWA AND R.G. MOYLES

The aim of this edition is to present a critical annotated text of the collected works of E.J. Pratt – complete poetry; selected prose and correspondence – fully collated and with a textual apparatus that traces the transmission of the text and lists variant readings.

E.J. PRATT

E.J. Pratt on His Life and Poetry

Edited by Susan Gingell

UNIVERSITY OF TORONTO PRESS
Toronto Buffalo London

© University of Toronto Press 1983
Toronto Buffalo London
Printed in Canada
ISBN 0-8020-5614-8

Canadian Cataloguing in Publication Data

Pratt, E.J. (Edwin John), dates.
    E.J. Pratt on his life and poetry
    (The Collected Works of E.J. Pratt)
    Includes index.
    ISBN 0-8020-5614-8
    1. Pratt, E.J. (Edwin John), dates. 2. Poets, Canadian (English) – 20th
    century – Biography.* I. Gingell, Susan, 1951–0000. II. Title. III. Series:
    Pratt, E.J. (Edwin John), dates. The collected works of E.J. Pratt.
    PS8531.R37Z53 1983   C811'.52   C83-094089-8
    PR9199.2.P73Z463

For my parents,
Betty and Brian Gingell

Contents

PREFACE xi
INTRODUCTION xv
EDITORIAL PRINCIPLES AND PROCEDURES xli
BIOGRAPHICAL CHRONOLOGY xlvii

GENERAL COMMENTARIES
'Highlights in My Early Life' 3
'Memories of Newfoundland' 5
'Newfoundland Types' 9
'Introduction for a Reading' 17
From 'A Profile of a Canadian Poet' 18
'The Relation of Source Material to Poetry' 18
'On Publishing' 28
'On Macmillan' 36
'My First Book' 36

INTERVIEWS
Interview by Ronald Hambleton on 'An Experience of Life' 41
Interview by Jed Adams on 'First Person' 47

COMMENTARIES ON SPECIFIC POEMS
'Carlo' 55
'In Absentia' 56
The Ice-Floes 56
'The Ground Swell' 59

'The History of John Jones' 60
'The Shark' 60
'The Toll of the Bells' 60
'The Fog' 61
'Come Not the Seasons Here' 61
'On the Shore' 61
The Cachalot 61
'The Sea-Cathedral' 67
The Great Feud 68
'Cherries' 73
'The Lee Shore' 73
The Iron Door: An Ode 74
'Sea-Gulls' 75
'The Child and the Wren' 75
The Roosevelt and the Antinoe 76
'To Angelina, An Old Nurse' 86
'Erosion' 87
'The 6000' 88
The Depression Ends 88
'Putting Winter to Bed' 90
A Reverie on a Dog 90
'The Way of Cape Race' 92
'A Feline Silhouette' 92
'Like Mother, Like Daughter' 94
'The Prize Cat' 94
The Titanic 95
'Silences' 108
The Fable of the Goats 109
'The Submarine' 112
'Old Harry' 113
'The Dying Eagle' 113
'The Radio in the Ivory Tower' 113
Brébeuf and His Brethren 114
Dunkirk 126
'The Truant' 132
'The Stoics' 133

Behind the Log 133
'The Deed' 145
Towards the Last Spike 145
'The Haunted House' 153

APPENDIXES
A The Fable of the Goats 155
B A Reconstruction of 'The Haunted House' 156
C 'The Loss of the *Florizel* Off Cape Race' 158

NOTES 161
INDEX 209

 # Preface

The materials gathered in this volume consist of the prose notes and other kinds of commentary E.J. Pratt wrote about his own work. The first part of the book contains general comments about his life, particularly his early years in Newfoundland, as well as remarks of a general nature about his poetic theory and the business of publishing poetry. A middle section, comprising the texts of two interviews Pratt gave on the Canadian Broadcasting Corporation in the late 1950s, provides further details about his life and work. The final section includes commentaries on specific poems, arranged chronologically according to the first known publication date of the poems. Information gleaned from Pratt's notes has allowed the reconstruction of an unpublished poem, 'The Haunted House,' which appears in the appendixes along with an unpublished version of 'The Loss of the Steamship *Florizel*' and a version of the difficult-to-find Aesop's fable Pratt apparently used as the source for *The Fable of the Goats*. My own remarks concerning the textual editing of the commentaries can be found on pages xli–xlv.

Many of the commentaries presented here have not been previously published, and those that have are now available only in sources that have long been out of print. The compilation was undertaken in the belief that the material brought together here provides a considerably enriched context for the understanding of Pratt's poems, both individually and as a corpus. The volume makes possible a greater knowledge of the man who wrote the poetry as well as giving us a better understanding of his creative process, from the conception of an idea for a poem to its ultimate publication.

Pratt wrote the commentaries for use in a variety of ways and in a number of media. Some were intended as lecture notes, some as broadcast texts, some as introductions for readings of his work, and others as notes appended as explanatory material in books of selected poems published during his lifetime. Pratt usually gave a series of readings after a new book of his poetry had been published, and his introductory notes to individual poems have been preserved among his papers in the E.J. Pratt Collection of the Victoria University Library.

I would like to thank the many people who have contributed in different ways to the preparation of this volume. Frank Watt served as my first adviser when I was working on the commentaries as a thesis project. Sandra Djwa has offered assistance of many kinds both at that stage and subsequently; her *E.J. Pratt: The Evolutionary Vision* (Vancouver: Copp Clark 1974) was the first work to make extensive use of the materials collected here, thus alerting scholars to their value. The staff at the E.J. Pratt Library, Victoria University, have greatly facilitated my research, especially Lila Laakso, whose familiarity with the special collections in particular and Pratt's work in general was generously shared. Claude Bissell and Northrop Frye helped me to verify certain facts and augment details, while Mrs Viola Pratt and Claire Pratt shared their own necessarily unique understanding. Thanks also to Margery Fee for her comments on the manuscript, to Gordon Moyles for his suggestions about the arrangement of materials in the volume, to my editor Gerald Hallowell for his patience and professional advice, to Michael Beckmann for encouragement and help proofreading typescripts in the early stages, and to Bill Robertson for support of many kinds.

The President's Publication Fund of the University of Saskatchewan provided assistance with typing costs, the College of Arts and Science awarded me a Released Time Grant to enable me to finish work on the book, and the Canada Council generously supported my Ph.D. research. This book has been published with the help of a grant from the Canadian Federation for the Humanities, using funds provided by the Social Sciences and Humanities Research Council of Canada, and with assistance from the Publications Fund of the University of Toronto Press.

S.G.
Saskatoon
September 1982

# Introduction

The prose writings of E.J. Pratt provide a variety of information about the life and work of this pre-eminent Canadian poet. Pratt's good humour, sincerity, and extraordinary capacity for friendship are highlighted in these pages, and the great significance of his formative years in Newfoundland, especially in his lifelong orientation towards the sea and in his respect for the human spirit, is confirmed. His view of human nature unfolds here, as does, in particular, his concept of heroism, focusing on the forces of faith and fate, which combine to create the ironic enigma of human existence. The commentaries and interviews that follow throw light on the literary tradition and the context in which Pratt worked, while influences on his verse and specific sources are acknowledged in his own words.

For the first time, Pratt's genius as a raconteur – a quality evident in his narrative poetry and long attested to by friends and acquaintances – can be documented. No better example can be found of the story-teller at work, modifying and selecting his facts to suit the effect he wishes to create, than Pratt's four versions of an introduction to his poem 'A Feline Silhouette.' In the first account the poet throws slippers and shoes at the offending cats, fires an airgun loaded with B.B. shot, and reads from his window an already composed poem, not necessarily of his own authorship. In version two he has added lumps of coal to his armoury of missiles; he fires an air rifle and composes a poem to read to the cats from a window to scare them away, though the poem is not necessarily 'A

Feline Silhouette.' The battery of version three has been enlarged to include rubbers and golf balls and his airgun has become a popgun. To this point, the claim each time is that the poem is based on a personal experience he had had in Toronto. But by the fourth recital his Methodist background has made its influence felt, and he admits: 'This is part fiction, but mainly true. Something must be left to the imagination here. It was the way I felt anyway but I have forgotten the poem which was written in the spirit of fun the next day and it is anyone's guess whether it was read from the window' (p 94). Anyone's guess indeed!

Pratt's sense of humour was frequently turned on himself. On one occasion he quipped about the effects of his reading on his audiences: 'There was a time years ago when in my callow enthusiasm I used to read verse hours on end, and though I was often in a state of exhaustion myself, I rarely realized the condition of my audience' (136). And before one reading of *Brébeuf and His Brethren* Pratt jokingly invited his listeners 'to join the roll of the martyrs' (114), pointing out that he had previously provided lifeboats to rescue them from his great disasters of *The Titanic* and *The Roosevelt and the Antinoe*.

While his delight in anecdotes, jokes, and character-revealing stories is made clear in many of the commentaries, his relish is perhaps greatest when he is yarning about the people and history of Newfoundland. The addresses on 'Newfoundland Types' are fascinating repositories of folk tales and folk characters from the land of his childhood and youth. He attributes much of the richness of his language to the speech he heard all about him in the outport communities in which he grew up. His youthful experiences shaped an idiom or a way of viewing life that, by his own admission, 'crops out in my work in the most unexpected places, in subjects which might at first glance appear to be outside of the area' (4). The maritime images that emerge in such patently non-marine poems as *Towards the Last Spike* are striking examples of this idiom at work.[1] Expanding on Blake's original metaphor of a sea of mountains, for example, Pratt writes of peaks 'With crests whiter than foam; they poured like seas, / Fluting the green banks of the pines and spruces.'[2] Pratt's prose also provides evidence of such use of idioms and images associated with the sea, as his comment about the difficulties he encountered in writing *Brébeuf and His Brethren* attests: 'I was moving in the mists of theology where I had to be exceedingly careful for here were many shoals and breakers' (124).

From these documents we can also learn many more biographical details.[3] A strong sense of the goodness of the man emerges from these pages, as does the sense of mutual love and support between himself and his wife, Viola. His capacity for friendship, which amounted to genius, is seen to have extended to include people from many walks of life: scientists, professors, politicians, priests, broadcasters, company presidents, students. He alludes frequently to the ways in which such contacts enriched his verse.

Mrs Pratt, at the official opening in 1964 of the E.J. Pratt Room of Contemporary Poetry at Victoria University, spoke of her hope that a balanced legend would grow up around her husband, a legend that would remember him not only as an 'absent-minded professor, the host of innumerable stag parties, the exuberant teller of tales and the hail fellow well met'[4] but also as the great and creative teacher that he was. Although the commentaries give us only brief glimpses into Pratt's career as a teacher, they do clearly establish the good-humoured relationship that existed between himself and his students. One evening saw him joking with an audience that included many of his former students, remarking that they had managed to survive the experience of his teaching by the law of the survival of the fittest. And when the roles of student and teacher were reversed during research for *Behind the Log*, Pratt spoke with affection of 'my own former students who now in their reversed role did their best to kittle up my notion upon matters pertaining to the operations of His Majesty's ships in the Royal Canadian Navy' (137).

The commentaries and interviews also establish the basis and development of Pratt's fatalistic perspective on life,[5] revealing at the same time the modification of this bleakness by the qualities of a broad humanity and good humour. In the interview with Ronald Hambleton that follows, Pratt affirms: '... my earliest years formed in me a tendency to ... fatalism, tempered with humanity. We were always close to death' (42). Fatalism, tempered with humanity, is what Pratt learned in large part from his father's teachings and experiences, as he goes on to explain: 'My father was a Methodist clergyman, and he seemed rather moderate in his views in a community with a strong Calvinistic affinity. Oh, the preaching I listened to as a boy! We got heaven and hell drummed into us. At seven or eight years of age, I listened to the actual crackling of the flames' (42). One sees the basis for the revolt of little genus *homo* in 'The Truant' already being laid here, but it is also true that the tempering humanity associated with Pratt's fatalism led to the less strident revolt and lavish generosity that lies behind *The Depression Ends*.

The philosophic and religious conflict that is a central preoccupation of Pratt's work from 'Clay' onwards also has its basis in his childhood. 'We were brought up in the belief of the goodness of God,' Pratt tells Hambleton, 'and yet we had to reconcile tragedy with it. We were always under that shadow' (43).

These writings confirm that tragic personal experience stands behind the poems 'Erosion,' 'The Fog,' and 'The Toll of the Bells,' and that Pratt's special interest in the wreck of the *Florizel* resulted from the fact that many of his own school friends had perished when that ship went down. But his childhood was not one long darkness, and memories of a happier kind were drawn on for such poems as 'To Angelina, An Old Nurse' and 'The History of John Jones.'

Pratt's satiric talents first emerged in schoolboy lampoons on his teachers. While admittedly transitory stuff, these beginnings were apprentice work of a kind, for two important lessons were learned: 'that there was something about rhyme and rhythm which acted as a very superior substitute for the blasphemous clichés which easily fall from student lips' and that there 'was a quality about a really well-turned line which [could give him] a great internal satisfaction' (37).

The somewhat dubious business enterprise and the more respectable, if no more characteristic, missionary work that financed

Pratt's undergraduate university education are disclosed here, as are the chief influences on his thought during his days as a student. His college studies tended to reinforce his disposition to fatalism: 'I went to study philosophy, and in those days [the professors] were mostly fatalists. Lectures were full of determinism – nothing in life could be altered ... I got a tremendous dose of Hardy in his prose and novels. This was another addition to my philosophy. Because he says: over all coincidences, there is a universal will determining the outcome. There were two kinds of philosophy being taught at the university thirty years ago: idealism and determinism. I scarcely got a whiff of idealism, though I liked it and wanted it. It was a desire in me, a deep wish. Later on, I got rid of most of this stuff in a five-act verse play I wrote called 'Clay.' A deadly thing to read now. I unburdened myself of all the philosophic cargo I'd amassed at college' (44).

These documents tell us, too, of some of the people who most affected Pratt's life, individuals like his colleague Pelham Edgar, and his high school science master R.E. Holloway. Incidents that significantly influenced him are also recorded here. One of the most monumental was his meeting in 1901 with Guglielmo Marconi, on the eve of the latter's history-making transatlantic broadcast from Signal Hill in St John's to Lizard Point in Cornwall. Living in Newfoundland afforded him this opportunity, but it also meant a chillingly close contact with the disaster of the sinking of the *Titanic* in 1912. These two events in Pratt's life, it seems, although they occurred eleven years apart, were mainly responsible for his very strong sense of the ironic.

Though there is little, if any, reflection of an ironic voice in the prose style of the commentaries, 'ironic' is a word Pratt uses over and over again to describe aspects of his poetry. The role of Jurania, the volcano in *The Great Feud*, is seen by Pratt as one of 'prophetic irony' (73) at the beginning of the poem, and of straight irony at the end, since it brings catastrophe to both of the warring factions, rendering the whole feud irrelevant. *The Titanic*, of course, is 'a study in irony, probably the greatest single illustration of the ironic in marine history' (95). So many of the occurrences Pratt narrates in this poem are ironic, but for him the 'profoundest irony was the shortage of the lifeboats when the weather was absolutely ideal for the launching' (99). Irony is also a principal concern of *The Fable of the Goats*, as Pratt reveals in discussing the Aesop's fable on which the poem was patterned: 'I wondered if this brief fable could be made the basis of a rather elaborate poetic symbolism which would reflect *in an ironic manner* [my emphasis] contemporary world conditions' (109). Pratt even finds his measure of irony in the Brébeuf story, here in the torturing and mocking of an Iroquois captive, for the poet was fascinated with the degree of sophistication in 'the sense of irony shown in the treatment of the prisoner – the sarcasm and the sense of the *double entendre* in addressing the victim' (119). And Pratt saw as one of the ironies of the Second World War 'that tons of plasma sent across the ocean to replenish veins should have been sunk in the North Atlantic before it could replenish the veins on European battlefields' (144). This irony found its way into *Behind the Log* in the lines (121–4): 'And blood mixed with the sea-foam was the cost / Of plasma safely carried in the holds / Across an ocean to a continent, / There to unblanch the faces on the fields ...'

The previously unknown geneses of many poems, and what drew Pratt to certain subjects, are also recorded here. *The Depression Ends*, we learn, grew out of the challenge of Pratt's mentor and friend, Professor Edgar, to incorporate the single, odd word 'prognathic' into a poem. *The Fable of the Goats*, it is revealed, is based on a little-known fable of Aesop, so obscure in fact that it is only with great difficulty that readers will find a collection that contains it. Further, we discover that 'The 6000' resulted from Pratt's accepting the invitation of a friend to ride in an old steam-engine from Toronto to Montreal (he only endured the dust and smoke to Belleville),[6] though he later transferred the run to a prairie location for his imaginative description of the event. According to Pratt, this experience was also to help him later in the writing of *Towards the Last Spike*.

What drew the poet to the story of the *Titanic*, besides his own proximity to the incident, is also revealed in the commentaries: 'The appeal of the story is akin to that which holds our minds when we read about a perfect plot, where every contingency is supposed to be safeguarded, and where the defence has repaired the vulnerable spot in the heel' (96). The Hardyesque sense of fate that Pratt perceived as the spoiler to the perfect plot was also part of his fascination: 'Was there ever an event outside of the realm of technical drama where so many factors combined to close all the gates of escape, as if some power with intelligence and resource had organized and directed a conspiracy?' (99–100).

It was the epic stature of both Captain Fried and the crewmen of the rescuing ship that attracted Pratt to the *Roosevelt* and *Antinoe* story: 'The whole affair was designed in the councils of the gods to be sung. My one regret is that I didn't do it better. It should have had a Homer. For Fried had all the noble qualities of Ulysses' (79). Similarly, it was the epic grandeur of the railroad-building task that interested the poet in the material of *Towards the Last Spike*: 'I was interested in the subject because of the magnitude of the pioneering job, and because of the scepticism of many statesmen and engineers as to the possibility of its achievement' (205, n2).

That Pratt was a painstaking researcher has long been recognized, but the commentaries allow us further insight into the methods and depth of his research. *The Cachalot*, like all of Pratt's sea stories, is based partly on personal experience – that of rowing around dead whales at Moreton Harbour, Newfoundland, where he was teaching school – and partly on his reading and research. Pratt's notes to the poem, published in *Verses of the Sea*, indicate at least two sources of material: Alpheus Verrill's *The Real Story of the Whaler: Whaling, Past and Present* (1916) was consulted for details of whaling expeditions and the object of their enterprise, and Frank Bullen's *The Cruise of the Cachalot: Round the World after Sperm Whales* (1897) is, as Sandra Djwa has argued, almost certainly the source of the conception of the fight between the kraken and the cachalot, and may well have suggested the title for the *Titans* volume since Bullen refers to this battle as a 'titanic struggle.'[7]

Early drafts of *The Cachalot* can be found in a notebook also containing copious notes on *Moby-Dick*, a fact that supports Sandra

Djwa's view of the relationship between Pratt's poem and Melville's novel. So too do the striking structural similarities and many other 'coincidental' likenesses,[8] such as Melville's *Pequod* meeting, in chapter fifty-two, a whaling boat called the *Albatross*, the name Pratt chose for his whaling vessel in *The Cachalot*.

But in addition to personal experience and literary sources, *The Cachalot* also benefited from the poet's consultations with Frederick Banting regarding 'data about the internal constitution of marine mammalia' (67). One humorous result of this relationship was the mock-heroic passage of the poem on the cachalot's pancreas and liver, written because of the widespread current interest in those organs resulting from Banting's research. The notebooks show that Pratt's own research for the poem included a lot of fact-hunting about early explorers, whalers, and whaling, as well as the assembling of a great deal of information about whales, krakens, and other forms of marine life.

Pratt says very little about the genesis of *The Great Feud*, beyond noting that the fictional Tyrannosaurus Rex of the poem owed its existence to a skeleton of a real dinosaur he had seen in a Chicago museum[9] and its resurrection to a number of petrified eggs dug up in the Gobi desert. The notebooks containing drafts of the poem testify to a massive amount of research on geologic ages, flora, fauna, geography, diseases and disorders of a dietary origin, and weather patterns in Southeast Asia, to mention just a few topics.

The Roosevelt and the Antinoe also grew out of a combination of experience and research, though in this case printed sources preceded Pratt's personal contact with the ships and men involved in the incident. The poet's initial interest was generated by Toronto newspaper reports, which stimulated his imagination enough to cause him to send for New York and British newspapers in order to read their versions of the story. After an abortive attempt to versify the tale in 'a light mode of verse, the faster tetrameter in which *The Cachalot* was written' (77), two more sources of stimulation were needed to make him return to the task: first, technical articles in *Blackwood's* and *The Scientific American* on the new and exciting invention, the radio compass; and, secondly, the renewed interest of the press in Captain Fried after his second great rescue, this time of the *Florida*. This revived attention to the captain manifested itself in such ways as the *Literary Digest* cartoon of him in conflict with Davy Jones, who is pictured as irate over Fried's preventing so many from reaching his locker. Convinced of the epic stature of the event by this time, Pratt arranged to do some first-hand research on board the *Roosevelt* in New York harbour and in the offices of the United States Steamship Lines.[10]

Pratt's geographical proximity to the sinking of the *Titanic* has already been noted. His decision to write a poem on the catastrophe gave rise to another flurry of research that took him to the *Periodical Index* for articles on the disaster, to books by survivors,[11] and to a checking of the minutest details such as the menus of the steamship line's dining rooms. A very different kind of research lies behind the wholly imaginative sections of the poem such as the poker game. To write this to his satisfaction, Pratt, a poker *aficionado*, claims he had to go to Pelham Edgar and other card-playing friends to verify the technical jargon of the game. His iceberg, as well as being related to A.Y. Jackson's painting 'Iceberg, at Godhaven,'[12] owes something to Sir Charles G.D. Roberts's poem 'The Iceberg,'[13] though, Pratt claims, 'I have tried not to steal Dr Roberts's thunder here' (186, n10).

The commentaries on *The Fable of the Goats*, as well as informing us of the fable on which the poem was based, tell us of Pratt's consultation with a geologist in order that he might 'construct aright the structure and strata of the mountain range on which the duel ... took place' (111).

An enormous amount of research went into the writing of *Brébeuf and His Brethren*, though the critical attention this poem has attracted has made known most of Pratt's sources, both literary and otherwise. However, as well as providing documentary evidence that Pratt did indeed use these sources, the commentaries reveal his invaluable relationship with Dr Wilfrid Jury, the archaeologist in charge of the excavation site of Ste Marie-among-the-Hurons. They also make reference to '... a number of visits to the shrines and the sites of the ancient missions to get some knowledge of the topography, of the flora and fauna, of the rocks and trees, the trails, the waterways, the edible roots, and the proper names, personal and geographical' (123).

Pratt's unstrained use of technical and scientific terms in his verse, which constitutes one of his major stylistic innovations and achievements, resulted not only from his personal exposure to theology, psychology, and science but also from research of a very specific kind. A commentary on 'The Truant' provides one such example: 'Some of the words used in this poem I didn't know myself until I began searching for scientific terms in the unabridged dictionaries' (132).

The primary source of information on Pratt's research for *Behind the Log* is his correspondence with Pelham Edgar, which has been preserved in the Pelham Edgar Collection of Victoria University Library, but the commentaries supplement this and provide as well Pratt's reactions to the research and writing process. On 2 August 1945 Pratt wrote to his friend: 'The Admiral (Jones) has given me top priority – everything practically at my disposal. I have passes for every place and everything. In fact, it is a bit embarrassing. It makes my own job ahead such a personal obligation ... I haven't written a line yet, have nothing but data, data, data. The task of selection and elimination is tremendous. I may get at it in early fall ...'

The commentaries reveal consultations with Dr R.W. Boyle on matters related to radar and asdic, the examining of navy records, and the interviewing of the Naval Control Shipping Officers, captains, and crews involved in convoy s.c. 42. They also disclose the pains Pratt took to have the Norwegian commander's words translated from Pratt's own English into Norwegian so he could then modify the unintelligible foreign language into a mixture of Norwegian and English; all this was done to give an air of authenticity to the commander's words and yet allow an English-speaking audience at least an intimation of what the captain was saying. The commentaries further suggest how the research process shaped the poem, for, in addition to collecting 'facts, stories, moods,' part of his research involved familiarizing himself with the language of the navy and, more specifically, the convoy, the 'technical terms, and the ever-maturing crop of nautical idioms' (134). One of the pervasive themes of the poem is language and communication, for Pratt found that 'language constituted a genuine problem in the early hectic months on the sea' (141). The style he discovered in the naval logs, 'brief, concentrated expressions, the very anatomy of speech' (143) and often naturally poetic, is reflected in the style of the poem. In fact, Pratt tells us, occasional phrases and expressions were taken straight from the log.

The theme of language – or in broader terms 'communication' – as Northrop Frye has pointed out,[14] is central to Pratt's work. Time and again Pratt shows himself fascinated with the subject of language, but nowhere is his attitude to speech better expressed than in the lyric 'Silences' and in his commentary on it: 'This bit of verse is based on the idea that speech, whether it is the speech of language or just inarticulate utterance, is meant not only to convey thought but to express emotion, and that expression in itself has a social value independent of both the thought and the emotion' (108). What Pratt meant by expression having a social value independent of both thought and emotion is made clear by the poem itself. There he sets out the position that any communication, even of a hostile kind, is preferable to silence, because man's humanity is defined by his ability to communicate in words.

Two men may end their hostilities just with their battle-cries.
'The devil take you,' says one.
'I'll see you in hell first,' says the other.
And these introductory salutes followed by a hail of gutturals
       and sibilants are often the beginning of friendship,
       for who would not prefer to be lustily damned than
       to be half-heartedly blessed?[15]

As he did research for *Brébeuf and His Brethren*, Pratt noted with delight the resonance of the personal and place names of the Indians as well as the strength and character of those of the French. He became fascinated with the nature of the Huron language and in one of the commentaries draws an analogy between the effect of the lack of labials in the Huron language (which resulted in war harangues being delivered with the mouth wide open) and modern totalitarian oratory, an observation that should remind readers that *Brébeuf and His Brethren* is a wartime poem.

Further evidence of Pratt's interest in communication is the fact that the building of the greatest communications link in early Canada became the subject for one of his narratives, and once drawn to the subject his process of research took its usual thorough course. Once again Pratt familiarized himself personally with the settings of his poem, spending five summers in the Rockies and on the west coast, even undertaking six weeks of climbing with an alpine club. Once again he consulted a whole host of personalities and experts, from Scotsmen (to capture their essential character and habits), to dieticians and physiologists (for the passage on the effect of oatmeal on the blood), to a physical education instructor (for the technical terms associated with a tug-of-war that he used in the section 'Sir John revolving round the Terms of Union with British Columbia'). Pratt also tells us that to supplement his reading he went 'to the historians, the financiers, and economists' (151), as well as to 'geologists and engineers and surveyors' (145).

As all this information on Pratt's research suggests, the commentaries are rich in technical and background information about the poems. To introduce *The Ice-Floes* Pratt once described at length the whole process of seal-hunting, just as before reading *A Reverie on a Dog* he provided his audience with the history and characteristics of the Newfoundland breed. And today, when the facts about the incident of the *Roosevelt* and the *Antinoe* are unknown to a new generation of readers, one can go to the commentaries on the poem to see what kind of incidents Pratt selected and what kind he omitted from the mass of material he collected on the subject.

Though on occasion the recounting in the commentaries of the narrative line of some of Pratt's longer poems may make these documents at first appear to be surrogates for the poems themselves, a comparison of such commentaries with the poems will, in the final analysis, only serve to highlight the stature of Pratt's poetic achievement. Such a comparison would reveal the fascinating qualities of his poetic language and the heightened dramatic effects that result from the judicious selection of detail and the careful structuring of incidents in the narrative poems.

The recounting of the narrative line in this way might also suggest that these prose pieces are in fact prose drafts of the longer poems, but two factors undermine such an assumption: the location of the prose after the drafts of the poems in the notebooks and frequent evidence of Pratt's addressing an audience or relaying background information that would not likely appear in a prose draft. In the one or two isolated instances, such as commentary 2 relating to 'The Truant,' in which the possibility of the commentary's being a prose draft would otherwise remain, the very isolation of these cases makes it unlikely that Pratt is varying from his standard practice of writing prose commentary on a recently or nearly completed poem.

The emphasis Pratt placed on factual research and the use of authentic detail should not be allowed to obscure another important facet of his work. In 'My First Book' he speaks of 'a hidden desire to mix phantasy with realism – a desire which has never left me' (40). This unique blend came to be the formula for much of Pratt's work. Thus, amid the general factual accuracy of *The Cachalot* we have the highly exaggerated account of the magnitude of some of the whale's internal organs, and interwoven with the historical documentation that forms the warp of the fabric of *Towards the Last Spike* we have the fantastic weft of the passages devoted to the North Shore lizard.

Furthermore, the reader of these documents occasionally comes upon a precise *explication de texte.* No better example of this can be found than Pratt's explanation of the metaphors of 'In Absentia,' which relate to his academic experience at Victoria College. A general illumination of many of the lyrics is another advantage the commentaries afford us. To have the context of the lyric 'Come Not the Seasons Here' fixed by Pratt's simple comment that it was 'a picture of a countryside devastated by war' (61) is most helpful; likewise, a reading of 'The Radio in the Ivory Tower' is enriched by the knowledge that behind the generalized character of the persona of the poem stands the particularized case of the American poet Robinson Jeffers.

Pratt even alerts us to certain stylistic features of his writing, such as the abundance of subjunctives and questions in *Brébeuf and His Brethren*, which are, according to the poet, a witness to his attempt to reconcile the facts of the case with the imaginative demands of verse composition. And, responding to Jed Adams's observation that his poetry is usually spare and without frills, Pratt agrees that he used few adjectives and explains the reason why: 'When I started writing in the twenties there was a magazine that you know, *Poetry* (Chicago), that went out full blast against adjectives, the archaic adjective especially ... it was felt that the adjective was there as a filler and hence ... in 1912 when *Poetry* came out, they were out against the adjective. And I feel that the adjective is often a filler, just a filler' (52–3).

Comprehensibility is another feature of his writing Pratt acknowledges as important, though he also comments to Adams on the desirability of a certain element of ambiguity or difficulty to stimulate interest and provoke thought: '... there are some poems where the objection comes that the symbolism is obscure, but I think that refers mainly to individual passages, not to the whole content. I believe in the whole content being luminous as possible, and at the same time I don't want it to be *absolutely* clear in every passage. I believe in a certain amount of difficulty here and there as a stimulus. But I think the whole content ought to be fairly free of shadow' (53).

There is much to be said for D.H. Lawrence's stricture that we must trust the tale and not the teller in matters of interpretation, but in assessing some of the controversies that have surrounded the interpretation of Pratt's poetry we cannot overlook the information provided by the commentaries. The specificity of the reference to the 'Abyssinian child' in 'The Prize Cat' seems fixed when Pratt categorically states that the poem refers 'to Mussolini's attack on Ethiopia just before the Second World War' (95), but we would do well to remember that this is the same raconteur who provides four versions of the details of the genesis of 'A Feline Silhouette.'

The question of Pratt's religious position, especially as this relates to *Brébeuf and His Brethren*, is at least partially answered by his statement that 'whether one is Protestant or Catholic, one may feel as I did when I stood with Mr Wilfrid Jury, the archaeologist, within a few feet of the place where Brébeuf offered up his life. It was indeed sacred ground' (121). His feelings towards the priests are largely admiring: 'In respect to certain expressions of the human spirit – courage, faith, self-effacement, endurance – that sheer holding on at solitary posts in the darkness of an approaching catastrophe which had all the earmarks of material failure – those twenty years of the Huron Mission can stand with any of the blazing periods of history' (114). He is even at pains to point out, both in the commentaries and in the poem itself, that the priests were broadly humanistic: '... in the course of their religious endeavours they never ignored the humane and social side of their ministrations. They strove to reduce disease in the villages, to improve sanitation and hygiene, to mitigate, if they could not abolish, the torture of captured enemies. They taught new methods of cultivation ...' (116). Yet Pratt also felt that the almost superhuman qualities of Brébeuf needed some careful handling if the priest were to remain credible, and so Pratt writes of his desire 'to humanize, as far as possible, the priest' (124).

The Iron Door, which is often read as a statement of Pratt's convictions about the afterlife, has a different emphasis in the poet's view, for he describes it as being 'based upon the opposition that the human will or hope presents to Death or extinction' (74–5). To read this poem as confessional verse representing Pratt's definitive view of eschatology may be somewhat misleading, then, but in a long letter to William Arthur Deacon, dated 27 August 1927, he specifies the concern of the poem as being the problem of immortality when he discusses its genesis, development, and themes: 'It originated in a dream where my mother, who was a woman of the profoundest faith in the life to come, was standing before a colossal door – the door of Death – and expecting without any fear of denial whatsoever, instant and full admission into the future state where she believed other members of the family had already entered. This was the nucleus of the poem. From there I elaborated it into a general conception of the problem of Immortality, starting with the feeling of despair and inevitability which faces one at a grave-side. That is, from a particular experience, I tried to universalize the idea ... I do not aim at solutions. I only wanted to give an imaginative and emotional interpretation of what I feel myself because I have never done anything which put the same compulsion on me for expression.'

In this letter Pratt makes clear that the character with whom he most closely identifies is the mother described in lines 187–211 (not his own mother; she is described in lines 116–31). Having explained that his characters 'all but one – the last – are drawn from persons I had known in life,' he continues: 'The last one, to my mind, sums up the problem, partly biological, partly environmental, of injustice and inequality in the moral order, and she presents the case in its glaring enigma.'

Like the controversy over Pratt's religious convictions, the question of his social philosophy has led to a great deal of critical speculation. While his heroes may tend to be collective in the best Canadian tradition of survival, there can be no doubt that Pratt honoured the individual voice.[16] His comments on the fractious masters of the convoy conference in *Behind the Log* speak eloquently to this point: 'All of them jealously guarded their democratic birthright of grumbling, the antidote to the Fascist lockjaw. That is one feature which we like to claim as part of the Anglo-Saxon tradition, the long-fought-for right of free expression of opinion ... The right to grumble is as sacred as the right to worship' (139).

Furthermore, the theme of 'The Truant,' Pratt states, is 'the revolt of the human individual against tyrannical power.' And of man he writes: 'He has developed concepts, a will of his own, a moral sense and a spirit of adventure *which refuses regimentation* [my emphasis] ... The free personality is something immeasurably greater than mere bulk and power and physical motion' (132–3).

In a balanced light, then, Pratt is seen to recognize and value man as an individual with all the rights and responsibilities attendant upon that status, but he also understands the need of individuals to band together in the face of overwhelming odds in order to survive as individuals.

Man is emphatically at the centre of Pratt's universe. He writes: 'Our harbours, hills, landscapes, seas, bays with their ever-changing colours and moods invite the best that can be offered by pencil, pen, brush, and camera, but it is the people who live and work in the harbours and on the seas who supply the finest material in their daily lives. The beauty of deeds is more difficult to describe and assess. It has to be estimated in terms of other than the physical senses. It calls for the highest spiritual approach, and nature herself as an inanimate existence must ever be a background against which a life is lived' (5).

Pratt was always seeking for the human implications behind the momentous events that are the physical 'stuff' of his poetry. His statement of his purpose in writing *Behind the Log* provides just one example. Speaking of the style of the log, he notes how it provides only bare, objective reports of death that do not touch on the implications for the living. But, he continues, the 'task of the writer is to suggest those implications, to show how behind the cryptic phrase or the unemotional statement there was blood, nerve, flesh, pulse' (143). In the same vein he records this about *The Titanic*: 'My interest in the loss of the *Titanic* was always more than a desire to record a story, a concern more with the implications of the disaster than with the factual side of it ...' (101).

What one can comment on further here is Pratt's conceptions of the heroic and the dramatic. In striving to understand the spirit behind heroic action, Pratt concurrently reveals the strong influence on his writing of his wide reading in English literature: 'Some of the greatest passages in our literature have been built up around great personal decisions to initiate action when the odds against survival were ... ninety-nine to one. It is the sling and the pebble against the spear and armour, where the impulse of the heart acts against the logic of the brain, where the ultimate value of the human soul is assessed in critical sacrificial moments ... There can be nothing more dramatic than a conflict which represents a last stand, a fight with the back to the wall; on the one side nothing but courage, on the other side unlimited power and a ruthless purpose; the flesh and blood and bare hands against the machine-guns, the forlorn hope with nothing left but the will against the overwhelming battalions' (127–8).

Though Pratt never specifically mentions the work, one wonders whether Bryhtwold's famous rousing of the remnants of the Anglo-Saxon army against the invading Danes in the Old English poem *The Battle of Maldon*, does not stand behind this formulation of the heroic. Bryhtwold's words were: 'Thought shall be the more resolute, heart the keener, / Courage the greater as our might lessens.'[17]

That men from all nations and walks of life are capable of heroism is repeatedly stressed in Pratt's verse. In describing the *Roosevelt* and *Antinoe* incident he refers to the 'inter-racial character of the life-crews' as one of the 'outstanding features of the incident' (81), and two points of interest for Pratt in the Dunkirk episode were, first, that 'Practically every trade, every profession, and every rank were represented on the decks of the nine hundred boats that went across the Channel' (126), and, second, that the boats of the rescue force were of an equally varied sort, for he speaks of the 'motley composition of the boats from the palatial yachts to the luggers and barges' (132). In the same vein, part of his fascination with the convoy conference of *Behind the Log* rests in the internationality of the assembly: 'I thought here was a chance to show the bewildering composition of the audience' (141).

Pratt's concept of the heroic has a twentieth-century flavour, for he believed that a combination of sacrificial heroic action and intellect under the aspect of science were the keys to an optimistic view of the future. 'Science in league with good will; individual courage and humanity behind the machine. It is that sort of thing, and only that sort of thing, which is the hope of this world' (85–6).

The commentaries also contain information useful in the establishing of a reliable Pratt text. One such example is the information

Pratt gives on the poem now titled 'The Dying Eagle.' He suggests two alternative titles, 'The Old Eagle' or 'The Old Eagle Has His First Sight of an Aeroplane,' pointing out: 'It is entitled in the collection "The Dying Eagle" but that is an error' (113).

A study of these documents allows us, as well, some insight into the way Pratt structured his poetry readings, invariably introducing the element of contrast, ever aware that the dark and pessimistic must be balanced by the light and optimistic. He therefore set the atavism of 'The Prize Cat' against the innocence of the lyric originally dedicated to his daughter,[18] 'The Child and the Wren'; and on another occasion he relieved the grimness of *The Ice-Floes* by the humour of 'A Feline Silhouette.'

This aesthetic principle of contrast was one Pratt also observed in the writing of his verse; thus, for *Behind the Log* he recalls 'searching for an action which would combine dramatic intensity with the eternal tedium of convoy' (134). He settled on the convoy conference to provide an 'interlude of relief much needed as the destruction in ships and life was tremendous' (139). To a similar end he introduced Tyrannosaurus Rex in *The Great Feud* to be a counterpart to the female anthropoidal ape, thereby balancing limited strength but advanced intellect with colossal might but minimal intelligence.

The commentaries, in alerting us to Pratt's intention that the poker game section of *The Titanic* be read as a 'short play' (99) suggest that his interest in writing verse-drama did not entirely end with the disaster of 'Clay.' Frequent dramatic readings of his work must have helped to keep this interest alive, and Pratt became deeply involved with a dramatic production of *Brébeuf* for which he collaborated with the composer Healey Willan and his friend Pelham Edgar.[19] Furthermore, an examination of the earliest drafts of 'The Truant' suggests that Pratt may have been considering a dramatic structure for that poem, as the phrases 'Off-stage' and 'On the stage' appear in the manuscripts.[20]

Just how Pratt worked from the research process to the submission of a poem for publication is another thing we can learn from the commentaries. Pratt found that 'the conclusion of a poem is the most important part and hardest to write.' He 'always had a fear of anti-climax' as it can 'ruin an otherwise fairly good poem.' To guard against such an eventuality, he would write the ending first and then would 'generally keep a poem in cold storage for weeks or months before publishing' (60).

In an account of his publishing career here entitled 'On Publishing,' Pratt significantly avoids mention of his first published work, *Rachel*, and begins with another work he viewed as an artistic failure, 'Clay.' The verse play is remembered more for the lessons it taught him than for its intrinsic worth. After a critical re-reading, Pratt tells us: 'I came around to the conviction that philosophical and ethical insights whenever they find their way into poetry should be emotional renderings of experiences actually lived or imaginatively grasped' (31).

Newfoundland Verse, too, is viewed as 'a bit of apprenticeship,' but it also provided verification that 'poetry blossomed more healthily out of the concrete than out of abstractions. It came best out of the imagination working upon the material of actual experience.' His method at this time he describes as one of trying 'to get the emotional effect out of the image or the symbol operating on the facts of sense perception' (33).

In 'On Publishing,' *The Witches' Brew* is described by its author as 'an experiment in technical adventure' (33) and one to which he attached no importance at the time of writing or at the much later date of the address. Finally, with 'Clay' received as too serious and *The Witches' Brew* as too absurd, Pratt turned to the great field of relatively unexplored material in science, something that would require 'some research and give body to poetry' (35). *The Cachalot* was the first result of this new process. 'On Publishing' unfortunately deals with his career only to this point so that his reaction to the reception of the rest of his poetry remains unknown.

Pratt's relations with his publishers, from Lorne Pierce of Ryerson Press to John Gray of Macmillan, seem to have been uniformly congenial and conducive to creative activity. Similarly, his reaction to the vast majority of his critics was a positive one, and he firmly believed in the vital connection and similarities between creative writing and critical appreciation.

At the time that Louis Dudek and Michael Gnarowski asserted that there was 'almost no developed literary theory from E.J. Pratt,'[21] their claim seemed legitimate, but from the commentaries and interviews there emerges a very definite personal theory of poetry. Pratt talks about the process of poetic creation from inspiration to publication in terms of organic metaphors. The decision to write on any given topic is, he says, one that is made for him, and once 'infected' by the 'germ' of an idea, the only 'cure' is a purgative one: '... I don't think I'd undertake a thing that I didn't feel under compulsion to do. You'd give up lots of things; you start things and you give them up and you find that there isn't the inner breathing or fire. But I always think of the distinction between an opinion and a conviction: that you take hold of an opinion but that a conviction takes hold of you. That's what I believe in the selection of topics for poetry and the writing of poetry. You have to do it. You feel you must get that out of your system. It's like an organic disease if you like. It has to be cured by being written out' (48). Then, mixing his metaphors somewhat, Pratt goes on to talk about the creation of a poem in terms similar to the midwifery metaphor Socrates used to talk about bringing an idea into being: 'I write a thing and it's like a child, you see, you're just dandling the child on your knee and running your fingers through his hair and you think this is the most wonderful thing ...' (48–9).

In discussing 'The Deed' Pratt suggests that his verse contains elements of both the realistic and the romantic, with the emphasis on the former. He sees nature as the environment in which people live and his understanding of the realistic is conditioned by that fact: 'The realistic in the broad sense represents a setting which may be drab or forbidding or commonplace but may contain an element of the beautiful or sublime from the nature of the human action' (145).

Deeds are the backbone of his poetic subject, but he writes with the hope that he can inspire his reader to reflect along more philosophical lines – on man's place in the universe and on the true meaning of beauty, as his comment on tragic literature intimates; like so many writers, Pratt, when he wrote of literature in general, was writing of his own work in particular: 'Whenever tragic literature, in staging the conflicts between man and nature or fate, brings out the refinement upon his face, the exaltation through suffering, it forces us to give our interpretation of life deeper implications, to make the pattern a nobler and more comprehensive one. This constitutes the main problem for idealistic literature: to get the anomalies explained, to find a place for man in a setting that makes sense to our baffled understanding, and the more we find ourselves in the presence of sacrificial deeds, the closer we get to the heart of life and the heart of the universe' (128).

Seeing the danger of two great lines of intellectual pursuit violently diverging, Pratt devoted much of his poetry to reconciling science and art, for he believed scientists and artists should be fellow workers in the supreme feat of engineering – getting humanity over the gulf between the present and the future: 'The reaction has set in against a clash of interest – between the scientific in the broad sense and the artistic in the same broad sense – for the very good reason that we cannot afford to let the two intellectual paths diverge, and go independently' (25). He declared himself to be preoccupied with '... the role that physical science is playing today in the construction and destruction of life, its relation to the bare elemental fact of existence ... I know nothing which, as material, offers a sterner challenge to drama and poetry' (137).

Thus, he made a conscious decision to write of machines, giant locomotives, asdic and radar, always setting them firmly in their human context: 'At first sight it might be said that an object such as a bulldozer could not be regarded as a thing of romantic beauty, but it is our neglect of the functional side of a machine which is responsible for that limited conception. Relate it to a deed and it takes on a life colouring' (27). He held that three elements were necessary to make a thing suitable for poetry: '... so long as human interest and wonder and feeling exist in regard to any material of life, poetry may find its source for expression' (26).

But in Pratt's view, science could provide more than a subject for poetry. The science and technology of the twentieth century had new rhythms to teach; a new *Weltanschauung* to express; in fact, possessed a poetry of their own: 'Science has always been to me, as a layman without any expert knowledge, a form of poetry, a system

of symbols and formulations which may look abstract and colourless enough on paper but when explained to our lay minds have the
power to put new rhythms in our pulses' (26).

Pratt does not have a great deal to say about style, but he
articulates more than once his objections to the obscurantist
tendencies of some modern literature.[22] 'I believe in communication,' he explains, 'in an experience which you have felt yourself
and you want to communicate to another. And if a poem is couched
in terms which are utterly difficult, unintelligible, half the value is
gone for me' (18). He maintained that a poet writes for an audience
and that he therefore has a responsibility to that audience to
communicate simply and directly.

Pratt's preference for the poetry of W.B. Yeats over that of T.S.
Eliot no doubt derives from the feeling that Yeats communicates
more simply and directly with his audience than does Eliot. Yet it is
clear that Pratt found something of value in Eliot's view of literary
history and development as it was set down in 'Tradition and the
Individual Talent.' Asked by Jed Adams to comment on the
relationship of past and future, Pratt responds: '... the logical
development of an art is from tradition into a modification of that
tradition, a change of that tradition. We belong to the past as surely
as we belong to the future. I certainly believe that a developing
tradition is the most logical and sensible direction in which to move'
(54).

There are few poems and virtually no aspects of Pratt's poetic
process that are not in some way illuminated by his comments in the
addresses, interviews, and introductions collected here. This is not
of course to imply that the poems cannot stand alone, but rather to
suggest that a reader's understanding of individual poems and of
Pratt's entire corpus can be considerably enriched by reading this
prose in conjunction with the poems.

1 See note 8 to the 'Newfoundland Types' commentaries.
2 *The Collected Poems of E.J. Pratt*, ed. Northrop Frye, 2nd ed. (Toronto:
  Macmillan 1958), 371
3 So far only Carl Klinck, in his outline of Pratt's life in the book he

co-authored with Henry Wells, *Edwin J. Pratt: The Man and His Poetry* (Toronto: Ryerson Press 1947), has made more than a little use of the commentaries for biographical purposes.

4 Mrs Pratt's remarks were reported in M.V. Ray, 'The Dedication of the E.J. Pratt Room of Contemporary Poetry,' *Victoria Reports* (Nov. 1964), 16.

5 Sandra Djwa, in *E.J. Pratt: The Evolutionary Vision* (Vancouver: Copp Clark 1974), 16–20, draws frequently on the texts of the commentaries and interviews to delineate Pratt's views on the roles of fate and free will in determining human action.

6 At a dinner at the York Club in Toronto, given to celebrate the publication of *Towards the Last Spike* (see commentary 2 on that poem), Pratt cited Brockville as the terminal point of his endurance.

7 Verrill, *Real Story* (New York: D. Appleton and Co. 1916); Bullen, *Cruise of the Cachalot* (New York: Crowell 1897); Djwa, *E.J. Pratt*, 71–2

8 Cf. Sandra Djwa with Robert Gibbs, 'The Living Contour: The Whale Symbol in Melville and Pratt,' *Canadian Literature*, 40 (Summer 1969), 17–25.

9 A postcard Pratt sent to W.A. Deacon, postmarked 14 June 1926, identifies the museum as the Field Museum of Natural History and includes this comment: 'Spent all day in this Museum getting acquainted with the animals of *The Great Feud*.' (This and all other correspondence between Pratt and Deacon subsequently cited is in the W.A. Deacon Collection, ms. coll. 160, Thomas Fisher Rare Book Library, University of Toronto.) Pratt's comment would seem to suggest that he visited the museum after the first drafts of the poem were already written. That his first title for the poem was 'The Great Schism' also supports the contention that the visit came after writing was already under way; but Sandra Djwa believes Pratt acquired a copy of Frederic Lucas's handbook *Animals of the Past: An Account of Some of the Creatures of the Ancient World* (New York: American Museum of Natural History 1901) before his visit to the museum, and this book may well have helped to provide the inspiration for the poem.

10 All this information can be found in commentaries on the poem, but additional facts concerning the research, such as Edgar's canvassing friends to raise money to finance Pratt's trip to New York, can be found

in a letter Pratt wrote to Edgar on 2 August 1945 from Halifax, where Pratt was doing research for *Behind the Log*. This letter is in file 12.16, Pelham Edgar Collection, Victoria University Library, University of Toronto; all correspondence between Pratt and Edgar subsequently cited is in this collection.

11 A letter to Deacon, dated 8 April 1935, identifies some of these: 'I have Beesley and Shaw and Lightoller (only surviving officer) and others.' For an account of how Pratt adapts his many sources for *The Titanic*, see Djwa, *E.J. Pratt*, 77–91.

12 To my knowledge, this was first suggested in print by Sandra Djwa in 'Litterae ex Machina,' *Humanities Association Review*, xxv, no 1 (1974), 22–31.

13 Sandra Djwa notes in a letter to me, 6 June 1979, that Roberts's poem owes something to Pratt's own earlier poem 'The Sea-Cathedral,' first published in *Acta Victoriana*, 51, no 3 (Dec. 1926), 17, and again in *Canadian Forum*, 7, no 80 (May 1927), 237. This poem in turn is based on a description in Lewis Legrand Noble, *After Icebergs with a Painter: A Summer Voyage to Labrador and around Newfoundland* (New York: D. Appleton and Co. 1861).

14 Frye, *The Bush Garden: Essays on the Canadian Imagination* (Toronto: Anansi 1971), 168–9 and 223

15 *Collected Poems*, 77–8

16 For a differing point of view, see Frank Davey, 'E.J. Pratt: Apostle of Corporate Man,' *Canadian Literature*, 43 (Winter 1970), 54–66, and 'E.J. Pratt: Rationalist Technician,' *ibid.*, 61 (Summer 1974), 65–78.

17 Translated from the Old English in *Bright's Old English Grammar and Reader*, ed. F.J. Cassidy and Richard Ringler (New York: Holt, Rinehart and Winston 1971), 371

18 The poem appeared in *Poetry of Our Time: An Introduction to Twentieth-Century Poetry, Including Modern Canadian Poetry*, ed. Louis Dudek (Toronto: Macmillan of Canada 1965), with the dedication 'To Claire.'

19 A great deal more information about the 'Oratorio' can be found in the Pelham Edgar letters to Pratt. A recording entitled *Brébeuf and His Brethren* was produced by the Department of Tourism and Information of the Province of Ontario and made by TBC Recording Ltd. of Don Mills, Ontario.

20 See S.A. Beckmann, 'From Java to Geneva: The Making of a Pratt Poem,' *Canadian Literature*, 87 (Winter 1980), 9–10.
21 Dudek and Gnarowski, *The Making of Modern Poetry in Canada* (Toronto: Ryerson Press 1967), 155
22 In a now generally forgotten essay, 'The Fly-Wheel Lost,' *Open House*, ed. William Arthur Deacon and Wilfred Reeves (Ottawa: Graphic Publishers 1931), 246–55, Pratt complained: 'There is a good deal of talk about the tyranny of words, of punctuation, of sentence conventions, but, whatever the substitutions, the newcomers must in time establish their own habits of control. Syntax is as much an evolution as the human larynx, and, under violent wrenches, as much subject to hemorrhage' (250–1).

Editorial principles and procedures

E.J. Pratt's commentaries exist both in typescript and in manuscript form. For the most part he wrote these commentaries on cheap school notebook paper and very often in pencil; the paper is now yellowed and crumbling and the writing is frequently faded, and in some places completely effaced. He wrote hurriedly and for himself, so his script is, regrettably, small and often illegible. The difficulty is compounded in certain instances by his frugal habit (more often observed in the draft versions of his poems than in the hand-written prose commentaries) of putting two lines of writing in the space of one. Though the texts of all the commentaries have been checked several times against a magnified original, some words and passages are completely illegible and what others say can only be guessed at: wherever there is a reasonable degree of doubt about a word or passage, attention has been called to this fact by placing an asterisk in the text immediately following the doubtful phrase. Since many of the manuscripts are in extremely poor condition, the form of the source (manuscript or typescript) has been clearly identified for the reader because of the greater likelihood of error in the transmission of the holograph commentaries.

The reader who peruses the volume from beginning to end will find certain information repeated several times, for Pratt was not averse to telling a good story more than once. Since he seldom presents the material in exactly the same light, however, and since he adds different details to the basics of a story on various

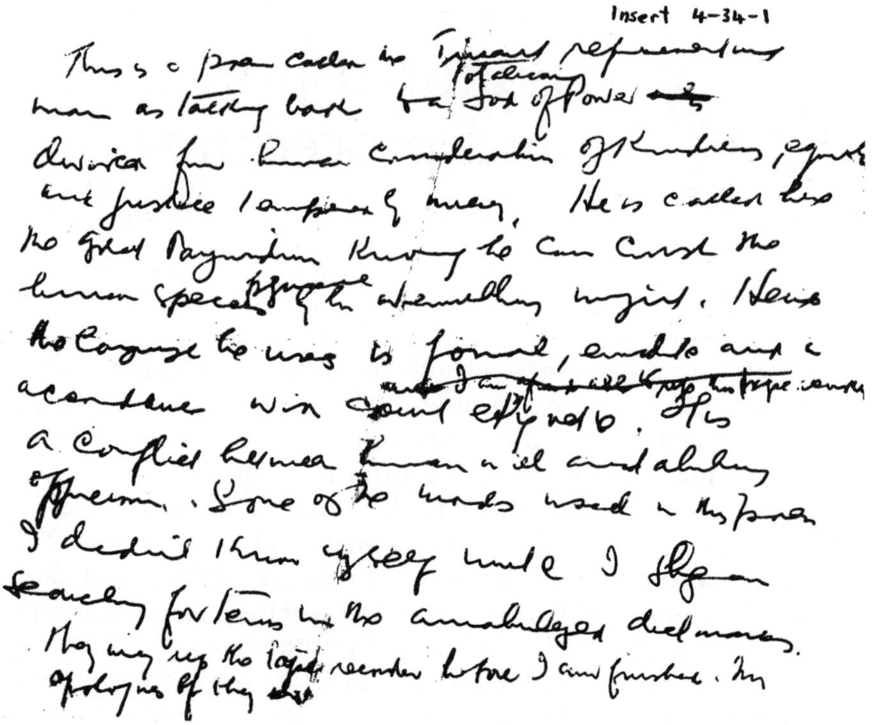
Insert 4-34-1

This is a poem called the Truant representing man as talking back to a God of Power and [illegible] from human consideration of kindness, equity and justice, compassion & mercy. He is called here the Great Panjandrum knowing he can crush the human species by [illegible] the overwhelming might. Hence the language he uses is formal, erudite and in accordance with [illegible] etymology. It is a conflict between human will and ability of freedom. Some of the words used in the poem I [illegible] until I began searching for them in the unabridged dictionary. They may keep the [illegible] reader [illegible] before I am finished. My apologies of [illegible]

Holograph commentary on 'The Truant'

occasions, the repetition has been allowed to stand unless it is virtually verbatim.

As Pratt had no intention of publishing the majority of these commentaries, punctuation is sparse and the text sometimes degenerates into a kind of point form. The commentaries have been lightly punctuated where necessary to facilitate reading, but fragments of thought have been allowed to stand, except in those cases where expansion from point form involved the addition of no more than one or two simple connecting words that could not possibly affect the sense of a passage. Many obvious spelling and grammar errors have been emended, while abbreviations have been expanded and capitalization modernized and made generally consistent without comment. Line or page references recorded in the texts have not been included, unless they are vital to sense, as they seldom refer to an easily available edition. Similarly omitted are Pratt's instructions to himself at various points to read aloud passages from his poetry.

All titles to the commentaries are Pratt's own, as they appear in his notes or in published form, with two exceptions: for reasons of clarity and grace Pratt's title 'Highlight Associations in My Early Life' was emended to 'Highlights in My Early Life' and two originally untitled commentaries were given the titles 'Introduction for a Reading' and 'On Macmillan.'

The texts of the interviews in the middle section of the book have been prepared by transcribing tapes in the Canadian Broadcasting Corporation archives and checking them against published sources where possible. Generally, the same procedure was followed as was used in editing the commentaries, though here an attempt was made to reflect in the punctuation the flow of, and pauses in, Pratt's conversation.

Notes to the commentaries and to the interviews appear at the back of the book. Information concerning the provenance of each item is given in a headnote at the beginning of each section of notes pertaining to a particular set of commentaries. In order to facilitate the task of scholars wishing to work with the original texts, box and file numbers have been cited: unless otherwise stated, these numbers refer to the E.J. Pratt Collection of the E.J. Pratt Library, Victoria University, Toronto. Where variant forms of commentaries exist, published sources have been placed first because of their greater textual authority.

DATING

From internal evidence we can be reasonably sure that the commentaries assembled here were written over a period of approximately a quarter of a century. Commentaries 3 and 4 on *The Cachalot* are probably the oldest, and because they were transcribed from pencil holograph notes following drafts of the poem in a notebook the composition date can be estimated at *circa* 1925. The commentaries on *Towards the Last Spike* are likely the most recent, and since in one of these Pratt refers to the poem as a book the commentary must have been written after the volume was published in 1952. When commentary transcribed from tapes is taken into consideration, the date of origin of some commentary is seen to be as late as 1958.

The difficulty of providing dating for most of the commentaries results largely from Pratt's habit of using his addresses repeatedly, adding or discarding material as the occasion required, so that many of the surviving typescripts are fragmentary. Occasionally, however, a typescript will be marked with a partial date, as is the case with one address, 'The Relation of Source Material to Poetry,' which is prescribed for release 'after 1 p.m. June 14th' – the year is regrettably missing. At other times an internal reference to the occasion on which an address was presented makes it possible to fix the exact date and year: the addresses made at the Macmillan dinners given for Pratt by his editor Hugh Eayrs on the occasions of the publishing of *The Titanic* and *The Roosevelt and the Antinoe* fall into this category because programs for the evening have been preserved amongst friends' papers. Where a date can be associated in any way with a text from external evidence, this information is provided in the notes.

Even when accurate dating information is impossible to provide, the reader can sometimes estimate the date when commentaries on individual poems were written, because an examination of Pratt's working notebooks reveals a common pattern with regard to the drafting of commentary. After virtually every collection of poems was published (*Newfoundland Verse* is the likely exception, for little commentary on the poems of this earliest book survives, if in fact it ever existed), Pratt gave a series of readings of these poems for which he prepared introductory notes, drafts of which usually follow the drafts of the verse. Sometimes longer poems such as *The Ice-Floes* would be read alone, and perhaps such readings of the commentary and poems were made after periodical publication of the verse.

From the time Pratt began to publish his major longer poems separately, he would prepare introductory material for them upon completion or sometimes before the narrative had reached its final form. The only surviving commentary on *The Iron Door*, for example, comes from a pencil description of the poem that follows drafts of the verse in notebooks. Some commentary on *The Titanic* must have been written before the poem was itself finished, for the texts of the two addresses refer to parts not yet completed or polished.

The majority of the commentaries on individual poems seem to have been written and presented in the period between the time Pratt was finishing the poem and before concentrated work had begun on the next project. As Pratt's fame grew, however, it seems likely that audiences would call on him to read from special favourites that would not be his latest work, and unless some internal clue makes dating possible such occasions are virtually impossible to identify.

It should be noted that the date given in the text alongside the title of commentaries on specific poems is the date of the poem's first publication; in most instances the actual date of writing of the commentary itself is impossible to establish.

Biographical chronology

1882	Born at Western Bay, Newfoundland, 4 February; third child of eight of the Rev. John Pratt, Yorkshire-born clergyman, and Fanny Pitts Knight, daughter of a Newfoundland sea captain
1888–1902	Educated in outport schools and at the Methodist College, St John's, with a three-year intermission, 1897–1900, as a clerk in a dry-goods store
1902–4	Teacher at Moreton's Harbour, a fishing village in Notre Dame Bay
1904–7	Probationary minister in the Methodist ministry at Clarke's Beach—Cupids and Bell Island—Portugal Cove
1907–11	Student in philosophy, Victoria College, University of Toronto, BA 1911
1912	Received MA degree, University of Toronto
1913	Received BD degree; ordained into the Methodist ministry
1913–20	Demonstrator-lecturer in psychology, University of Toronto; assistant minister in a number of churches around Streetsville, Ontario
1917	Received PhD from University of Toronto – thesis, *Studies in Pauline Eschatology and Its Background*, published in Toronto; *Rachel: A Sea Story of Newfoundland in Verse* printed privately in New York
1918	Married Viola Whitney (BA Victoria College 1913), 20 August

1920	Joined Department of English, Victoria College
1921	Birth of only child, Mildred Claire
1923	*Newfoundland Verse*, first commercially published book of poems
1925	*The Witches' Brew* published in London
1926	*Titans* published in London; *The Witches' Brew* in Toronto
1927	*The Iron Door: An Ode* published in Toronto
1930	Appointed professor, Department of English, Victoria College; elected Fellow of the Royal Society of Canada; *The Roosevelt and the Antinoe* published in New York; *Verses of the Sea*, with introduction by Charles G.D. Roberts, published in Toronto
1930–52	Taught summer school at Dalhousie, Queen's, and the University of British Columbia
1932	*Many Moods* published in Toronto
1935	*The Titanic* published in Toronto
1936	One of the founders and first editor, from January 1936 to August 1943, of *Canadian Poetry Magazine*
1937	*The Fable of the Goats and Other Poems* published in Toronto, winner of the Governor-General's Award
1938	Appointed senior professor, Victoria College
1940	*Brébeuf and His Brethren* published in Toronto, winner of the Governor-General's Award; awarded the Royal Society's Lorne Pierce Gold Medal for distinguished service to Canadian literature
1941	*Dunkirk* published in Toronto
1943	*Still Life and Other Verse* published in Toronto
1944	*Collected Poems* published in Toronto
1945	*Collected Poems*, with introduction by William Rose Benét, published in New York; *They Are Returning* published in Toronto; received D. Litt. from University of Manitoba, first honorary degree (others: LL.D., Queen's 1948; D.C.L., Bishop's 1949; D. Litt., McGill 1949; D. Litt., Toronto 1953; D. Litt., Assumption 1955; D. Litt., New Brunswick 1957; D. Litt., Western Ontario 1957; D. Litt., Memorial 1961)

1946	Created Companion of the Order of St Michael and St George in the King's Honours List
1947	*Behind the Log* and *Ten Selected Poems* published in Toronto
1952	*Towards the Last Spike* published in Toronto, winner of the Governor-General's Award; awarded the University of Alberta Gold Medal for distinguished service to Canadian literature; member of the editorial board, from 20 December 1952 to 13 September 1958, of *Saturday Night*
1953	Retired from Victoria College; appointed professor emeritus of English
1955	Elected honorary president of the Canadian Authors' Association
1957	Received Canada Council award on 75th birthday
1958	*The Collected Poems of E.J. Pratt*, edited by Northrop Frye, published in Toronto
1959	Received Civic Award of Merit from the City of Toronto
1961	Received the Canada Council medal for distinction in the field of literature
1963	Elected honorary member of the Empire Club of Canada; elected first honorary member of the Arts and Letters Club
1964	Died in Toronto, 26 April

E.J. PRATT ON HIS LIFE AND POETRY

General Commentaries

'Highlights in My Early Life'

I feel very much in a reminiscent mood today. Memories come crowding back and I am going to pick out a few highlight associations in my early life – the things I can never forget and often wonder why I remember ... the first day I went to school in Cupids, a blustery day in January. Why it was in January and not in the earlier September I do not know except that I was four months older and more able to stand up against the wind assisted by my two brothers, Will and Jim. I remember the first time that discipline was administered to me. It was at Brigus. I've forgotten the misdemeanour though I remember the schoolmaster whom I have always held in affectionate remembrance ever since. I remember the big fire at St John's, the bank crash, the *Greenland* disaster on the ice-floes, the homecoming of the ship and the great memorial services. My total recollection is a medley, the trivial and the incidental joined with the dramatic and significant. I remember the first snowslide that was built for me by my grandfather, Captain William Knight. I remember my birthday February 4th when I was thirteen years old, when my father at Fortune gave me a catamaran as a present. That catamaran cost one dollar. I had it painted a cobalt blue. I had wanted it above everything else as a birthday present so that I could go out into the woods and haul home firewood. When my brother Jim asked me what I should prefer if I had my choice, a gold watch or a catamaran, I replied a catamaran, and his one remark was – 'That's what I call ambition.' In any case the gold watch was about as much out of my grasp as Buckingham Palace.

The main memories are those of my father and mother who have ever been the sustaining forces of my life. My father being an itinerant clergyman, changing his circuit every three years or so, the family naturally had the opportunity of seeing many phases of the life of the country. Those first twenty-odd years of my life gave me a wealth of experience which will never completely be drained. In fact, it crops out in my work in the most unexpected places, in subjects which might at first glance appear to be outside of the area. It is like an idiom or an accent from which one could not, and would not if he could, dissociate himself. Such subjects as storms, marine disasters, rescues, sacrifices, all the way down from the high heroic to the sharing of bread and the little nameless unremembered acts of kindness and of love – these seem to be the natural subjects for the thought and expression of Newfoundlanders. They certainly possessed the minds and hearts of my most loved father and mother in their combined ministrations extending over twenty-five years.

Newfoundland has always been for me the place of great deeds which have been traditionally the texture of its seafaring life. The people are accustomed to taking chances – great gambles, if you like – with the highest stake of all, life itself. There is always something profoundly moving and dramatic in decisions where the odds are against you, where the issue is fought out on high ground, where the end is noble, where the battle is joined with the wind and the stars against you, and especially when the risk is taken on behalf of the lives of others. There isn't one person among us who, having witnessed a fine sacrificial action, hasn't felt like hoisting a flag to the masthead bearing the signal – 'Let no one do a mean deed today.' That is the influence of conduct shaped by character.

It is not only in war where the great deeds are done. We know that this country went through the two world wars with sterling moral credit. Treasure of life and money was poured out without stint. That is now a record which belongs to history, but the quality which was shown through those two periods of four and six years also belongs to a less sensational extent in the regular struggle of life. The other war.[1] This kind of war has ever gone on against the elements which never make a peace treaty with man and it is out of that kind of conflict mainly that the Newfoundland spirit has been forged.

A good deal of the material of Romantic literature, particularly of Romantic poetry, is made up of nature description and quite properly. Nature herself is a storehouse not only of power but of beauty. Our harbours, hills, landscapes, seas, bays with their ever-changing colours and moods invite the best that can be offered by pencil, pen, brush, and camera, but it is the people who live and work in the harbours and on the seas who supply the finest material in their daily lives. The beauty of deeds is more difficult to describe and assess. It has to be estimated in terms of other than the physical senses. It calls for the highest spiritual approach, and nature herself as an inanimate existence must ever be a background against which a life is lived. The beauty of a great act has the beauty of a moral law or the beauty of the physical universe. In fact, it is the only way in which the strength and significance of a law can be measured or expressed.

'Memories of Newfoundland'

To write an article on memories of Newfoundland is like trying to pick out one duck to fire at from a flock of thousands. The mind is bewildered at the task of selection. So, possibly, the best plan is to do what as youngsters we invariably did while out after game – close the eyes and drive both barrels into the processions. I should prefer to call this a letter rather than an article.

Being the son of a clergyman whose mission it was to migrate every three years from one town to another, I had a good opportunity of getting acquainted with the heart of the country, which is essentially the outport life. So distinctive is the Newfoundland type that it is only with the greatest difficulty that one may translate it in foreign terms or communicate it even to Canadians. When a half-dozen of us Newfoundlanders gather together in Toronto to smoke and yarn, the foreign born, if he happen to be invited to the company, finds himself only on the fringe of the charmed circle.

The conversation, once it has lapsed into dialect, is a closed book to him. He may know that haggis is a Scotch dish, or a particular hybrid of stew is Irish, but has he ever eaten brewis? No. His palate for dried cod is limited to a few tasteless fillets which the proprietor of a meat-and-fish store in the city claimed to have been cut from genuine cod. Has he ever eaten whorts? No, only blueberries – a fundamental error. Or bake-apples, or capillaire, or partridge berries? Never heard of them. Had he ever been stimulated by the smell of kelp after a northeaster had lashed the shores – a tonic like strychnine to the blood? Or by the smell of caplin three days after the tonnage had been deposited on the cabbage beds? No. Then he was forever excommunicate, a stranger to the true faith. How did he pronounce the name of the country? With the accent on the second syllable. That was enough – the final heresy.

And for the rest of the evening, while our friendly alien tilted his head over the back of an armchair and dozed, we reminisced about Newfoundland dogs, the departure and return of the sealing and fishing fleets, the gargantuan meals of flippers in the spring, partridge coveys, the size of the trout we almost landed, school thrashings, snowdrifts, fore-and-afters, the late arrival of trains and steamers, and the stories of old salts who knew life as it was in the sixties and seventies. Two of us present remembered a summer in St John's, when every fine afternoon we went swimming in 'The Hole' off 'Sliding Rock' in Rennie's Mill River. We tagged some of the names – Ayre, Macpherson, MacNeilly, Knight, Higgins, Parsons, Bond, Baird, and many others. Slim and active we were in those days; but the years have added weight and dignity, changing us into greying teachers, furrowed businessmen, worried trustees, and portly lawyers and justices.

These are the light and happy memories of Newfoundland, the casual ones which belong to the excursions from the main highway, and which form the usual subject of chat when a few of the native-born are grouped around a stove.

In a more serious vein I might refer to some outstanding experiences which can never be erased from my mind. One was a dramatic event of significance not merely to Newfoundland, but to the world, which occurred when I was attending the Methodist College in 1902. Principal Holloway, one of the most remarkable teachers I have ever known, and one of the most gifted and thorough despite the physical handicaps under which he laboured, was demonstrating to us in his laboratory the nature of the x-ray, which had just been discovered. To see through an opaque object was a marvel like listening for the first time through a telephone or hearing the reproduction of a voice on the gramophone; but that experience, absorbing as it was, faded before an event which took place a few days later.

Mr Holloway told us that he had arranged for the class in physics to go down to the House of Assembly to see Marconi in person. This was not to say a surprise, but a shock – like coming into the presence of Deity. The world had known of the invention some time before this, but it was our first experience of witnessing a message transmitted from one closed room to another, from key to key without a wire. This was shattering enough in all conscience, but it again was only another prelude to what occurred the next day. No one knew precisely why Marconi was in town. We had a general idea that he was still further experimenting, and that he needed Cabot Tower for research. But imagine the thrill the following morning when the newspapers headlined the statement that Marconi had bridged the Atlantic from Signal Hill to Lizard Point in Cornwall with wireless telegraphy!

Those of us who remember the announcement may recall the sense of conquest over Nature that visited the hearts of men, the trust in science for the prevention of the grosser human calamities. Wireless had not only given a richer meaning to the phrase 'the brotherhood of the sea,' but it was considered as having eliminated forever the horror of the huge tolls after collisions and storms. And the sensation it was for us lads to be in close to the actual discovery, to be in the field, watching the inventor finishing, as it were, the last lap of his achievement! It was not long before the claims began to be vindicated with growing impressiveness as the stations were multiplied on the coasts and the apparatus installed on the ships. The years 1910 and 1911 were the banner years of rescue – steamers answering calls through winter gales, with thousands rescued, and the post of a Marconi operator took on a touch of heroic drama. He was the sentry of the ocean, not less than the captain himself the symbol of duty and loyalty and watchfulness. That morning will always remain one of the big moments of existence.

Another experience, a tragic one, was the loss of the *Greenland*. I was very young at the time, but it seems merely as yesterday when the ship came to St John's with her freight of frozen bodies. The great memorial was held in the Anglican cathedral, with several representative clergymen speaking messages of consolation to the immense congregation of mourners. The words burned into our souls as they described the struggle of the men on the floes, the pitched battle with the elements at their worst, and the ironic enigma of Nature and its relation to the Christian view of the world.

Less in magnitude, obviously, than this disaster, but sharing in some of its qualities, were many events witnessed along the coast, which illustrated the heroic stuff out of which human hearts can be made. This was brought home to my own family by reason of the long pastoral ministrations of my beloved father. It was a source of perpetual wonder to him, illuminating his faith, to observe the native courage and devotion with which men would set out to accomplish a task of rescue involving sacrificial effort. Often the drama was a short one – a matter of a few hours – where the mind was not concerned very much in assessing the slim chances of survival or in weighing the issue with the risk, but where the blood naturally counted on its iron for the job. And when the deed was done, whether in failure or success, it came back on the village, raising the moral temperature of the community. It had the effect on us as if a flag had been run up to the masthead bearing the signal – 'Let no one do a mean deed today.'

I often think of the public attention which is given by our Canadian newspapers to exploits undertaken on behalf of life. This is, of course, as it should be. It is the finest material for notice anyway, but the impression derived from the Newfoundland scene is that the process of rescue is a normal part of life's routine. It is taken for granted, like the action of the heart-valves. Some of the sublimest deeds I have ever known did not get outside the local records. They are enshrined in more imperishable tissue. They have a beauty about them more than the fragrance of roses, more than the music of nightingales, and they are part of the spiritual heritage of Newfoundlanders.

'Newfoundland Types'

1. I have been asked to speak on some aspects of Newfoundland life, and I shall try to do so by portraying some of the types that make up the bulk of the population on the fishing coasts, and to indulge in some reminiscences of my own.

There wasn't one of the British Dominions which was more essentially British than Newfoundland. Being situated on the other side of the Atlantic, being in the past neither a part of Canada nor of the United States, its isolation tended to preserve that British connection. Until recent times its currency was English, until the time when, to use a proverbial phrase down there, the dollar and the devil came in together.[1] Its import trade was largely English, its government, its customs, its sport, its newspaper editorials, its education, English in character. Its principal school teachers in the city schools, its preachers were imported from England. Its matriculation examinations in my day, though written in St John's, were sent to London and marked by London examiners. Much of that of course has changed in the last generation, but the stock itself hasn't changed, and I mean by that particularly the sailor stock, the ordinary everyday life in the outports, which has preserved the ancient heritage when much of that heritage has been lost or modified beyond recognition in other parts of the British connection. One reason is that there has been practically no immigration into Newfoundland other than English, Scotch, and

Irish, and a long distance back French to a less degree. It is thus easy to see how the strain has been perpetuated. The little villages lived to themselves. In such a place as I lived for two years before coming to Canada, a steamer would call once in two weeks at the harbour, bearing freight from St John's and the newspapers would carry news belated to that degree. The church services naturally remained the same; the Irish communities still had their funeral wakes with their unconsciously humorous remarks upon the dear departed: they had the same wedding jigs and the practical jokes played on the groom just after the wedding, but, above all, the people have preserved their mode of speech, their accents, their social, one might say, their tribal or clan customs, the same sort of life which the fishermen lived centuries ago long before the founding of Québec. Those Elizabethan qualities of character and expression are richly grained in the present stock. Devon blood, Cornish blood, Yorkshire blood, Irish and Scotch blood still runs tumultuously in their veins, and I know that were a certain type of sailor today in the Newfoundland outports brought face to face in conversation with a resurrected Devon man, the two could find more common ground of intelligible speech and emotional outlook than say such a Newfoundlander would with a present-day Anglo-Saxon from Canada or the United States.

Now as I am not an economist or a politician and much less a financier, Lord help me, I am going to restrict my remarks to a few reminiscences and to an account of the people themselves, particularly the sailors with whom I spent the first twenty years of my life. A year ago I returned from a visit to Newfoundland. I had been invited down by the St Andrew's Society to propose the toast to Robert Burns on Burns' nicht, January 25. I thought it was a rather crazy notion to go such a long distance to propose a toast and deliver a speech, but it was their funeral, not mine, and the invitation was just another characteristic of Newfoundlanders, and that was their loyalty to a tradition. Scotchmen in St John's, where they mostly reside for obvious business reasons, are in a very small minority, numerically, but they make up for their smallness of numbers by their compactness and their tenacity of national feeling. Burns is almost a god to them. They take their Burns neat. When I had finished my speech, the governor, Sir Gordon Macdonald, had to propose the toast to the then British Commonwealth of Nations. We were all expecting a political speech, but he scarcely touched the Commonwealth in the large general sense, except to say that Burns had done more for the Commonwealth as an idea than all the politicians that ever lived. It was a Burns nicht, and a Burns nicht it was going to be. He said that Newfoundland was the only country in the world where the people declared a public holiday on the anniversary of Robbie's birth, or on the anniversary of anybody's birth, except that of the King. All the banks and the trust buildings were closed and that meant a lot when the name of every manager began with a Mac. The public buildings were closed, and all the stores, even though one might surmise that double pressure the next day would be put on the sales clerks to make up for the financial loss caused by the holiday the day before. But the point I wish to make is that same tenacity of heritage belonged to the people generally.

I want now to refer to their idiom as one mode of illustrating that linkage with the past. When I got down there, I was delighted to hear some of the old delicious expressions. Instead of 'You're looking fine today' spoken to a lady who might, let us say, be on a reducing diet, I heard 'You're lookin' immense today,' a remark of course intended as a compliment, and if the lady wasn't feeling immense, in that sense, she might reply not with 'I'm just feeling fair' but with 'I'm only in the middlins for I have a wonderful head,' wonderful being generally a synonym for terrible or awful. I have a wonderful head or a wonderful tooth, when the toothache was sending the woman crazy. And instead of 'I was nearly killed today,' it was 'I had a like to be killed today.' And a housemaid explaining that a starched shirt wasn't quite finished, might remark to her mistress 'It'll be all right, ma'am, when I get the congregational side done,' congregational referring to the starched bosom. That's one of the best of them all. A cup of tea in between whiles is a mug-up and a snack between breakfast and the midday meal is an elevener, more obvious, of course. A Newfoundlander is spotted by another Newfoundlander by his terms. Fish is never halibut or herring but codfish, better cod, and blueberries are always whorts. When a doctor wants to rush a flu patient to the hospital and there is likely to be some delay, he can always get immediate action by saying that his patient's face is as blue as a whort.[2]

I should like to spend a long while doing nothing but going through the villages in the outports renewing my acquaintance with the vigorous salty language. So distinctive is it[3] that it is only with difficulty one can translate it in foreign terms, especially when the conversation has lapsed into dialect. It has an Elizabethan root, for, as I have said, those people in the small villages are the descendants of the Devon men and the Cornish men, and thousands are the descendants of Irish ancestors who have kept the brogue so rich and pure that Irish people from Southern Ireland might very well today go to southeast Newfoundland and learn how their forefathers spoke Irish three centuries ago. Sometimes I heard a mixture of all dialects in the same conversation and some of [my] Canadian friends, after paying a summer visit to Newfoundland outports, told me that they couldn't catch the meaning of much of the conversation. Here is one bit of conversation which I once overheard between the skipper of a herring skiff and his wife who was waiting for him on the wharf in the harbour. She wanted to know whether he had caught any herring. Now in plain literary English, this is what would be spoken, the wife shouting out – 'Are there any herring this morning?' The answer from the skipper would be – 'No, there are not any herring this morning. There might as well be no herring as any herring, because if there are any herring, they are not at all big.' What she really shouted out was – 'Any arn dis marn?' – 'No, dere ain't any arn dis marn. Might as well be narn as arn, cause if dere arn dere nar a bit big.' That's the pure McKoy.

There is another expression that I have never forgotten. When my father was a minister in a town on the south coast, an Anglican bishop came to our parsonage and told us a story of how he was received in a little village on [a] visit to his straying flocks along the coast. It was a great occasion for the village and there was considerable excitement and nervousness over the proposed measures for his entertainment. The obvious place to go was the home of the local magistrate, but as that gentleman was away on his official duties the decision was reached that the bishop should stay at the home of the local dealer. The wife was instructed that as soon as the bishop entered he was not to be addressed as Bish, or Bishop, or even as Mr but as my lord. She spent several days rehearsing the salutation, with the appropriate gestures, in a state of extreme nervousness. The bishop came over in [an] open boat escorted by his officials, and as soon as he entered the house the episcopal gravity was thrown off its base by the salutation of the old lady – 'O Lord, will you please lower your holy and sanctified starn on that bench.' The salutation was delivered with the utmost reverence and seriousness. The bishop told the story to my father with great gusto – the humour of it was so unconscious. No one could fail to detect the delightful nautical flavour of the expression, as distinct from the rather pallid conventionality of – 'How do you do, my lord, will you please come in and be seated.'

The Newfoundlanders have a native eloquence, a fervent, if rough, type of speech, whether seen in a political oration, a sermon or prayer.[4] The preachers in my day, whether local preachers or ordained clergymen, could lift their congregations out of their pews by the most gorgeous descriptions of heaven or else shake them under the planks by painting hell with colours never seen on land or sea. We, as youngsters, would creep under the seats until the time came for the benediction. We would come out from our hidings when we were sure the colours were dry. One might dispute the gospel truth of the message but no one could deny the power. It was a real heaven and a real hell we saw. The cinders were in our eyes on Sunday night. Only the morning put out the nightmare fires, and not always then.

In addition to that eloquence is a quick-wittedness which the Americans today particularly enjoy. Two stories were laughingly related to me when I was down there. An American airman, pointing to the letters NFLD on the tunic of a sailor, jokingly asked what they stood for, and the sailor immediately replied – 'Not found lying down as you were at Pearl Harbor.' The other concerned an American in a motor car nearly running down a Newfoundlander in a blackout. The American shouted – 'Why can't you get out of the way?' and the pedestrian shot back – 'What's the hurry; you're here for ninety-nine years anyway.' When the Americans were constructing their great base at Argentia, they decided to build a first class road to St John's through Holyrood. An American officer wanted to find out what kind of a road was there already, and began making inquiries from some of the people. On an excursion of his own down a rough road, he asked a boy whether the road ran to St John's. All he got was a grunt – 'Eh?' 'Can you tell me, my boy, if this road leads to St John's?' 'Eh?' 'Well, can you tell me if this road runs through Holyrood?' Again, 'Eh?' The officer, quite vexed, said, 'You don't know much, do you?' The boy replied – 'I ain't lost.'

There is another kind of humour which sometimes appears in the daily newspapers and gives the appearance of being unconscious. I am indebted to *The Book o[f] Newfoundland*[5] for these examples. Sometimes, the humour is unintentional due to neglect of the syntax on the part of the writer and unobserved by the editor before it gets into print. Occasionally ...[6]

2. I should like to speak for a few minutes upon the relationship between my life as a Newfoundlander and the work I have tried to do as a writer, and I may say just here that even in dealing with[7] subjects that belong to the dry land the sea has a way of despatching a wave to wash the doorstep or spray the sills.[8] A man cannot get far away from his heritage, and the memories of my boyhood seem as fresh today as they were more than forty years ago. Some of those characters in the outports have remained with me as very vitalized recollections – one or two it may be in a village who by reason of some pronounced idiosyncrasy stood out among their fellows, characters we talk about in reminiscence decades after. Those are the dramatic individuals who really form the subjects for painters, short-story tellers, novelists, and writers generally. We may smile when we refer to some of the character

points but such are the points which make the individuals memorable.

The appeal of this subject never seems to wear out. I have been asked to prepare next winter some broadcasts over the CBC for Ontario high schools and the director suggested that as far as possible I introduce a number of poems dealing with eccentric persons slightly off balance, not in their minds exactly, but in their tastes, hobbies, and preoccupations. Part of a writer's job is to collect and describe such characters. All of us have gone through periods of hero-worship in the manner of *Tom Brown's School Days*. Strong men, men of action, men of emergency have been our demigods. Our local strong men formed our circle of heroes pretty well on the same footings as one Horatio Nelson and the Duke of Wellington. We did admit a few such into the charmed circle, or perhaps it was the men with one specialized skill – the sleight-of-hand man, the magician who made us gape with astonishment. A short while ago I spent an evening with John Masefield and Laurence Binyon who told me of their early experiences. Mr Masefield spoke with relish of his life in New York when he was a very young man. I asked him what was his most vivid recollection of New York and he told me that the man he admired most was a bartender who could take two glasses each containing a liquid which shall be nameless and toss the contents over his shoulder and back again without losing a drop of the mixture. Not a very worthy object of admiration, let us concede, but a friend of mine, Professor George Herbert Clarke of Queen's University, Ontario, who was writing a monograph on Masefield, took the story so much to heart that he paid a visit to New York to find out if the tale were true and he had it verified by the saloonkeeper who was Masefield's boss. I do not wish to indicate here that such matters are the chief concern of academicians in Canada or poets laureate in England, but at least it does reflect some light upon a boy's capacity for astonishment, and much of that experience in New York was woven by Masefield into his poem *The Everlasting Mercy*. Those qualities of manual dexterity always excited us. Then I turned to Laurence Binyon, the keeper of the Egyptian section of the British

Museum. Mr Binyon was one of the ablest literary critics in England and one of the most serious, perhaps solemn, men of my acquaintance. My wife, who may have thought the conversation was becoming too flippant, asked him if he had ever had such an experience as a boy and to our astonishment he said that his youthful hero was a man whose hobby was spitting for incredible distances and with incredible accuracy. He used to make bets that he could drown a fly on the wing. He always won. Binyon had written a poem on the man but he couldn't find a magazine to publish it. You may understand what an edifying evening we had at our dinner table with Masefield leading off with an account of his life in New York.

I then said to him – 'Would you care to know what men stand out like pikestaffs in my youthful experience?' He said he would. So I told him about a man, I think it was in Fortune or Grand Bank, who spent years trying to beat the *Harlaw*'s whistle. I don't know where the old *Harlaw* is now but I remember how the inhabitants would swear at her when she woke them up at dead of night with the screams of the most infernal siren ever installed on a ship. Well, this man could put his first and third fingers in his mouth and drown out the *Harlaw* in power and vibrancy. And he used to do it in the middle of the night when the *Harlaw* wasn't in port just to wake up the inhabitants out of a sound sleep. He was only deterred from doing it every night by the threat of tar and feathers.[9] Masefield said that such a man was just made for a poem, for boys if you like.

I tried my hand, not at him indeed,[10] but [at] a few other types that were known to me, one a fisherman down north where I was teaching school, who had none of the sensational talents referred to but who was known or believed to have sworn only twice in his life, a negative accomplishment which practically amounted to genius in its own way. The poem is just a thumb-nail biography in thirty lines or so and is called 'The History of John Jones.' When that poem was published I received a letter of mild criticism from a Newfoundlander living in Vancouver who claimed that the allowance of two oaths in a lifetime must have been made under a system of rationing unknown either to war or peace – that I must have slipped up on my quota or the old salt must have come down from a generation of Puritans who were taught to put a watch on their lips. But I was just describing a phenomenon just about as hard to find as the competitor to the *Harlaw*.

Another type that is familiar to some of the older members here is the one who was always called upon to take charge of an emergency which might arise in a local community. In fact, that adaptability to varying conditions, that canny knack of knowing what to do in a crisis, that turning of the hand to multiple tasks, has generally been ascribed to Newfoundlanders as a native peculiarity. It is something I suppose which develops over a long time through people in sparsely settled communities being thrown back on their own resources. Every village has such an individual. It was a matter of – 'Go and get Uncle Joe at once. Tell Aunt Sally to come over. She'd know what to do.' Such people still elicit my respect and affection every bit as much as a great scientist or a great physician. It might be the blacksmith who would set a bone or take out a tooth. The job would be done effectively if roughly, provided toxaemia didn't set in or half the jaw didn't come off with the extraction. At least the tooth would be out. I speak from very feeling memories. I tried to describe an old nurse known to our grandmothers – a nurse who might be first aid and final aid, a dentist, apothecary, housemaid, housekeeper, cook, and possibly a doctor all in one. Angelina.

To come back to the more general theme of conflict on the sea with which I have been absorbed the most of my writing life, I should like to read a poem called 'Silences' ...[11]

'Introduction for a Reading'

I am going to spend this short session in reading some extracts from a few poems which deal with human action. I have always been interested in deeds, especially those which are performed for the saving of life – deeds which involve risk and sacrifice where the chances are piled up for death and the chances for survival are at a minimum – deeds done where there is no commercial equation, without a thought of getting anything out of it – nothing but a life to be saved or hearts to be resuscitated in an anxious home; and again deeds where there is certain death for the doer, and perhaps injury or death for those for whom the effort is made.

I do not need to emphasize this quality in Newfoundlanders for there is scarcely a point on the coastline which doesn't have its memories of rescue. The search for the lost is particularly a characteristic of the Newfoundland tradition[1] as it is part of the Christian tradition. I remember reading the account of the search for Sir Frederick Banting when his plane crashed in the woods off Musgrave Harbour.[2] When people referred to the search I replied that it was just Newfoundland routine – an instinctive impulse ...

From 'A Profile of a Canadian Poet'

Always in my mind is the importance of having the ending right; that's the reason why I write the end first. Then I go back over it. I want to make certain that the third act of the tragedy is in due form, proper form, and I gradually weave my way back to the beginning rather than [working] from the beginning to the end. I find that's more satisfactory because I have a terrible fear of anti-climax ...

We have moved away from clarity of expression into obscurity which I think is a bad drift. I believe in communication, in an experience which you have felt yourself and you want to communicate to another. And if a poem is couched in terms which are utterly difficult, unintelligible, half the value is gone for me.

'The Relation of Source Material to Poetry'

1. I have often had to combat a widespread impression that whereas in prose, especially of an historical or scientific character, a writer has to respect his sources, in verse he may be as cavalier as he pleases. What have the Muses to do with facts, with dates, with the commonplaces of this humdrum world?

If poetry just meant warbling, or just spinning fancies out of one's inner consciousness, there would be some force in the question. A bird does the first; a spider the second.

In subjective poetry – lyrics, songs, hymns, odes, personal sonnets, and the like – factual considerations are not regarded as of prime importance. It is the mood and the music, the turn of the phrase, the magic of words, that we look for. But when we enter the realm of objective poetry, descriptive, narrative, epic, dramatic, the knowledge of the subject is related to the aesthetic value of the result.

Let it be pointed out first that the communicated mood or the emotional response is fundamental in every variety of poetry, but that response is a very unstable compound influenced by a complexity of factors and one of these is the mastery of the subject achieved by the artist.

Of course, all of us know that there are some errors or anachronisms in poetry which do not, and should not, to any extent affect the evaluation. It depends upon the character of the errors, and I suppose that if one were to choose between a perfectly accurate but dull and an inaccurate but thrilling composition, one would prefer the latter.

But why offer the choice? The knowledge of the material should accompany the workmanship of the lines. When a writer composes an ode to Polaris and through ignorance locates the star somewhere in the vicinity of the Southern Cross, the reader receives a jolt which affects the aesthetics.

Naturally, the point does not apply to burlesque, parody, and some forms of light satire or extravaganza, for, when we realize that a writer is chuckling to himself while committing an intentional mistake, we chuckle with him, not at him. The point applies mainly to serious writing.

When Bridges brought out *The Testament of Beauty*,[1] readers and critics were struck not only with the nobility of the structure but with the scholarship and the eighty years of life and experience that lay behind it. Observation, reading, reflection, and knowledge of natural history were the components that, together with the form, constituted the achievement.

'Gie me a spark o' nature's fire. That's all the learnin' I desire'[2] expresses just one-half a truth – the necessary inspiration which Burns indubitably possessed in the highest degree. But he would never have reached his heights if he had logically followed out the romantic nonsense implicit in the stanza. The Muses breathed upon him or blew through him unquestionably, but the spark became a conflagration because the knowledge of life and literature was in his mind as abundant fuel for the blaze.

I remember the thrill I received a few years ago when Benét brought out his poetic reconstruction of the American Civil War in *John Brown's Body*.[3] In spite of the criticism of its changing metres and the introduction of so many stylistic forms such as ballads, songs, and prose insets which to some critics threatened the unity of the construction, it struck the world as a magnificent historical projection alive with poetic fire.

The passion was there fusing the facts, indeed. The battles were presented with the most thoroughgoing research, the fields visited, the geographical and topographical features painted with the fidelity of an eyewitness, the issues of the North and South objectively laid bare, the mind of the plantation owner and the mind of the slave imaginatively realized, the varying fortunes of the struggle portrayed with an amazing detachment, and the dramatic elements blended in the moving section towards the close.

I wonder how much of the triumph of the poem would have been reduced if the reader were continually frowning at the lazy slipshod exhibitions of an unhistorical sense. I have also in mind the toil of underbrushing, the sifting of material, before the constructive capacity really began to operate in the work of Edwin Arlington Robinson.

This obviously does not mean that, in writing a romantic poem based upon remote historical events, the writer is deprived of the invention of incident. If he may abridge or expand or select, he may under certain conditions transpose situations or invent particular characters, granted the dramatic or poetic purpose is thereby served.

But in most of the long poems I have read in the contemporary output, I have noticed that, wherever such alterations are made, the author takes pains to explain in a preface that he is making his departure and asks his readers to allow him the concession. He does not want to be convicted of ignorance. A self-conscious transposition or distortion may be acceptable provided the stand-point is conceded, but an unintentional error may be so comic as to become tragic.

Hence in a very fine poem by Archibald McLeish – *The Conquistador* – the author serves notice on his audience that if they find certain incidents in his story not vouched for by history, he has simply made them up. Legitimate, of course. But any preface like that is an explicit avowal that respect for the integrity of a source does not need justification whereas a violation does.

2. I have given as a title to this address 'The Relation of Source Material to Poetry.' It is a broad and ambitious title for it might have been called 'The Relation of Poetry to Knowledge or Its Relation to Science and the Humanities.' I had a feeling of presumption in the mere statement of the subject, as my own personal acquaintance with science is limited to what I can gather from my scientific friends who help me so kindly and liberally whenever I am engaged upon a task of beating a group of facts and impressions into verse.

I have often had to combat a widespread idea that whereas in prose, especially of an historical or scientific character, a writer has to respect his sources; in verse, he may be as cavalier as he pleases. What have the Muses to do with facts, with dates, with the prose commonplaces of this humdrum world? If poetry just meant warbling, or just spinning fancies out of one's inner consciousness, there would be some force in the question. A bird does the first; a spider the second. In subjective poetry – lyrics, songs, hymns, odes, personal sonnets, and the like – factual considerations are not regarded as of prime importance. But when we enter the field of objective poetry, descriptive, narrative, epic, dramatic, the know-ledge of the subject *is* related to the artistic value of the result. Communicated moods are dependent upon a large variety of factors as all of us know – turns of phrase, rhythms, unity of impression, a common area of experience and understanding, and the feeling on the part of the reader that a segment of life, however small the focus, has been mastered and presented. This is not to say that there isn't a huge difference in the quality of errors which might be committed. There is, and some mistakes are relatively insignificant, but a writer must always be on guard to see that there is no disturbance of the mood by a sloppy inadvertence. Sometimes in an otherwise fine artistic production an error may creep in and have the same effect on a listener as if, for example, a clergyman should perpetrate a blasphemous joke in the midst of an evangelical sermon or a prayer. Even if the joke were unintentional, the more profane element in the congregation would detect the aesthetic flaw within the moral edifice. All writers are aware of the dangers of anti-climax. When it is used consciously for given effects by such masters as Pope, Dryden, and especially Byron, it becomes a most effective weapon in satire, but if it is used unintentionally it boomerangs on the writer himself.

The necessity of research in dealing with historical subjects was brought home to me by many an experience and I discovered how the laugh could be turned against a writer even in the field of verse, as it has been turned against myself occasionally. In the writing of a poem on a sea rescue I had to learn something about the operation of directional wireless: so I decided to have a chat with my friend Professor Gilchrist of the Department of Physics in this university. He told me a story of what occurred several years before when a professor of history came to him to get the names of some recently discovered gases. The historian said that he was asked to write a poem to be read at a banquet in celebration of the twenty-fifth academic anniversary of the professor of chemistry. So the physicist named a number of gases rather casually not knowing to what use they were to be put – krypton, helium, zenon, argon. The historian thought argon sounded well – he was interested mainly in the sound: it suited his needs, and nothing further was said about the subject until the banquet was held and the chairman called upon the historian to deliver himself of his stanzas. After a few introductory lines the historian began to glorify the chemist by comparing him to argon. The chemists and physicists commenced to laugh, all but the chemist in whose honour the dinner was being held. The laughter became almost hysterical as the face of the chemist moved over into purple and violet zones, while the historian's voice became more and more liquid as he advanced towards his fiftieth Spenserian stanza. The other historians, the professors of English, and the laity generally, were at a loss to explain such hilarity from a reading which was after all meant to be a simple tribute to the chemist's alleged buoyancy and volatility, until it was whispered around that argon was the most inert gas that chemistry had discovered, that argon wouldn't unite peaceably with the other elements, let alone explode. The chemist, who was in reality quite the reverse of the chemical substance, shook his fist into the face of the innocent historian and the banquet almost became a riot. The incident is remembered today only on the ground of a scientific absurdity, while the Spenserian stanzas went into oblivion.

Well then, if we assume that, having committed himself to a definite source of material, a writer should respect the validity of that source, must he be limited in the kind of material he selects for poetic treatment? The treatment limitation, if it exists, depends more on the capacity of the writer than on the nature of the material. A history lies behind this question. There was a time when writers, the dramatists and the poets, relegated scientific material to prose out of a strange prepossession which was bound up with theories of inspiration and poetic diction, and with the belief that anything so mundane as a machine should be treated only in textbooks and manuals on experimental procedure. It is curious to observe the duration and intensity of the hold which that Romantic fallacy had upon the minds of writers. I suppose that the opposition between science and poetry was a phase of the conflict between science and religion. Most of the nineteenth-century writers were obsessed with the fear that physics and mathematics would take the soul out of the creative imagination. Rationalism had had its day in the eighteenth century, and the great name, above all names revered in that age, was that of

Newton. The veneration was brilliantly reflected in Pope's lines: 'Nature and Nature's laws lay hid in night. – God said – "Let Newton be, and all was light."'[4]

With the coming of the nineteenth century the winds veered, not among the scientists, but among the imaginative writers. They reacted against the Newton worship. I have always had a curious interest in that famous dinner which the artist Haydon gave to his friends including Lamb, Keats, and Wordsworth, and I should give a lot for a verbatim account of the conversation and speeches that preceded and followed the toast to Newton and Confusion to Mathematics. Coleridge didn't turn up, but it was known that he, too, moderated his enthusiasm for Newton by remarking that it would take two or three Galileos and Newtons to make one Kepler. At that dinner, however, there were three Romantics and the toast was proposed, 'Confusion to Mathematics.' I wonder what Wordsworth said. Did he drink the toast? Or did he just sip it? Was he hovering between his theory of the equation of analysis and murder and his admiration for the bust of Newton on which he was to forge[5] a glowing passage later in his career? We don't know. By the time the toast came round he may have been so far sunk in tranquillity as not to recollect his favourite emotion. But had Shelley been present, he might have pointed out the irony of the speeches, for the moment that they lifted their glasses to toast the confusion to science, Newton's principles were being beautifully demonstrated as the white light from Haydon's candelabra was being rainbowed through the best vintages brought up from Haydon's cellar. Most of the Romantics could admire a rainbow after rain, and they could describe it as a triumphal arch or the promise of God or what not, without knowing what caused it, but it is very difficult for realists (shall we call them?) to see that[6] a knowledge of origins should affect the beauty or otherwise of the results derived. Here the prism was just doing in a room what the vapour was doing in the sky.

That revolution is taking place today. I am not qualified to say how far the visual and plastic arts have gone in that[7] direction. All I wish to point out is that dynamos, lathes, drills, and turbines are just as much material for poetry as lilies and carnations and cuckoos, and they are humming their way into the measures of verse with the same ease and intimacy as the former reaping hook, the wheel, and the plough. The reaction has set in against a clash of interest – between the scientific in the broad sense and the artistic in the same broad sense – for the very good reason that we cannot afford to let the two intellectual paths diverge, and go independently. We are all making a common journey, a rough and dangerous one. We are reading every day about humanity at the crossroads. Every scientist is talking about the gulf ahead of us which must be bridged. It is at once a physical and spiritual gulf and all kinds of workers are needed in that supreme engineering.

If we were living in a Utopia, we should be building ivory towers along our coasts instead of lighthouses. The lighthouse is necessary because the sea is rough, and the harbour is not only a destination for trade but a haven for security. Life has become a sequence of calls and answers. Generations ago, captains, sailing along a coast in fog or darkness would blow their ship's whistle or shout and they might be answered by other captains, or they might [be] answered by rocks which might disclose their position in time, or too late. Men are always doing that on land or sea through instruments. A short while ago I spent an evening with an old Newfoundland student friend, Dr R.W. Boyle, formerly of the National Research Laboratories at Ottawa. We reminisced about our youthful days in Newfoundland, especially about our experiences with captains of coastal[8] steamers. When they were faced with some emergency, they possessed the knack of meeting it and generally overcoming it. When the regular mechanical aids were not at hand in a crisis, they could improvise substitutes. In a sense they picked up their navigation. When a captain came into port at night in a heavy fog, we might ask him the next morning how he did [it], when the usual maxim was 'When in danger or in doubt, stand out to sea.' His reply [would be] that he felt his way in. He blew the whistle and the echo hitting a rock or cliff would give him his location. Long after that my friend used to refer to science, or to this particular branch of it, as an elaborated method by which a practical device of the captain could be reduced to an exact system. Science has always been to me, as a layman without any expert knowledge, a form of poetry, a system of symbols and formulations which may look abstract and colourless enough on paper but when explained to our lay minds have the power to put new rhythms[9] in our pulses. What a road in the history of speech between the inarticulations of human beings thousands of years ago and the intricate communications summed up in words like telegraphy, wireless, radio, asdic, radar, and such like. There is still some meaning left in the definition of Romanticism as the expression of a sense of wonder, and certainly a good deal of the world's poetry has sprung out of that feeling of the unusual, for things that inspire awe, generally because they are not understood, or because, when they have been more or less understood by being brought under laws and principles, they maintain excited interests by reason of their critical and often unpredictable bearing on life. Even when we accept the inventions as contributing to our daily routines in entertainment and instruction we are caught by moments that shake our souls, as when we exclaimed during the war – 'Just think, that's a voice in Guadalcanal, or out of the jungles of Java, speaking this very second, or that is Churchill's voice, or, again, that's the voice of the dead – a disk containing a Roosevelt message.' We can hardly adjust ourselves to the statement of the rationalist – 'It's all physical of course; in a few years we will take it with as little concern as one another's voice in a room.' Perhaps so, but in those few years other events will be happening with new dramatic significance, constantly churning us up inside, making our hearts beat faster and our breathing harder. For myself I cannot get over the wonder of it, however old the invention. And so long as human interest and wonder and feeling exist in regard to any material of life, poetry may find its source for expression.

We know that any given fact is not a static object found to be self-contained at the moment of its discovery. It is alive and vocal, calling out for its immediate family, its blood relations. All its cousins, near and far removed, come in to take a look at its face to find out what position it should occupy in the family circle. It enters a world of functions and values. Starting, as it may, in a realm of abstract thought, it is soon led under the compulsion of its governing theory into the field of human deeds. And that field itself needs its own exploration and assessment. After the scientist in[10] theory and the technician in practice have launched their results, we ask what is the relation to human life. There should be no apology for the use of the abused word utilitarian when it is a matter of the abatement of human misery and the increase of human welfare. At first sight it might be said that an object such as a bulldozer could not be regarded as a thing of romantic beauty, but it is our neglect of the functional side of a machine which is responsible for that limited conception. Relate it to a deed and it takes[11] on a life colouring.

May I recall just here as an illustration an event which engrossed the hearts of us all three or four years ago which showed the fine stuff which has[12] entered into the composition of human nature, something so fine, so durable, that we have no descriptive terms adequate to its worth. Gold and iron, one precious, one strong, do not possess this kind of preciousness, this kind of strength. Our Western world just snapped to attention as to a salute during those three days in April, when the reports came in from San Marino, California, of the efforts made to save that little girl from the well-tomb. That the life was lost turned the drama into a tragedy but didn't dim the lustre of the effort. It was heartening to see the way the newspapers played up the event, crowding out the police court cases, the civil litigations, the tax evasions, even by-elections and political squabbles, to give a more just proportion to the most vital and valuable expressions of humanity. To have a whole state, a whole continent in fact, concerned with that boring-in to reach that fourteen-inch pipe; to put one-half a million dollars worth of mechanical equipment on the job and to have the diggers take the risk not for the money, but for the girl, for the life – that had the same effect upon us as if flags were flying all over the country, not at half-mast but at the masthead, bearing the signal – 'Let no one do a mean deed today.' One reporter called the action 'Operation Cathy' – which seemed to me a real inspiration, for an Operation with a capital O it was indeed, with the bulldozers, cranes, electric drills working by day, working by night under powerful floodlights as if it were a highway or a mountain tunnel. Outwardly it looked the same – only the motive was different. The scientists, the mechanics, the men of good will, the men of brawn and brain all joined hands in that high spiritual union. The operation carried with it a beauty as wonderful as that of a sunrise or a mountain range. The newspapers, the journals, the air and the ether went all out for the publicity of the action, and I have kept repeating to myself ever since the question, as I did at the time of the Moose River Mine Rescue[13] and at the time of the search for Banting in the woods off Musgrave Harbour, Newfoundland[14] – What are newspapers meant for anyway but to tell the world of those fine things? What are the air and ether made for but to transmit those glorious despatches of human valour and sacrifice not for the taking of life but for the saving of it. And all the more is it necessary when the age is so full of lamentation combined with cynicism over the insignificance of human life and its moral negations.

A great deal of our life is made up of those calls and answers where the machine, the product of man's hand, is put at the service of his mind and heart. And I am convinced that literature must make it a prime concern to explore that source of material. Men have been hailing one another across centuries and continents. The dead have chimed in with the living and the living with the dead, and to catch the rhythm is a legitimate function of poetry. I imagine that this is what in a fundamental sense Wordsworth[15] had in mind when he gave his inspired definition of poetry as the impassioned expression which is in the countenance of all science.

'On Publishing'

I feel very much honoured at being asked to give an address to this group this afternoon. My friend Mr Mackenzie[1] asked me if I would make a combination of an address and a recital. I am glad that he did not ask me to read verse and go on reading for fifty minutes. There was a time long ago when, in my callow enthusiasm, I used to read verse hours on end, and though I was frequently in a state of exhaustion myself I never realized how serious was the condition of my audience. With that in mind, I shall read only briefly and talk at greater length. I am going to talk about some efforts and failures to get into print some years ago, and I am telling it largely to illustrate how fallible and untrustworthy a writer's judgement may be about his own production, especially just after he has produced it, and I think it pertains more to the writing of verse than to the exercise of any other form of art. At least that is how it appears to me.

A number of questions were put to me by Mr Mackenzie and by others in the last week or so. Would I answer them? I may not be able to answer them adequately, so please take my answers as mere speculations. What is the connection between artistic finish and commercial publication? Would a person write better poetry and take more trouble about it if he knew that it was going to be published? Is he interested in publication anyway? In writing an historical poem what is the relation between source material and poetry? This last question is too involved to do it justice here. May one produce poetry out of propaganda? I suppose propaganda might be construed on such high and comprehensive grounds that poetry could issue from it, but generally I think that where the intention is so stated at the beginning, the propaganda becomes lost in the poetic construction. The *Paradise Lost* is the example quoted most often. The epic may be taken at its sublime level as poetry without any feeling that the ways of God have been vindicated to men. If, on the other hand, the intention is crassly stated on a low plane that a poem is going to be written to advocate high tariffs or the fitness of a candidate to run as a mayor for Toronto, we feel that the verse that follows may not get into the high brackets either morally or artistically. My own personal feeling about it is that whatever high merits come out of propaganda, they do so only as by-products and often as accidents.

May I attempt to answer the other questions by way of personal reminiscence and by way of acknowledged failures.

I started out most ambitiously and with a cocksure confidence that I would storm Parnassus with my first effort. I had graduated from the University of Toronto in philosophy; had, in fact, actually taken my Ph.D., and I was consumed with a desire to write a philosophico-lyrical drama in which all I had learned and taught in philosophy and psychology would be presented to the public in a verse composition. I spent two years upon it, which really meant two summers and two Christmas vacations, and in my chesty self-confidence I thought that in this full-dress, five-act play in blank verse interspersed with a few choruses I had something which was Elizabethan in character. It was certainly Elizabethan in carnage – in the number of persons despatched through their bloody exits. They were lying all over the floor with daggers and bullets through them, the dying and the dead in one awful mess.[2] I dignified this so-called poem with a title 'Clay,' but I had enough sense to submit it to a few of my friends who were also literary critics, particularly my honoured chief Professor Edgar.[3] I remember now their attempts to say something nice about it without betraying their critical integrity, but I detected a sober undercurrent of scepticism, [a] mood of 'This will never do' although it wasn't so bluntly articulated. I came to the bitter reflection that these critics, who were also personally friendly to me, did not like it. Then I went to see a publisher who said – 'Yes, we'll publish it but at your expense.' As my salary then was so low that it wasn't taxable, I said 'No.'[4]

I went home that evening and piled up the twenty typed copies of 'Clay' and I said to my wife – 'I am going to burn them.' She replied – 'If you think you must, all right, but before you do so, answer one question – Why did you call it "Clay"?' And my only answer was – 'Why not?' There was something ominously prophetic about the title. All the hopes of two years crashed, and I shall not forget the effort of the will as well as of the fingers, when I tore the tremendous manuscript to shreds in all its copies and sent it into the flames. It was like the strangulation of a child. I could feel the vertebrae creak and crack and the jugular get tighter and tighter. The only thing in the world that really wanted that poem was the fire. The flames caressed it, greedily licked it, and finally devoured it. In a few minutes the fire itself was dead.

When I recovered from my bereavement with the passage of time, I asked myself what was wrong. I discovered that Mrs Pratt, unknown to me, had salvaged one copy. I re-read the poem this time like a stranger with a cold, critical eye and found that although there were thousands and thousands of lines, yet it was only thousands and thousands of lines. It was full of theories and reflection of theories, ethical maxims, philosophical truisms, bald, very bald generalizations – practically the whole cargo of the department of philosophy and psychology as it existed twenty years or so ago in the University of Toronto. I came around to the conviction that philosophical and ethical insights whenever they find their way into poetry should be emotional renderings of experiences actually lived or imaginatively grasped. For the writing of that alleged poem all that was necessary was a fountain pen and unlimited paper.[5]

There is another point I might state just here. I think that the worst time to send a poem to an editor is just after it is written. A father never knows what the baby is going to look like after a few weeks or a few months. It takes time for the features to form. I remember the rather inept remark a man made when he came over to the house of a friend to see the newly arrived. The parents naturally were in a state of ecstasy but still were in some doubt, at least the father was, that the infant might grow into a John Barrymore, and they asked their friend for his opinion. He replied – 'All I can say is that the boy looks healthy.' A poet cannot even say that about a poem. He may have his opinion, but he had better defer getting the editor's opinion for a few weeks because the editor might not like either the health or the looks.

I determined that I should not make the same mistake about 'Clay' again so for the next two or three years I wrote a good deal of verse upon the seafaring life of Newfoundland where I was born and brought up, threw overboard half of the poems, and submitted the rest to Lorne Pierce of the Ryerson Press who decided out of the goodness of his heart to bring out a volume under the title *Newfoundland Verse*. It was generously received[6] by the reviewers, particularly by a man to whom I owe a great debt, Mr Morgan-Powell of the *Montreal Star*. The book sold moderately well and it gave me a confidence rudely shattered by 'Clay.' *Newfoundland Verse* had a lot of defects, a lot of immaturities, and now after twenty years I feel that only about one-third of the contents could properly be included in a collected edition, and this brings me to another point,[7] that is, the relationship between a writer and his audience. Sometimes you hear the remark on the part of young writers, 'Oh I am writing just for myself. If I satisfy my own high standards, that is the artistic achievement. I am interested more in self-expression than in communication. I don't care what the ignorant public think about it at all. What do they know about art and the expression of the inner moods of the sensitive soul?' I think there is a great deal of self-delusion and self-infatuation in that standpoint and the answer is to be found in the later behaviour of the artist himself. The behaviour contradicts the theory. I have mixed up a lot in my time with craftsmen of all the arts and I have never met one musician who did not want his score transmitted, not one song-writer who did not want to hear his song sung, not one painter who was uninterested in a gallery exhibit, not one sculptor who placed the sign 'No Admittance' on the door of his studio, and I may say not one serious writer, whether novelist, dramatist, essayist, or poet, who, despite his assumed indifference to public concern, did not at least once knock at the back door of a publishing house, or who did not get at least one rejection slip from the editor of a magazine. I said not one *serious* artist who regarded his work as an important part of his life's activity. I think we should concede that there is a place for the writing of poems that never see the light of day, that some poems should not, and I include a lot of mine own in that classification, that some poems exhaust their whole function when they furnish a psychological release for the poetic patient, that self-expression has a primary and fundamental quality, but to detach it as a general principle from any kind of social contact is like trying to start a fire by a lighted match without any fuel. The artist and the audience are complementary.

There are of course pitfalls in any unqualified statement. To say that the public at large and at any given time are the final authority upon the pretensions of art is as wrong as to say that the individual artist is the ultimate tribunal. Popularity itself is a very variable court of appeal. It happens to be right sometimes as when fiction and poetry, making their first appeal to the thousands and even to the millions, maintained that same appeal for generations and centuries both to the lay readers and the professional critics. And conversely it happens to be equally wrong when works which enjoyed an immediate response because of a tinsel brilliancy were later consigned to oblivion as the fashion went out of date, or the voice crooned or croaked itself into a sleep from which there is no awaking.

On the other hand, to say, as Ibsen remarked,[8] that the minority is always right, is itself an ambiguous proposition. Who constitute the minority? Do not the minority, if they live long enough to get the allegiance of the majority, point to the fact of that allegiance, and say – 'We told you so; we were right after all.' The whole question boils down to the matter of an audience and the constitution of that audience, to the time the audience takes to assemble and the time they stay to listen. Amidst all the complicated factors in estimating art, the audience is the constant. And the publisher's job is to secure that audience.[9]

That brings me back to my own personal experiences which I have been asked to relate. *Newfoundland Verse* was for me a bit of apprenticeship with large chunks of crude stuff where the axe cut in against the grain. But at least I discovered for myself that poetry blossomed more healthily out of the concrete than out of abstractions. It came best out of the imagination working upon the material of actual experience. My aim was to get the emotional effect out of the image or the symbol operating on the facts of sense perception, and my next effort was an experiment in technical adventure. I went back in my mind and ruminated upon the monstrosity called 'Clay.' Could I afford to spend another whole year for the sake of producing a dud, for I was sure that the scepticism of my critical friends and the more than scepticism of the[10] publisher was justified. So I embarked upon a thing called *The Witches' Brew*. I had recently completed a treatise for my Ph.D. upon a subject which I heartily disliked called 'Studies in Pauline Eschatology,' which traced the history of Paul's ideas on the soul and particularly on Hell. My friends say that *The Witches' Brew* was a psychological reaction against the doctorate, that I had to get hell out of my system before I could do anything worthy of serious consideration. I fear that I haven't it all out yet but that was their theory of the origin of the poem. It was one of the few poems that I wrote without any thought that it would ever be published. Not that I was averse to publication but I did not think it needed publication. It was done for an occasion merely. The occasion happened to be the fifth anniversary of our wedding day. My friend Professor Arthur Phelps[11] who was spending a holiday near us at Bobcaygeon on the Kawartha Lakes suggested that I write something to signalize the occasion, something that would be written for entertainment only, just for fun, if that was possible, without any thought of fixing up society or reforming the world, something which a few persons invited to the dinner might possibly enjoy after the last course. When my wife asked me about the subject I said that I was going to deal with the effect of alcohol on fish, an absurd topic unquestionably. I did not attach any literary importance to the production. I don't yet. Professor Phelps suggested that I send it to a publisher which I did, not expecting for a moment that it would be accepted. I sent it to a London (England)[12] publisher, who to my greatest surprise decided to bring out five hundred copies, this time at his expense. I may say incidentally that this publisher[13] went out of business three months afterwards, but not before I made the acquaintance of two critics, one in Aberdeen, the other on the staff of the *Edinburgh Scotsman*. Is it worth mentioning here that the only serious criticism I got in Great Britain was from Scotchmen? Both literary critics searched for hidden meanings and symbolism, but not finding them claimed that the book was a libel on the brands and therefore a temperance pamphlet, or that it might conceivably be an advertisement but exceedingly obscure. I was asked later by a theologian what I meant. My only answer was that I saw a unique opportunity of bringing together a strange assortment of individuals[14] – Milton and Paracelsus, Sir Isaac Newton and William Blake, Gulliver and Bottom, Byron and Pepys, John Calvin, John Knox, John Wesley, Johnny Walker – bringing them all together to discuss the nature of design in a mad universe over the bodies of inebriated fish. The answer did not appear to be quite satisfactory.

As the public did not feel disposed to buy many copies of the book I felt I had accomplished another failure. 'Clay' was too serious, *The Witches' Brew* too absurd. What was left? I came at last to realize that there was a great field of relatively unexplored soil ready for poetic handling, that is, the field of science. Not that science in some phase or other had not furnished topics for poems. It had, but when one considers the total output of verse in a given country or in a given age, scientific material has generally been neglected, probably out of a widespread and to my mind false notion that scientific or technical knowledge is unromantic. It is my conviction that in the years to come the great subjects for the imaginative writer will come out of science, and out of the humanization of science, taking that term in its wide and most cultural significance, where it stands as the ally of the human spirit in search of its finest goals. However, to come back to personal matters again, I began hunting for a subject which would require some research and give body to poetry and I thought of whale-fishing. I had seen whales alive and dead. I had seen them in the harbours of Newfoundland, particularly at Moreton's Harbour where I taught school for two years.[15] I rowed around them where they lay dead after capture prior to their manufacture into oil. I realized that at last I had a subject which could lend itself to research – to the digging up of the raw material which, while perfectly authentic, appeared absolutely incredible to people who had never seen a whale. The dramatic possibilities were enormous. Everything was drawn to the huge scale and yet the dimensions were accurate except where they were obviously and intentionally magnified (I believe I did enlarge the liver somewhat). Here, then, was material which had all the wonder of romance and yet [was] mathematically exact. That resulted in a poem called *The Cachalot* which I read to the Club at the request of Fred Banting because I had referred to the pancreas of a one-hundred-ton cachalot.[16]

'On Macmillan'

A year ago I had the good fortune to be honoured with an invitation to the Macmillan Annual Dinner. I consider myself doubly honoured this evening for I do not know of any aggregation of people sitting down at a table outside of our domestic circle where I can count so many personal friends. I do not look upon the Macmillan Publishing House merely as a great impersonal business concern which makes contracts with its authors and editors and tradesmen, but as a large family in a city community where I may visit very frequently, where I can always be assured of honest dealing, good faith, and, what is just as important, a large measure of good will and affection that one associates with a home. Not often have I made such a lasting and profound friendship as I have with the president of the house.[1] I count it an honour to include him and Mrs Eayrs amongst my most intimate and cherished companions and that esteem is likewise given to all the members of the staff ...

'My First Book'

One of the most common questions I am asked – culminated by the threatening demand of the editor of the *Canadian Author and Bookman* – is 'What turned you to writing in the first place?' Well, I really cannot answer that. I certainly cannot lay much claim to precocity. Fortunately there are no records to the effect that, 'This was written at six years of age, this at ten, this at thirteen'! I am very thankful that the reading world has been spared those juvenile and adolescent masterpieces. It is true that I scribbled bits of verse when I was going to public and high schools, but this was written generally as lampoons on the teachers, after being stood in the Fool's Corner for an hour. The result, however, was of some importance for I enjoyed the experience of a boyish retaliation, heightened by the fun my classmates got when I read the lines, and I soon realized that there was something about rhyme and rhythm which acted as a very superior substitute for the blasphemous clichés which easily fall from student lips, following the discovery of mischief.

Much of this stuff was satirical and transitory, but nevertheless it was a form of self-expression which could just as easily find an outlet through lyrical, narrative, and dramatic modes. There was a quality about a really well-turned line which gave me a great internal satisfaction.

I soon realized that my problem was one of communication. How could I transmit that pleasure to others? I felt that it was an all-important problem, for I have never seen the value of exclusive self-expression. There is too much implicit contempt for the reader if the poet compels him – after reading a poem – to ask, 'What is the writer thinking about? Is he attempting to describe a chimpanzee or a mushroom? Did he get paid for that line of asterisks? Do they represent personal profundities far deeper than the plummet of language can fathom – or are they just stanza divisions?'

There was a lot of that in the air less than a generation ago. Some of it has disappeared, for which we must thank the rational impatience of the reading public.

I was caught in this maelstrom myself. Fortunately, before I got close to the falls I was rescued. I suffered some damage before the rescue was affected but I did learn one lesson – to put a manuscript in a drawer for a few weeks or months before submitting it for publication. I began to realize that presenting a poem to a magazine immediately after writing was the same as displaying a day-old baby to the neighbours before the features took on colouring and formation. I discovered that neither editors nor neighbours react to a new-born prodigy in the same way as its parents! This took a long time to learn and many a brain-child was sturdily slapped on the stern by an objective examiner and promptly sent back to the progenitor for further care and decent apparel.

My first book was *Newfoundland Verse*, an attractively produced, chunky little volume which appeared under the Ryerson Press imprint in 1923. Lorne Pierce selected a number of poems out of a much more numerous batch, and put them into the collection.

But before submitting them I had spent two or three years in composing verses, long and short. One long poem was entitled 'Clay' – a tragedy in five acts which I thought was Elizabethan. It was that indeed – but only in the carnage which gave the characters their bloody exits![1] I did not offer it to a publisher but read it to a group of my critical friends who said 'No,' in unambiguous terms. The savour of blood and the dagger thrusts reminded me later of Webster at his worst. It never saw the full glare of day. There were other shorter poems marked by too much facility of language. These I sorted out myself aided by critics like Pelham Edgar who remarked only too often, 'This will never do.'

Nevertheless I had the satisfaction of seeing a few of them in the *London Mercury*, the *London Bookman*, the *Manchester Guardian*, and in several of the Canadian magazines. *The Ice-Floes* had a prior publication in the *Shorter Poems* edited by Professor Alexander[2] for the high schools of Ontario. There was no royalty here but the promotional value was far ahead of the few dollars which might have been extracted.

Critics have been good for me, as well as – on the whole – to me. I have always been grateful to the critics who, animated by no personal prejudice, and sincerely interested in the poetic art, returned rejection slips with the conventional regrets. Occasionally a poem was sent back which I thought, and still think, creditable, but on the whole the criticism was an invaluable spur to self-examination.

I feel that the art of criticism is vitally related to the art of composition. It is subject to the same caprices, temporary judgements, and fallacies. One critic may not like the subject matter; another, the treatment; another, the concern with the 'time-spirit' or the political and economic aspects of the age; another, the emphasis on 'art for art's sake,' and these prepossessions are bound to leave their stamp. But, as a rule, the critical assessment has an enlivening and helpful result. I have known writers who, imagining eternal absolutes in their work, have gone their own way, oblivious to all comment. I believe this to be a mistake, for one is apt to get one's head into the sand and become blind to what is going on in a world which develops in art as well as in science. The best that a writer can hope for is a fair number of critical readers who can find something exhilarating enough in his writing to read it, and be candidly reasonable about its merits and defects.[3]

I am afraid my relations with publishers lack any dramatic highlights. There have only been three of them during the thirty-year span from *Newfoundland Verse* to *Towards the Last Spike*. First was Dr Lorne Pierce, then as now the sympathetically erudite editor of Ryerson Press. Then came the late Hugh Eayrs, head of Macmillan of Canada, and his successor, at Macmillan's, my present publisher, John Gray.

I have no complaints of any publishers – quite the contrary! Loyalty and deep friendship always marked our relationship. Occasionally they may have looked a bit dubious over a manuscript. But whenever differences arose over the poetic merit or the market value of a poem, such differences were resolved through amicable discussion and never once through physical or verbal violence.

To return to that first volume, I realized that Lorne's exclusions in the majority of cases showed sound judgement, but he retained enough to make, from my point of view, a satisfying book. When it appeared, I had visions of transcontinental tours out of the royalties. I had, however, to be contented with the exhaustion of an edition of one thousand. The purchasers did not line up four-deep at the bookstalls and my projected tours were limited to more modest excursions from Toronto to Mimico or Whitby!

It is difficult to assess the effect upon me or my writing of the publication of this first book. It naturally had a stimulating effect, derived from the encouragement.

But the general tone of my work seems to have been subtly

altered. I cannot say that this sprang out of a conscious effort on my part for it was scarcely deliberated. It may have developed out of a hidden desire to mix phantasy with realism – a desire which has never left me. Be that as it may, my next volume was *The Witches' Brew*, published in England by Selwyn and Blount and in Canada by Macmillan's. My old friend, Arthur L. Phelps, suggested that I write a poem in hilarious celebration of an impending fifth wedding anniversary, and that it should be read aloud in the presence of my wife, with Art and Lal Phelps and a few others invited in to our cottage at Bobcaygeon. The theme was a wild one – the effect of alcohol on fish. The first draft was about fifty lines, but for some reason I couldn't stop and the final draft ran into several hundred lines, with the Shades coming up from Hades to observe and discuss the reflexes of the marines. It was mad stuff, indeed! Some reviewers wondered if the poem was a temperance pamphlet or the reverse.

This poem was followed the next year by *The Cachalot* and *The Great Feud*, the two long poems which make the volume *Titans*, which continue the phantasy but this time blend into it a strong dash of realism and research.

Interviews

Interview by Ronald Hambleton on 'An Experience of Life' 1955

HAMBLETON: A great many people have praised you, Mr Pratt – and rightly – for being a master of direct, swift-paced narrative poetry. But to me at least, you are also something more disturbing – which I am going to describe in a deliberately exaggerated way as a sad-voiced harbinger of doom.

PRATT: I'm not a harbinger of doom. I am mainly a writer of tragic situations relating to the sea.

HAMBLETON: It's as if you were forever conscious of sad mortality ... beauty that must die, and youth whose hand is ever at his lips bidding adieu.[1]

PRATT: Perhaps it is true that the note of direct optimism isn't sounded very often in my poetry, but I think you are going a little too far to describe me in terms of Keats, who hardly ever mentioned joy without mentioning at the same time that it was fleeting, slipping from his grasp.

HAMBLETON: And do you think the word 'doom' is too strong?

PRATT: I consider myself lucky you didn't use the word 'destruction.' I don't think my work is of the same order as the *Apocalypse*. Still, we should look at this observation of yours pretty closely, and perhaps by rephrasing it a little, arrive at my particular view of life – if I have one at all.

HAMBLETON: Will it be a view of life that has slowly matured, or did you undergo in your youth some violent conversion?

PRATT: Even a violent conversion in youth would change gradually over the years, I think – become modified. In my case, it would be truer to say that my earliest years formed in me a tendency to (perhaps you might call it) fatalism, tempered with humanity. We were always close to death.

HAMBLETON: You and your family, you mean? Was this a characteristic of your life in Newfoundland?

PRATT: Oh, yes. My father was a Methodist clergyman, and he seemed rather moderate in his views in a community with a strong Calvinistic affinity. Oh, the preaching I listened to as a boy! We got heaven and hell drummed into us. At seven or eight years of age, I listened to the actual crackling of the flames.

HAMBLETON: And this was a moderate viewpoint?

PRATT: There was no predestination, as the Calvinists believed. They insisted you were doomed at birth, damned without hope of redemption. But the Methodists had a relieving philosophy – there was [the] possibility of repentance. We grew up in this atmosphere. My father often quoted the line, I remember it so well: 'When the lamp holds out to burn, the vilest sinner may return.' 'Vilest,' you see. Sin was a malaise to be cured in all forms. When the fishermen came back from Labrador, they backslid of course. Had to go to the penitent form outside the church. Ask God publicly for repentance.

HAMBLETON: Your father had a ministry among the fishermen of Newfoundland. I suppose he was a native – he, and your mother?

PRATT: My mother was Newfoundland born, but not my father. He grew up amidst the English Calvinists. Five boys and three girls, big family – but my father never once gave us a crack that hurt. He radiated kindness. His view was moderate Methodism. Life was better than the creed.

HAMBLETON: But this doesn't suggest a strong atmosphere of death – you said you were always close to death.

PRATT: So we were. There was death at sea, in the terrible storms of the Atlantic. Often, my father had the task of breaking the news of yet another death to a new widow in the community. I remember him saying, 'How can I tell her? How can I tell her?' And my mother: she had strong faith, but she said, 'Why did God allow this?'

HAMBLETON: Of course, this is a principle of determinism: that no act of ours can hold back the tragedies of life.

PRATT: 'God did not ordain tragedy, but permitted it.' The first thing I ever wrote (a long narrative poem) concerns the loss of an only son at sea.[2] We were brought up in the belief of the goodness of God and yet we had to reconcile tragedy with it. We were always under that shadow.

HAMBLETON: Perhaps, then, it is not so much the shadow of death, or of doom, but the shadow of inevitable tragedy – and tragedy has many forms. This is nearer to what I was trying to say at the beginning: that the outcome of all is tragedy, and the tragedy is inevitable.

PRATT: I am tempted to believe at times very strongly in fate.

HAMBLETON: This is a kind of determinism too.

PRATT: No, it's different. I mean the convergence of the twain – after the fashion of Thomas Hardy – where two unrelated events or circumstances lead like converging lines to one end. Often, there is the convergence of the manifold: things we lightly call coincidences.

HAMBLETON: In ordinary life, it's not considered particularly ominous, to be afflicted with coincidences.

PRATT: I came out of my house not long ago and just missed the bus, by a fraction of a minute. Suppose for fifteen days or fifteen weeks I missed my bus by that precise margin of time each day? Wouldn't I have reason to think there was some design in the coincidences?

HAMBLETON: You could avoid it by leaving the house earlier.

PRATT: But then, the bus is ahead of schedule, and whizzes by still earlier. That looks like fate – it's one of Hardy's 'mood-dictated impressions.'

HAMBLETON: Of course, this kind of coincidence has little meaning, because nothing of importance hangs upon it. But what I detect in your poetry is the recognition of the importance in trivial things. You seem to say that the world is living an ironic drama.

PRATT: Irony is connected with fate – and cannot be extricated from it. My father, you see, often could not go directly to break the news of a death at sea. Sometimes he had to combine this heavy task with his ordinary pastoral visit. This is the purest irony.

HAMBLETON: He would be greeted with the ordinary carefree and smiling welcome, until something in his manner perhaps showed the woman that this was no ordinary visit.

PRATT: Yes, and from then on, his pastoral visits would be associated in that family with the tragic announcement he made then.

HAMBLETON: It would tend to predispose you, a sensitive child, to a recognition of the still sad music of humanity.

PRATT: At university I was plunged in even deeper than that. I went to study philosophy, and in those days they were mostly fatalists. Lectures were full of determinism – nothing in life could be altered.

HAMBLETON: No free will?

PRATT: None. And I got a tremendous dose of Hardy in his prose and novels. This was another addition to my philosophy. Because he says: over all coincidences, there is a universal will determining the outcome. There were two kinds of philosophy being taught at the university thirty years ago: idealism and determinism. I scarcely got a whiff of idealism, though I liked it and wanted it. It was a desire in me, a deep wish. Later on, I got rid of most of this stuff in a five-act verse play I wrote called 'Clay.'³ A deadly thing to read now. I unburdened myself of all the philosophic cargo I'd amassed at college.

HAMBLETON: Didn't you salvage any of it?

PRATT: The best things in it were some lyrics – in a minor key, very sad.

HAMBLETON: You seem to represent the convergence of the manifold about as much as anyone.

PRATT: In what sense?

HAMBLETON: As a, shall we say, tragic poet of the sea. You are Newfoundland born – in the middle of the Atlantic, so to speak. You were the son of a man whose task it was to express grief to others, share their sadness, but never to feel the same kind of grief himself. You happened to fall into a university at a time when a rather specialized kind of philosophy was being taught. There you have three lines of convergence. I suppose it was pure accident, coincidental, that perhaps your most representative poem, written in your most idiomatic verse, concerns the sea?

PRATT: *The Titanic*, you mean.

HAMBLETON: Yes. A tragedy at sea.

PRATT: This sea-tragedy is to me the most tremendous example of all we have been discussing. If I had not been predisposed towards fate already, the loss of the *Titanic* would have created a belief.

HAMBLETON: Were you personally connected with it?

PRATT: In a curious way. It was early in this century; I was taking junior matriculation, and some of us schoolboys were taken from college to the House of Assembly in St John's to observe a wireless experiment conducted by Marconi. He had gained permission to try an experiment from Signal Hill, his task being to receive a wireless signal from an associate in Cornwall. In 1901, it was. Well, when he was successful, the papers took it up like mad.

HAMBLETON: It opened up a new era.

PRATT: But the papers! I still remember the headlines: NO MORE LOSSES AT SEA! Great banner headlines – because now, you see, ships could be equipped with radio and summon help. Eleven years later, the *Titanic* went down. And it went down just south of the spot where the clicks of the instrument hit the ears of the scientists.

HAMBLETON: That's pure irony, too.

PRATT: The whole tragedy is.

HAMBLETON: In the strictest sense we have been adhering to?

PRATT: Without a doubt.

HAMBLETON: In that there were manifold circumstances converging on one event? I suppose also, converging on one geographical point in the Atlantic.

PRATT: There was a lot about that I didn't put into my poem. We're all familiar with the superficial details of the disaster: that this was the great unsinkable ship, the sea utterly calm, the night quiet and clear. The atmosphere radiated confidence.

HAMBLETON: And the ship was not in the northern latitudes, where icebergs are frequently found.

PRATT: Few would have dreamt of seeing an iceberg so far south in

April. And remember, not a man aboard was willing his own destruction or anyone else's destruction. Their volition was toward the living, but that volition was neutralized by ignorance.

HAMBLETON: How?

PRATT: Perhaps ignorance of danger. The *Titanic* was equipped with only one-third the regulation number of lifeboats – because she was known to be unsinkable.

HAMBLETON: But still, were men prompt to act when danger struck?

PRATT: Well, imagine. In that quiet water, a shock that passed away at once. There was no splintering crash, no terrifying inrush of water. Rather a shudder. When the wireless operator felt it, he delayed five minutes before he sent out his s.o.s.

HAMBLETON: Not to provoke uneasiness among the passengers.

PRATT: With good reason. There were hundreds in the steerage who couldn't understand English; they would be confused by orders from an officer. The captain wanted to avoid panic. These strands of circumstance leading the *Titanic* to its disaster. The *Californian* only twelve miles away – she could have reached the *Titanic* easily in the two and a half hours there were. An officer of the *Californian* actually saw the distress rockets of the *Titanic*, reported this to his captain, who refused to take it seriously. Said it was fishermen.

HAMBLETON: And all the while they were appealing for help.

PRATT: And there was the irony of the gaiety, and the Strauss waltzes, and the ship ablaze with light.

HAMBLETON: And as you say, 'the foxtrot's sublime irrelevance.'

PRATT: And, over all, this sense of security.

HAMBLETON: But how meaningless, this security.

PRATT: This is to me the terrible contrast between the tragedy of the *Titanic* and the tragedy of Brébeuf. When Brébeuf and Lalemant were destroyed by the Indians, it was they, the two Jesuits, who *chose* to be. It was free will entirely. But when two thousand people died with the *Titanic*, there was no free will.

HAMBLETON: It's curious, isn't it, that the sea-death is called an act of God, but not the other. 'God does not ordain a tragedy, but permits it.' Does that apply with equal strength to both, do you think?

PRATT: Brébeuf and Lalemant wished for death. They had asked themselves long before: shall I go through with this mission work in New France and take everything that's coming, or not? They were continually putting themselves into a condition of capture. They knew death by hatchets would come someday. There was an ecstasy in their hearts at the time of death.

HAMBLETON: Which is more terrible? The lives lost on the unsinkable *Titanic*, with everyone believing the best; or the lives lost in Huronia, with the martyrs believing the worst?

PRATT: To me, there is no hesitation. Two sorts and conditions of men: one with faith in their ship, faith in a material structure; the other with faith in Christ, faith in a spiritual heritage.

HAMBLETON: If we keep the hesitant definition of fate we arrived at a few minutes ago – that is, a series of coincidences that make for tragedy – then we have to admit that both these tragedies were fashioned by fateful coincidences. Except that in the case of the Jesuit missionaries, the coincidences were man-made. Made by man's free will.

PRATT: That is what elevates the tragedy of Brébeuf above the tragedy of the *Titanic*. It was a spiritual relief to me to get at *Brébeuf* after the *Titanic*. I was dealing not with fate but with faith. There is nothing very exalting about a tragedy like the *Titanic*, a disaster due to stupidity. I have in mind a personal consolation. To live eternally amid the *Titanic* disaster would be a depressant; but *Brébeuf*, even though a tragedy, was a spiritual stimulant.

Interview by Jed Adams on 'First Person'   1959

ADAMS: What do you answer when people ask you how you write? How do you go about the business of writing?

PRATT: Well ... an idea comes to your mind and it's nebulous at first and it takes shape by continuous reflection on it. And always in my mind is the importance of having the ending right. That's the reason why I write the end first.

ANNOUNCER: That was E.J. Pratt, Canada's epic poet, chatting informally with Jed Adams. This is *First Person*, a series dealing with autobiographies in sound of famous people. Tonight's *First Person* guest, E.J. Pratt, recalls events and experiences from his own life. Ned Pratt, who in his lifetime has written more than ten volumes of verse, is well qualified to continue his observations to Jed Adams on how to write.

PRATT: I gradually weave my way back to the beginning, rather than from the beginning to the end. I find that's more satisfactory because I have a terrible fear of anti-climax. That's the reason why I want the ending to be good, if possible. For instance, in *The Titanic* the conclusion is very important indeed. When she sinks, the only thing on the ocean, the Atlantic, is the presence of the iceberg. It's the master of the ocean now after this colossal destruction has taken place and it has the look of a face, an amorphous, I call it a paleolithic face, like a monster, a half-human and half, well, granite or ice, you see, remorseless and careless and indifferent to the tragedy. I want to make certain that that's on the ocean after the *Titanic* went down.

ADAMS: Another poet, Carl Sandburg, said once that a writer must write what he thinks; a poet must write what he must. How do you feel about that?

PRATT: Well, I think there's a great deal of truth in that, but I don't think I'd undertake a thing that I didn't feel under compulsion to do. You'd give up lots of things; you start things and you give them up and you find that there isn't the inner breathing or fire. But I always think of the distinction between an opinion and a conviction: that you take hold of an opinion but that a conviction takes hold of you. That's what I believe in the selection of topics for poetry and the writing of poetry. You have to do it. You feel you must get that out of your system. It's like an organic disease if you like. It has to be cured by being written out. I felt it all along, even with little poems, short ones of ten or twelve lines, a little vignette.

ADAMS: Ned, do you think your poetry, like Sandburg's *Lincoln*, will abide?

PRATT: Well now, hear ... I hope ... is all I can say. I've seen so many go over the falls and I'll be thankful if one out of ten does survive. Well, they've survived for twenty-five years anyway. I write a thing and it's like a child, you see, you're just dandling the child on your knee and running your fingers through his hair and you think this is the most wonderful thing, the features of John Barrymore. I did have the tendency first to rush into print with it. 'Oh, this must not be lost.' A little later, I looked at it in print and I said, 'Did I do that? Terrible! I hope nobody read it.' And, I got into the habit, fortunately, of writing a poem and putting it at once into cold storage. Slip it into a desk. Take it out in six months, or six weeks, and get the fresh impression which is pretty valid I think. You say, 'Did I do that?' Generally it's, 'I hope not'; occasionally, 'Thank heaven I did.'

ADAMS: Of your many poems, Ned, which is your favourite?

PRATT: Well, I think that of the long ones, *The Roosevelt and the Antinoe*, the great rescue, where everything was converged upon the rescue of life. *The Titanic* was a greater complex than the other because you had the heroic and the mean there. But in *The Roosevelt and the Antinoe* it was all heroic.

ADAMS: I know that three years ago, I believe it was, you wrote a poem called 'Magic in Everything' which was unpublished. Would you read it for us?

PRATT: Yes, I'd be glad to. This is a selection from the poem and [was] used as a Christmas card, decorations by my daughter, and it illustrates the development in the mind of a youngster who believed absolutely in Santa Claus until the discovery was made later on.[1]

ADAMS: No evidence of artistic success can equal the acclaim of one's contemporaries. Many have described you as Canada's leading poet. Would you agree?

PRATT: I'd raise a hornet's nest if I answered that. I'd say, one of them I hope. But I don't make a claim for leadership because it could easily be denied. I believe there's an originality about what I do. I think there is. I don't think anybody has written on the *Roosevelt* and the *Antinoe* and the *Titanic* exactly that way. And I don't bother much about leadership. Well, let the person be the leader who leads, and if I lead in one direction there may be others leading in other directions.

ADAMS: In your seventy-five years, Ned, you've amassed many

honours, a CMG [Companion of the Order of St Michael and St George], which is the next step below knighthood for a Canadian, twelve honorary doctorate degrees and three Governor-General's Awards for poetry. But do you recall a silver medal which once went to pay for a dinner party at the old Queen's Hotel[2] in Toronto.
PRATT: I do, but it wasn't silver, it was gold. A gold medal, and I didn't know what to do with a gold medal. You could stick it away in some closet and forget about it or you could sell it. So I had a lot of friends from Newfoundland mainly, who were always hungry, on just the verge of existence. So I thought it would be a rather gracious thing to sell the medal and buy a dinner for, say, twelve people, at the old Queen's Hotel, on Front Street. I got twelve dollars, fifteen dollars it was, for the medal, at one of the stores, and I called in my friends from the highways and the byways and told them that I was going to put on a dinner at the Queen's and they had to come hungry, which was the main condition, and the dinner would be late and we'd stay there for three hours. Well, we all arrived at the proper time, a little before the time really, and I went up to the waiter and I said, 'Give us the works tonight. This is a celebration.' So we sat down ... from half-past seven till ten o'clock and we had everything that the Queen's could offer. In fact, two main middle courses, one consisting of duck, roast duck, and the other of Yorkshire pudding and roast beef. There we sat till ten o'clock, twelve of us. In those days a dollar ... was the price. You'd get everything for a dollar. Well, three dollars were left over, and it was handed to the chef.
ANNOUNCER: Ned Pratt was born in Newfoundland in 1883,[3] the son of a Methodist parson and the third in a family of eight. Following in his father's footsteps, he became a preacher at Portugal Cove, a fishing village of a hundred people. Of this venture Pratt says, 'I married, baptized and buried, but I never felt at home in the pulpit.' This was no doubt partly because his mind was cooking up a plan, hardly becoming to a gentleman of the cloth. His method [sic] was above reproach; to raise the money to continue his education at the University of Toronto. Jed Adams asks Ned Pratt about this phase in his life.

ADAMS: Do you recall how you paid for your first year at Victoria College in Toronto?

PRATT: Well, you refer to the way I got up to Toronto by selling patent medicine? Oh, that's what you mean. Yes, I and another fellow belonging to Bell Island concocted a brew made out of cherry bark and the tops of spruce and some sarsparilla, and I must say that at that time though it was very unconventional a pretty strong lacing of rum, and we sold quite a number of bottles at a dollar, and two of us got up to Toronto with a hundred and fifty dollars and that paid all our expenses practically for the year in tuition and food and lodging. Well, we never repeated the experiment because we were afraid to go back to Newfoundland for a long time. Well it all came to a joke at the end and more laughs than sobs out of it, you know, and that's how I got through the first year. The second year, third year, went out under an organization called 'The Forward Movement of the Missionary Enterprise' and we had to present the Cause right out west and made two hundred dollars out of that. Well, that's the way we got through; by the skin of our teeth, you know.

ADAMS: As the grandson of a sea-captain, I can understand your preoccupation with the sea. Throughout most of your poetry, your critics say, there is a strong streak of death. Do you feel this to be a major preoccupation with you?

PRATT: Well, it is in a way because my father was a minister, an itinerant Methodist minister, who travelled every three years from one district to another, on the south coast and east coast. And the shipwrecks were numerous and he had to break the news to the widow if a ship went down and tell her that her husband or her sons were lost, and to get that – I remember my father going from the house to the widow's house bracing himself, and going in company with a doctor. He couldn't bear it going alone. He went with a doctor and they told the news. And the widow scented it ahead of time when she saw the two going together, you know. So naturally that became incorporated into the writing and the thinking. Though I was only a youngster at the time yet I never could forget the look on my father's face when he was just fortifying himself ... 'to break the news' ... which was a common expression. 'To break the news' – this meant the disclosure of death. You can't get away from that, you know. I couldn't. Especially if it was a big disaster such as the loss of a ship where the skipper who owned the ship went down with two or three sons. And the whole town would go into mourning. That can't escape you. And hence there is a good deal of preoccupation, and also there is a good deal of the lighter stuff which is there to counterbalance it. For instance, *The Witches' Brew* ... I don't know how that escaped me or got out. I think it was just an emotional release, 'Let 'er go, Gallagher!' When it came out I was at Victoria College, at the time a theological college, and some of the theological professors said, 'What does Pratt mean by writing a thing like that? And what is his idea? What does he mean?' And the chancellor,[4] who had a great sense of humour, said, 'Oh, he doesn't mean anything at all about it.' He said, 'It's just let 'er go. Let 'er go. Have a good time. Let 'er go.' It was written on the fifth anniversary of our wedding and so it had to be in the celebrating mood. Yes, that's counterpoint in a way, isn't it?

ANNOUNCER: Poet Pratt talks about his poetry, but only when someone asks him. Without attempting to make a cult or mystery of it. Words are his great love and he regards two hundred lines a year as his average output.

ADAMS: As a student of the English language, what, in your opinion, is the worst word?

PRATT: The worst word? Oh dear! Well I don't know; I could give you a dozen. Words like 'esoteric' I don't like. It just feels that you're removed from your audience, and from life. I could mention a lot of words that I'd rather have out of the *Collected Edition*, than in ... after a year's glaring at them.

ADAMS: How about adjectives? Your poetry is usually spare and without the frills?

PRATT: Yes, well I tell you something about that. When I started writing in the twenties there was a magazine that you know, *Poetry* (Chicago), that went out full blast against adjectives, the archaic adjective especially. And it's an old problem; it's not new at all. Sir Walter Scott started it, the dislike of the adjective, because the eighteenth-century people like Pope and Dryden put in the adjective of two syllables to make up the five accented line. And Scott went in at* the four accented. And it was felt that the adjective was there as a filler and hence in the early part of this century, in 1912 when *Poetry* came out, they were out against the adjective. And I feel that the adjective is often a filler, just a filler.

ADAMS: One feature of your writing, so your critics say, is its comprehensibility. Your poetry, they go on to say, can be enjoyed as simply as a good meal or a hockey game.

PRATT: Well, I'd like to believe that. And, there are some poems where the objection comes that the symbolism is obscure, but I think that refers mainly to individual passages, not to the whole content. I believe in the whole content being luminous as possible, and at the same time I don't want it to be *absolutely* clear in every passage. I believe in a certain amount of difficulty here and there as a stimulus. But I think the whole content ought to be fairly free of shadow.

ADAMS: Are you hopeful for the future of Canadian poetry?

PRATT: Yes, I am, in a way. I could mention some writers in Canada who are about as good as we've had in the past – for instance, [Earle] Birney in British Columbia. I have a great admiration for that fellow's work. He's a brilliant fellow, and he's very versatile in fiction and in satire and in poetry and in drama; he's about the best we have. And … I'm optimistic there. I'm dealing with people now, that are in the vanguard, you know, not those that are lagging behind, following and imitating and giving worse versions than what other fellows have written, that were bad enough at times. I think we're going through a transition, and a great number don't know where they are, that's true. They're in a cloud. They don't know their own minds and it's very flattering, self-flattering, to have people say – 'Oh, you're in the mainstream today' or 'You're a real modernist' and 'You're getting a lot of attention.' I see that all the time. Well, modernism, a wide term of course, can be anything. Sandburg was a great modernist about twenty years ago, but that was mainly on the basis of his subject matter I think. And Eliot today is the modernist, though he disclaims modernism and upholds tradition. It's a dickens of a medley of emotion and thought, out of which we'll pass in time I think. I'm a strong Yeatsian myself, great admirer of William Butler Yeats, who founded his own school and didn't yield to every gust and flurry.

ANNOUNCER: Some years ago Dr Pratt retired from his position as head of the English department at Victoria College. His study is reserved for him, however, and he is still a familiar figure about the college.

ADAMS: More than anyone else I know, you know a great deal of our past. Do you think that people today have forgotten where they came from? More explicitly, by forgetting their past, their heritage, they will not be able to know the direction they're going in?

PRATT: Yes, I think so. That's perfectly true, in my mind, that the logical development of an art is from tradition into a modification of that tradition, a change of that tradition. We belong to the past as surely as we belong to the future. I certainly believe that a developing tradition is the most logical and sensible direction in which to move.

ADAMS: Ned, you have had most of the honours and some of the abuse that comes to a man in public life. I was wondering whether you would have any words of counsel to give the youngsters of Canada?

PRATT: Well, I don't know that I could suggest much. Except this; that we've moved away from clarity of expression into obscurity, which I think is a bad drift. I believe in communication, in an experience which you have felt yourself, and you want to communicate to another. And, if a poem is couched in terms which are utterly difficult, unintelligible, half the value is gone for me. I don't mean to say that every poem should be *thoroughly* explicit, but there should be quite an area of intelligibility about poetry as there is about prose, only the language may be different. We've moved into almost an area of insanity in expression where I don't think the people who write understand what they're writing about, and I think that the swing back will take place someday, where people will get disgusted with attempts to understand something which was intended to be unintelligible.

Commentaries on Specific Poems

'Carlo' **November 1920**

The incident upon which this poem is based occurred a few years ago. The mail steamer *Ethie* was making her final trip for the season from Battle Harbour on the Labrador coast to a port on the southwest part[1] of Newfoundland. When she was within a few hours' run of Bonne Bay, she was caught in a great storm which prevented her from making the harbour, and at eight o'clock in the morning, after a night in which the waves stove in her hatches and flooded the stokehold, she went ashore on a reef. It was December with zero temperature. There were ninety-three persons on board, some of them women, and it looked as if there was not the remotest chance of a rescue, as the fishermen who had come down to the shore were unable to launch a boat in the tremendous seas. A line was shot from the steamer but it did not get any distance. Then a lifebuoy was attached to the line in the hope that the wind might drift it ashore but the weight of the line sank it.

A Newfoundland dog on the shore was ordered by his master to go for the line. The only words spoken were 'Fetch it, boy,' accompanied by a gesture in the direction of the ship. The dog, after being hurled back by the waves a number of times, managed to get outside of the rock-surf, covered the distance, took the line in his teeth and swam back to the shore.

A stouter rope was then tied to the line, pulled in, and secured to a boulder in a cliff. A boatswain's chair was quickly improvised and in an hour or so every person on board was drawn over in safety.

(The reference in the poem to the dog leaping over the taffrail of the ship is an error, the result of an earlier report that the dog belonged to the vessel.)

'In Absentia' June 1921

Thank you for your interest in the poem 'In Absentia.' I did not have in mind a *particular* person whom I could call by name, but rather any teacher who was off on a fishing holiday, let us say sometime in late May when he was getting very tired giving lectures or marking exam papers. He may be assumed to be an ardent fisherman and the emotion that seized him when he hooked a 'big one' was so great that the whole life-span of seventy years (in fact the whole universe)[1] is concentrated in the experience. The sun and the sky are mirrored in the water and are but minor ...* compared with that fish.

Obviously the man is a teacher of languages ('language-weathered face'). The whirling disk is the revolving trolling spoon. The asterisk or star attached to a subject in which a student has failed would bring an expression of excitement to the face of the student. I have transferred the expression to the face of the professor for there is the possibility of his failure to land the fish, but I have left it to the reader to regard that as momentary for the tug on the line indicates a pretty good hold.[2]

May, the time of examinations,[3] and September, the time of resumption* of lectures,[4] are now not on the calendar for the fisherman.

The Ice-Floes April 1922

1. The seal hunt of Newfoundland ranks next to the cod-fishery in industrial importance. On the fifth of March the fleet, consisting of ten or twelve ships, starts out from St John's and steams along the east coast for two or three hundred miles in search of the 'main

herd.' The seals, whose native home is in the Arctic, leave Melville Sound, Baffin Bay, and the Greenland regions in November, swimming, during the succeeding months, off the coast of Labrador, until in February they reach their whelping grounds on the ice-floes in the Gulf of St Lawrence and particularly in the eastern waters of Newfoundland. They come in vast numbers – a half-million or more – and bring forth their young on the ice in the latter part of February. The pup, which is five or six pounds at birth, grows so rapidly that in one month he may weigh fifty pounds. 'You can see them grow,' is the sealer's comment. The hair on this young seal is white and soft like wool but as it gets older it becomes mottled with brown and yellow spots. It is the young seals which the fleet are pursuing, on account of the superior nature of the skin and fat, though of course all types, old and young, are taken.

The ships try to get into the herd by the middle of March, because when the young seals are about a month old they 'dip' or take to the water, being shoved off the ice by their mothers, just as fledglings learn to fly by being pushed from their nests by the mother-bird. If the seals manage to get to the water before the ships arrive they are safe, for by instinct they swim 'true north,' and, with the surviving old ones, they migrate back to the Arctic for the summer, to resume their southern journey the following autumn.

The common seal, called the 'harp' because of a dark curve upon the back resembling a musical harp, is the most graceful and beautiful animal in the sea. It is intelligent, has large, almost human eyes, and can to some extent be domesticated and taught tricks like a dog. When it gets older it loses some of its beauty, and the names *rusties*, *bedlamers*, *saddlers*, and *old harps* are local descriptions befitting the advance of age and general depreciation of colour and appearance.

As soon as a ship gets into a patch of seals, and into very thick ice where further progress is impossible, she is said to 'burn down,' and the crew are ordered over the rails for the kill. The men proceed in different directions to cover as great an area as possible, under the command of the 'watches.' Each man is provided with a gaff, a sheath-knife, and steel, a coil of rope and some biscuit (hardtack), and his job from dawn till dark is the slaughter of the seals. A blow from the gaff on the nose of the seal stuns or kills it, a cut is made from the throat to the tail, and in a few moments the coat is detached from the body. Inside this coat is the fat, roughly two inches in thickness – the carcass being left on the ice. As soon as a man gets three or four pelts, he slips the rope through the holes cut near the edge of the skin, and takes them 'in tow' to a pile of seals on a pan of ice where the other 'hands' of his watch are drawing theirs, and thus over the ice-fields, many square miles in extent, scores of hills are being raised for the steamers to pick up, should the ice become loose enough for her to make any headway. If the ship is thoroughly fast, the men must drag the seals the whole distance themselves.

The hazards of the voyage are many and dangerous, and the greatest marine disasters of Newfoundland have sprung from the seal-fishery. In the course of a day's pursuit, the men may be separated from their ship by miles, necessitating hours to reach her position after the scream of the siren or the flag-signal had indicated a fall in the barometer. It must be remembered that the ice-pack is full of hummocks, pinnacles, and pressure ridges, making travelling difficult and slow, while crevasses and fissures are always in [the] process, under the impact of rising winds, of forming water-leads continually increasing in width. It then becomes a race against the gale and snow, the ship being blotted out, and the report of guns and the sound of the whistle being confused with the crack of the ice and the swoop of the wind around the great boulders. Sometimes, especially when the wind is off-shore, the pack gets broken up into fragments or pans and numbers of the crew may be borne out to sea.

2. My friend Father Dwyer[1] has asked me to talk about some of my Newfoundland experiences on which I have based a few poems, and I am going to talk quite informally before reading the verse.[2] There are two or three very dramatic events in the recent history of the island of which I had vivid personal experience, and one is in

connection with the great seal hunt which has always ranked as one of the major industries ...[3]

The blow-holes called bobbing holes are of great interest. They are holes in the ice which are kept open in the severest weather. A seal will dive down beneath the ice in search [of] food, coming up here and there to breathe and, although gone it may be for hours, will come back to its particular hole to suckle its whelp. It is a well-known fact that the mother will never mistake another pup for its own and will never suckle another, though to us they all look alike. If the mother should happen to be lost or killed the young harp slowly starves and dies. Such a starveling is locally known as a nogghead.[4]

The total catch for a year may be between two hundred and three hundred thousand. The greatest number brought into port in one trip by one steamer was by the *Florizel* in 1910 – approximately fifty thousand.

The event I referred to was the loss on the ice-floes of one-half the crew. I remember the homecoming of the ship with thousands of the population of St John's down at the docks when the frozen bodies were taken ashore, and later I remember the great memorial service[5] held in the Anglican cathedral where clergymen of all the Protestant communions took part ...

'The Ground Swell'   January 1923

This is a name given to the sound made by the waves suddenly coming up against shallow ground, and spending themselves upon the sand and pebbles of a shore. It is a steadier and more prolonged note than the thud against cliffs because the fall of the incoming tide upon the beach is followed by the suction of the sand during the ebb. It may be the result of a distant sea-storm which has not visited the land; and this sibilant note heard in the dead of night, when there is no wind or noise of any kind, produces an eerie feeling often associated with the thought of disaster.

'The History of John Jones'   **January 1923**

1. I shall begin with a thumb-nail sketch of a sailor who was believed to have sworn only twice in his life. When the poem was published I received a letter from a Newfoundlander living in Vancouver who said I must have slipped up on my quota, for an allowance of two oaths in a lifetime must have been based on a system of rationing unknown to peace or war. But I was dealing with a moral phenomenon whose economy of speech practically amounted to genius.

2. I knew a man like that, though there is a touch of exaggeration...

'The Shark'   **January 1923**

... This doesn't need an explanation, except perhaps this remark, that the conclusion of a poem is the most important part and hardest to write. I have always had a fear of anti-climax. It can ruin an otherwise fairly good poem. Sometimes I have succeeded in avoiding it, I think, and sometimes I have not.[1] That is the reason why I generally keep a poem in cold storage for weeks or months before publishing and then take it out and say to myself – 'Well, look at that last line: the poem has turned on its beam-ends or perhaps it has reached port more or less under its own canvas.' I hope that the poems to be read have been reasonably successful in that respect.

'The Toll of the Bells'   **1923**

The next is a couple of sonnets which, though written long after the event of course, yet commemorates, however inadequately, a great church service held here in St John's when the *Greenland* came in with her survivors and her dead. Some of the older people will remember the event. I was only a boy at the time but it is an ineffaceable memory. No part of the whole ritual that made up the formal side of the service seemed able to the same degree to bring home to our hearts as the bells did the solemnity and desolation of the tragedy.

'The Fog' 1923

Fog on the Grand Banks can be very treacherous, especially when the fishing dories get separated from the mother ships. Occasionally a steamer, even going at slow speed, might run one down, and not know it till long after. I remember a story describing such an incident; the feeling of helplessness and loss of all direction. This could happen even close to shore.

'Come Not the Seasons Here' 1923

[This is] a picture of a countryside devastated by war.

'On the Shore' 1923

The next [is] 'On the Shore,' dealing with a tragic incident towards the close of the First World War.

The Cachalot November 1925

1. The definition of whales as a species of fish is a rough popular description based upon the fact that they are wholly aquatic. Such a classification, however, is obviously inadequate, as the zoological account of a fish is that, in addition to its being a vertebrate animal which lives in water, it breathes by gills and has cold blood.

The whale is a mammal – a warm-blooded creature which suckles its young. It possesses lungs which require it, after a period of sounding, to come to the surface to discharge its breath from a spiracle or 'blow-hole' on the top of its head. This spouting is never, as is sometimes imagined, sea-water, but simply vapour like human breath condensing when it emerges into a cooler atmosphere. Its fins resemble, at first sight, those of a fish, but close anatomical inspection reveals them to be rather the rudiments of legs – a fact which supports the theory of the whale being formerly a land animal that reverted to the sea. Moreover, its fins, which it uses to hold its young to its sides for protection, are not used to any important degree in swimming, beyond helping to maintain balance, the whole propulsion coming from the tail. This is of enormous size and strength, capable of hurling a boat with its crew of six men many feet in the air, or of driving an eighty-ton whale through the sea at the rate of twelve or fifteen miles an hour. Another fact of interest is that the tail is horizontal, not vertical, as in the case of all true fish.

The best-known of all the varieties are the Greenland or right whale and the sperm whale or cachalot. The former is distinguished primarily by the presence in its upper jaw of a structure called *baleen* or whalebone, which consists of solid plates terminating in hundreds of fibres, as fine and flexible as the ribs of an umbrella. This fringe serves as a sieve to strain out the water after the whale has engulfed in its jaws myriads of small fish like pilchards, sprats, and caplin, and the lesser crustacea (shrimps, crabs, mussels, etc.) – no larger fish being devoured since the throat is only a few inches in diameter.

The cachalot is differentiated from all other types by a number of obvious characteristics. Its head is like a huge block with an almost square front, while that of the right whale is curved. The lower jaw is straight and slender and contains approximately forty teeth, each eight or nine inches long, and so firmly embedded in the jaw that they need block and tackle for their extraction. The throat is so large that half-a-dozen Jonahs might find an easy and simultaneous passage into the interior.

The outstanding quality, however, is that, besides the blubber-oil which is contained in all whales, it possesses spermaceti, a pure, transparent liquid which takes on the appearance of white wax upon contact with air. This substance, several hundred gallons of it, is enclosed in a section of the skull called the 'case' which is cut open by the whalers – a quite delicate operation – and drawn up in pails attached to ropes rove through the blocks.

The mode of capture today is very different from that prevalent fifty years ago and has become an altogether unromantic procedure. The whale is overtaken by a steamer and pierced by a harpoon shot from a gun on the fore-deck. The initial plunge of the whale releases a trigger which fires an explosive, and the whale in the majority of cases is killed immediately. But a generation ago, a ship might leave New Bedford or Nantucket and remain at sea for three years on a continuous cruise, engaging whales in battles which as often as not resulted in the loss of boats and the destruction of crews. Directly the whale was sighted, the boats were lowered and rowed to within fifteen or twenty feet when the harpooners plunged their irons into his body. The whale was never killed by the harpoon, he was merely held fast by it, and when, after hours of sounding and of dragging the boats, he had slackened his pace sufficiently to allow the crews to overtake him, he was killed by the lucky thrust of a lance in his heart.

2. The term *kraken* strictly refers to a mythical sea-serpent alleged to have been seen by superstitious sailors off the coast of Norway, but is used commonly as a designation for the gigantic squid or devil-fish. That such a monster as the squid is not a fabulous creature but an actual inhabitant of the sea is abundantly attested, for several have been discovered dead on the beaches of the North Atlantic, and huge fragments of their bodies have been found within the stomachs of cachalots. The squid may attain the weight of tons; its eight tentacles, sometimes fifty-feet long, protrude from the head (hence the name cephalopod), and are armed with rows of round, concave, claw-rimmed discs which act as a sucking vacuum when applied to the body of their prey. It also possesses a peculiar

inky substance called sepia, which can be expelled from a sac to darken the water at the approach of an enemy. The closest parallel to the octopus in structure is the common squid, a diminutive decapod used as bait in the cod-fishery, which, when pulled over the gunwale of a boat, has an uncanny precision in discharging its irritating secretion right into the eye of a fisherman.

It may at once be assumed that, with the exception of the whale, there is no form of marine life which can successfully resist the grasp of an animal such as this. The bigger sharks would be helpless, and there are instances of the finding of dead whales where the fissures and stripes on their bodies indicated death through only one kind of encounter.

The squid then becomes the natural foe and prey of the cachalot. Frank Bullen (one of the most authoritative writers on the whale-chase), in referring to the killing of a great sperm, states that amongst the masses of food ejected from its stomach just before death was one block of squid estimated to be 8 × 6 × 6 feet. A very thrilling part of *The Cruise of the Cachalot* is Bullen's description of a fight between a whale and a squid actually seen over the rail of the vessel:

At about eleven p.m., I was leaning over the lee rail, gazing steadily at the bright surface of the sea, where the intense radiance of the tropical moon made a broad path like a pavement of burnished silver. Eyes that saw not, mind only confusedly conscious of my surroundings, were mine; but suddenly I started to my feet with an exclamation, and stared with all my might at the strangest sight I ever saw. There was a violent commotion in the sea right where the moon's rays were concentrated, so great that, remembering our position, I was at first inclined to alarm all hands; for I had often heard of volcanic islands suddenly lifting their heads from the depths below, or disappearing in a moment, and, with Sumatra's chain of active volcanoes so near, I felt doubtful indeed of what was now happening. Getting the night-glasses out of the cabin scuttle, where they were always hung in readiness, I focussed them on the troubled spot, perfectly satisfied by a short examination that neither volcano nor earthquake had anything to do with what was going on; yet so vast were the forces engaged that I might well have been excused for my first supposition. A very large sperm whale was locked in deadly conflict with a cuttle-fish, or squid, almost as large as himself, whose interminable tentacles seemed to enlace the whole of his great body. The head of the whale especially seemed a perfect net-work of writhing arms – naturally, I suppose, for it appeared as if the whale had the tail part of the mollusc in his jaws, and, in a business-like, methodical way, was sawing through it. By the side of the black columnar head of the whale appeared the head of the great squid, as awful an object as one could well imagine even in a fevered dream. Judging as carefully as possible, I estimated it to be at least as large as one of our pipes, which contained three hundred and fifty gallons; but it may have been, and probably was, a good deal larger. The eyes were very remarkable for their size and blackness, which, contrasted with the livid whiteness of the head, made their appearance all the more striking. They were, at least, a foot in diameter, and, seen under such conditions, looked decidedly eerie and hobgoblin-like. All around the combatants were numerous sharks, like jackals round a lion, ready to share the feast, and apparently assisting in the destruction of the huge cephalopod. So the titanic struggle went on, in perfect silence as far as we were concerned, because even had there been any noise, our distance from the scene of conflict would not have permitted us to hear it.

3. I have attempted to picture a cachalot or sperm whale in his critical conflicts with his greatest[1] enemies. It is a very ordinary experience in Newfoundland to see in some of the harbours a steamer towing in dead captured whales. Nowadays, however, the romance of the whole fishery has passed, in so much as they are killed very quickly by harpoons and explosives fired from a gun in the bow of the ship. There is very little danger. But this is a description of a fight in the old harpoon days when a ship might be out on a continuous trip for three years[2] and any given fight might take a day or twenty-four hours before the boats killed their victim or the whale destroyed the boats. A large cachalot might be around a hundred feet in length, weigh one hundred and fifty tons, and [be] capable of remaining down with rope attached five or six thousand feet under water for an hour. The sperm whale is

different from the Greenland whale in that he has teeth and an enormous throat. The grey prey of the sperm is the kraken or cuttlefish[3] or giant squid or octopus. Krakens [are] not a myth as some people think.[4]

4. I feel very honoured indeed in being asked to talk to you and read to you about some phases of seafaring life in Newfoundland. The subject has an absorbing and perpetual interest to me as I had the good fortune to be born and brought up there and also because it was the home of my stock on my mother's side since the time of Gilbert.[5] I thought that the best thing I should do tonight would be, instead of giving sketches of Newfoundland history, to give some description of the life there, the habits of the people, and the risks to which they are exposed upon the sea. That is material which has always had a dramatic and poetic appeal to me. The first thing I should like to read would be the account of what an American writer has called the greatest* hunt in the world.

5. ... But one may ask what liberties are allowed a writer in both the manufacture and arrangement of his material. I should claim that such liberty is greatly restricted in historical poems or in those poems where scientific facts are the essential basis, and wherever there are important deviations there should be a recognition on the part of the writer either explicit or involved in the poem that such departures are being made. If the change is made for the sake of comedy or fantasy there would be no objection as a general principle. But the reader must be taken into the writer's confidence at some stage of the game. I had one illustration of this in writing *The Cachalot*. I had spent two years teaching school[6] at a whaling station in Newfoundland and I had the opportunity of seeing a number of those huge mammals as they were towed into the harbour and moored belly up for days before they were conveyed to the factory for their manufacture into oil. I used to row around them and measure their length, which seemed absolutely incredible to people who had never seen a whale. People gasp yet with incredulity when the fact is stated that a large whale might at birth

weigh well over a hundred tons,[7] (and the delivery accomplished without the aid of anyone but Nature as obstetrician). The dimensions given in the poem are accurate except in a few instances where they are obviously and intentionally magnified in a mock-heroic way. I believe I did enlarge the liver somewhat. And as the poem was written at the time of the discovery of insulin I did take liberties with the pancreas.[8] I had read it at a medical banquet[9] at which my friend Dr Fred Banting was chairman. Fred had supplied me with some of the data about the internal constitution of marine mammalia, and he remarked that if he could find an animal with a pancreas as big as the one I described, he could supply not only this world but the next with all the insulin needed for a decade. And he suggested that I should write a poem on a dinosaur with a bad pancreas which might be read at the next annual banquet. The poem was written and read but it never got into print.[10]

'The Sea-Cathedral'   December 1926

1. Icebergs seen in the North Atlantic are colossal fragments of Arctic glaciers which have descended from the higher positions of the mainland to the sea. They may be observed drifting south with wind and current, some of them five hundred feet long and two hundred high, and weighing many millions of tons, for they are approximately seven-eighths in volume under water. Upon reaching a coast they may stay a whole season aground, breaking up and slowly dissolving under the impact of waves. No more beautiful sight is afforded on land or sea than a towering berg reflecting the sunlight in all the nuances of green and blue, or revealing itself after dark under the searchlight of a passing steamer.

2. One of the most majestic sights of nature is an iceberg either afloat or aground. The North Atlantic icebergs have their homes in the nine glaciers. They glide down into the ocean and move slowly down with the tides and get stranded off the Newfoundland coast where they break up gradually under the wash of the sea and

dissolve. Some of them are of immense size towering two hundred feet in the air and [having] nine times that mass under water. They weigh many millions of tons, may be a quarter of a mile in circumference, and possess all the colours of a sunset. At night when they are disclosed by the searchlight of a steamer they are amazingly impressive.

The Great Feud   1926

1. The method of the poem is to take an evolutionary theme and work it out in terms of an imaginative symbolism. I want to show how colossal a catastrophe [might result][1] if certain natural instincts and passions such as self-preservation, a sense of family and racial pride or even the feeling of honour or adventure or the desire to possess and retain were given absolutely free rein.

It is the account of the development of a feud between the land and the sea put away back in the pleiocene age long before the coming of man. The scene is laid in Australasia on the littoral border of an isthmus joining Australia with Malay, a geological fact about a million years ago. It is the most fertile place in the world – the nursery for fauna of the earth and water.

In a blind, dumb way the fish had come to realize that the land and air had become an insidious menace to their very existence. It had taken aeons for that realization, but it had come. They had felt, first of all, that a migration had taken place. They are threatened with depopulation due to many adventurous species getting up on the intertidal flats, developing flippers and feet and lungs and so forth. And again they had seen sea-birds pouncing on their young and on the smaller tribes and carrying them into the air. And they had seen animals on the shore, like bears for instance, swimming out and catching them: that's invasion of their homes. All these facts have increased the sense of unrest and hate which is rendered all the more acute because, limited to their environment they cannot adequately[2] avenge themselves upon their foes.

Parallel with this the same sense of hatred and hostility has developed in the land tribes. They too have seen the sea tribes kill and devour their own species, for instance when they had been marooned at high tide on islands and when they had been swimming in the rivers crocodiles had seized them, and particularly on the shore. That is the great disputed area bordered by the high and low water marks. The land claim the strip because it is dry when the tide is low and the sea claim it when the tide is high, but as the tides are always in motion the variable and mobile* indefinable boundary becomes the bitter arena[3] of contest.

Now what is going to bring* this feud to a fight* and explain this by ...* natural solidarity ...* It is a crisis in the world's history and evolution is making a jump. The air is electrical. Even winds are behaving strangely. Any kind of miracle may happen. Nature herself takes a hand in the feud and impartially overwhelms both sides at the end of the conflict in the form of a deluge of lava from a volcano ...*[4] The volcano is a kind of spectator watching the progress of the fight and finally getting into it herself.

In the first draft of this I had the idea of making the presence of the volcano felt by a number of choruses and refrains but I felt that it cluttered up the ...* of the poem. I had this difficulty too. The culmination is one of unrelieved disaster, almost complete [but] not quite. There is one survivor, a female anthropoidal ape that is just on the threshold of reason and morality. But I had to escape from too great an effect of horror by injecting a hale salt of the grotesque* into it.

2. I have chosen as a subject for this address a verse fantasy[5] called *The Great Feud or a Dream of an Armageddon* away back millions of years before the appearance of man upon the earth, a description of a worldwide battle between the inhabitants of the land and the inhabitants of the sea. The idea was to present a fantastic picture of some stage in the evolutionary struggle for existence, and to show how near to extinction a race might come, if the instinct to attack and to retaliate upon attack were given absolute rein without any moral considerations. I have called the poem a dream though it might more fittingly be called a nightmare.

The scene is laid in Australasia on a three-hundred-mile coastline joining Australia with Malay – one of the most fertile regions of the world and the great nursery for life on land and sea. The fish are represented as half blindly and dumbly conscious of hostility on the part of the earth. In the first place they have lost large numbers through the lure of emigration to unknown regions. Many have adventured onto the muddy flats to develop lungs and flippers and feet and have been destroyed. Many have been attacked at the shoreline by beasts of prey; many have been seized by birds,[6] and they have been possessed by a desire for revenge to get back at a foe which, in the natural order of things, is out of reach.

The main idea of the feud crystalizes around a boundary question. Both sides claim possession of the shoreline and some justification is given by the ambiguous nature of the coast through the flow and recession of the tides. 'This is mine,' says the sea. 'Some of my nationals are here and have occupied territory.' 'No,' says the land, 'We were here first.' Patriotic feelings are appealed to with equal and fiery insistence. Wherever aggression takes place, there is retaliation. Life for life is exacted. But here is the practical problem. As the land animals had to be united for conflict against the fish, the carnivores had to refrain from eating flesh until the time came for the attack upon the marines. That meant that the land carnivores had to become vegetarians in that supreme interval covered by the entente cordiale. I had no trouble with the herbivores, naturally, for plants, grasses, and herbs and berries were ready at hand as their natural food, but the carnivores had somewhat hard going on rice and celery and rhododendrons and so forth. Still, they agreed to try it out and there wasn't anything wrong in making carnivores vegetarians for a short while because it had the effect of increasing their rage and hunger when the hour came for their onslaught on the fish. That was an orthodox point of grand strategy. And there was no artistic problem any more than in changing the queen in *Snow White* into a hag. *Snow White* could be taken to illustrate the point. There is an internal logic in this fantasy. The birds sing and fly; the deer run like the wind; and the tortoise manages to reach the top of the stairs when all the rest are on their way down. The tortoise is true to his nature. He has been scientifically observed. If Disney had made him outrun the hare – not merely outwit, but outrun the hare – it would have been an artistic as well as a scientific blunder, unless there was something in the original design to explain it. If the tortoise had discovered an elixir of life, a stimulant, and had drunk it, then such amazing activity and speed might have been made credible.[7] Scientific matter-of-factness would have to be made aesthetically acceptable as an initial assumption. But unless so designed the facts of existence should be respected.

I had to skate around a number of difficulties here. How were all the beasts of the earth to be organized for the fight against the fish and the mammals of the sea? I had to get a leader to explain to them the nature of the war, to raise their martial rage to a white heat and to direct their strategy as soon as the beasts arrived at the shoreline. I asked myself the question – What would be the most intelligent animal that life had evolved up to that time? So I selected an ape, a female anthropoidal ape. I had to endow this ape with speech, though I left the matter of dialects, *et cetera*, to the imagination of the readers. Then how would she be visible to the countless hordes? That was the second question – What was the tallest animal in the world? Obviously, a giraffe. So I put the giraffe on a high monolith and made the ape climb up on the neck of the giraffe from which she could harangue the multitudes. Bifocals were not invented then, so I left that knotty point alone. This is the account of the speech. Read.[8] One reviewer, commenting on that line, said I must have been a Methodist or an evangelist of some sort. Well, I was a Methodist, at least at that time.

The next point was how would the fish be apprised of the invasion and its time. I wanted an amphibian, which could speak a common language. Naturally, that would be a turtle which might leave the water and go along the flats and up to the great amphitheatre. Her first purpose is to lay her eggs, but her second purpose is to find out what caused a huge spiral of smoke in the distance. This smoke issues from an active volcano called Jurania which later is to play an ironic part in terminating the fight by a general catastrophe for both sides. Jurania broods over the whole event. The turtle having heard the ape's speech tumbles back to the sea and informs the marines.

The next question was – Could I find an animal which might act as a counterpart to the ape, something low down in the scale possessing colossal strength joined with the minimum of intelligence? I came across such a one when I visited the museum at Chicago some years ago. I went to the zoological section and noticed that a whole floor was occupied by the skeleton of a carnivorous dinosaur named Tyrannosaurus Rex. I looked at a number of the dinosaur's eggs which had been dug up in the Gobi desert,[9] petrified of course through age and of enormous size. I said to myself – 'What a monster to introduce into the fight.' When I finished writing this, I read it to Vi[10] who remarked – 'I suppose you know that dinosaurs were extinct by the time that mammals were introduced.' I said 'Yes, but I have to get him in somehow to lay around him with his pinpoint brain and his immense size when the Great Feud got going.' He wouldn't have enough intelligence to know which were his allies, which his foes, so he would attack both in the crisis creating a panic and getting badly mauled in the process. That would add to the excitement. He is the only one who doesn't observe the vegetable diet. There isn't enough protein in it for him. But how introduce him at all since he would come on the scene millions of years after his species had vanished? It was easy enough to handle an amphibian turtle. But to get through a subway which took several millions of years to build was another matter. To assume he was there at the time would have a zoologist laughing at the inaccuracy provided such a scientist would be in the reading audience.[11]

In fact, after the poem was published, [a critic of] the *Edinburgh Scotsman* pointed out an inaccuracy. He said – 'It is a little hard for us to adjust our minds to tigers living on celery or lions on rhododendrons, but since they had to be vegetarians for a short time for strategic reasons, we'll let that pass merely with a question mark, but,' he added – 'does this writer, in handing out tapioca to the hyenas, not know that tapioca is a prepared product usually done up in cartons, and being a prepared product, it would indeed take a hyena to sniff it out?' I admit that the Aberdonian[12] made a home run. I was telling this story on myself at a literary club in Toronto some time ago, and the editor of a magazine,[13] who hated tapioca as a table dish, remarked that he didn't see anything irrational about the poem because tapioca was the perfect food for hyenas anyway.

Now Jurania, the volcano, is important. It came in at the beginning with prophetic irony, and it must come in at the last to round out the catastrophe. All the combatants that survived the fight are buried under the lava, except the intelligent ape who scents the danger and avoids it by going back to her brood ... One reviewer was quite pleased at this survival for he said, if the ape had been destroyed, where would we be? Well, here we are.

'Cherries'   October 1927

This is a dialogue between a boy and a girl who have quarrelled one of those quarrels which are going to be eternal but are always made up the next day, sometimes the same day, possibly in five minutes, but while it lasts – oh boy!

'The Lee Shore'   October 1927

1. The word *lee* has two meanings. To be 'under the lee' of a ship or an island is to be under its shelter; so the lee bulwark of a ship is the side opposite to the *weather* side. But a lee shore is that part of a coast *against* which the wind blows and hence dangerous to ships, especially sailing ships.

2. A lee shore as you know is the shore against which the wind is blowing. In a storm it is the dangerous shore for both steam and sail, particularly for the latter. [It is] the shore where the light-houses are placed and the signal lights established. The harbour

then becomes the difficult place to enter and no matter how heavy the sea and how inviting the port the ship has to move back into the storm for its own safety.

The Iron Door: An Ode   1927

The idea of this poem, as the title suggests, sprang out of a dream but it underwent a good deal of elaboration later. The subject is an iron door which has been hung by the hand of Death in great granite cliffs supposed to represent the barrier between this world and the next. The atmosphere is one of storm and gloom[1] in which there is very little light. The door has all the appearance of finality. It has no latch on it suggesting that it is not meant to be opened. It has no knocker, hence the futility of banging away at the panels. The crest of Death has been fashioned on the lintel and it looks down ironically enough upon the door which is cruciform in construction. A multitude of human souls appear before the door and out of the large number appear half-a-dozen persons who represent various types of earthly life and belief. Some of them demand to know what is on the other side, if anything. They symbolize many states of emotion. Some are in a state of fear and bewilderment, another of profounder confidence, another is cynical or indifferent, another clamorous and so forth. Is this all the Creator has to show for himself at the end of a human life; a gravestone in the form [of] a closed door? An old seaman pauses at the side[2] and as he does notices a basalt crag that in the motion of the fog takes [on] the character of a moving hull. For a moment he takes it to be a ship belonging to the unknown hintersea and he halloes the unknown admiral asking for his bearings and whether the traditions of the service here in this world are observed on the other side, whether the stars and the sextant may be trusted over there; whether duty is a word to him like fire in the veins, as three of his sons were drowned in an heroic manful effort to save the crew of a sinking ship. Then a little boy is there looking around for the face of his father. The whole subject really is based upon the opposition that the human will or hope[3] presents to Death or extinction.

The last case is that of a woman who makes an assault upon the door to know why she should carry the burden of a [species]* which is part [biological, part ideal]* and for which she holds no moral responsibility.

A young man appears[4] who gave up his life in a brave but hopeless attempt to save the life of a man whose name he did not know when there was no human eye to watch the deed. He puts the problem before God of[5] ... the reason for a double sacrifice which is more than the Bible exacts for its doctrine of redemption. A little boy asks for the presence of his father, does not state any argument but merely makes the appeal.

'Sea-Gulls'   December 1930

Sea-gulls would continually be on the sea and above it in great numbers. I thought that one of the loveliest sights in nature was a flock of sea-gulls just about to alight on the waters. The wings were white; the sea was blue. Was there anything more white, anything more beautiful? What image could be used? Before reaching it I had to dismiss certain objects or symbols of whiteness and beauty as not quite adequate. I found what I wanted in the last line.

'The Child and the Wren'   1930

1. Now 'The Child and the Wren,' selected to show a complete contrast to the poem just read ['The Prize Cat'] in situation and mood.

2. This is founded on an actual observation of an attempt on the part of a little girl[1] to entice a wren to come close enough to pick a crumb of bread from her hand.

The Roosevelt and the Antinoe 1930

1. The American liner ss *President Roosevelt* left New York for England on January 20th, 1926, and, when three days out, encountered one of the greatest storms the Atlantic has ever known. At dawn on Sunday morning, in a blizzard, she received an s.o.s. call from the *Antinoe*, a little British grain freighter, which, with bunkers flooded and steering gear out of action, was not able to tell her own position. The *Roosevelt* started at once to look for her, with all the chances against success; sighted her in eight hours; lost her in a snow squall; picked her up again nineteen hours later; and then spent three days in an attempt, which finally succeeded, to rescue the twenty-five members of the *Antinoe*'s crew. The rescue is regarded by both American and British authorities as the finest episode of modern times in the saving of life upon the Atlantic.[1]

2. I am just about overwhelmed by your hospitality tonight. I had some idea of course conveyed to me of the nature of this occasion[2] but I didn't think it was going to be quite so elaborate, so magnificent. It looks more like a convention, or an international peace conference or the inauguration of a shipbuilding plant, but the thing which gives me most exhilaration is, above all, the presence of so many of my personal friends around a dinner table. Some of my oldest pals are here tonight, some of fifteen years standing like my old bosom friend Clare Hincks,[3] some of shorter time but still friends whom I cherish and love as I love life itself.

My friend ...* publisher, and host Hughie has asked me to give a brief description of the origin of the poem. It isn't very easy for me to say just when I began it as there was quite a long incubation period of straight amazement at the magnitude of the rescue without any formulated intention on my part to write about it. I first saw the account of it headlined in our Toronto papers and was so struck by the heroic outlines that I sent for and obtained copies of the New York papers and later of the English papers which for more than a week seemed to have no space left for anything else but the *Roosevelt* and *Antinoe*. That was in January 1926. I did think that possibly during the following summer in the university vacation – the only time I have for writing – I would make an attempt at it, which I did, but I realized that I was making a failure of it. I had selected a light mode of verse, the faster tetrameter in which *The Cachalot* was written. I saw it wouldn't go, the material broke the mould, and so I abandoned it. But a little more than a year ago I noticed that the magazines of England and America were frequently recurring to the event, alluding to it as the greatest example of seamanship in the rescue of life since the discovery of steam as a motive power, and I also noticed in the *Scientific American* and in *Blackwood's* articles upon the weird almost miraculous function of the radio compass in the location of ships in distress. About this time too, or possibly a little later, Fried had repeated his great deed by his rescue of the *Florida*,[4] which attracted world attention, the *Literary Digest* drawing a cartoon of Fried being reprimanded by Davy Jones for restraint of trade. Davy Jones feared he would have to close up his locker. Fried was becoming a national or international figure, and yet as splendid an achievement as the *Florida* rescue was it was used more as a means of refreshing the American memory upon the magnificent achievement two years before.

I wanted to go down to New York to get the facts at first hand so I wrote Mr O'Brien, the general manager of the United States Steamship Line and he gave me the most cordial invitation to spend as much time as I wished aboard the *Roosevelt*. The ship had just come into the harbour when I got there New Year's Eve but I managed to get on board at once even before she was out of quarantine. O'Brien notified the officers of my purpose and requested them to furnish me all the information I needed – which they did in full measure.

First I secured the logs of the *Roosevelt* and *Antinoe*; the exact messages which passed between the two ships during the four days of the event; all the wireless and flag signals, all the morse blinked out by the little dollar flashlight, the only means of communication which the *Antinoe* had on the last three nights. I went through the contracts between the sailors and the master signed before the sailing. I spent a couple of hours in the wireless room with the chief and his assistant while we went over the calls from the *Antinoe*, then a considerable time in the pilot house as they operated the direction-finder. Two or three of the crew started the winches, lowered a lifeboat and pulled it up again and showed how the releasing gear was worked. I had heard also that one of the most moving experiences of the rescue was the attempt of a Roman Catholic priest to administer the last rites to the sailors who were drowned. So the second officer and I selected a hypothetical stateroom which the priest might have occupied and then went up the flights of stairs to the main deck, along the passages and ladders to the boat-deck and over to the davits where he stood. I got the exact position of the barometers on the wall of the pilot house. I discovered a diary written by a passenger[5] during the voyage, which was full of particulars. A clerk in the office of the line gave me the reports of the officers ...* and so on and so on.

When I returned to Toronto I had to leave the job alone till the spring but in the meantime I realized I had material that just clamoured for treatment. The big task was to select and emphasize the high moments of the four days and of those moments there were many. I never heard of anything on the seas that was so shot through with drama. In nearly every hour there was a peak or a crisis and the matching or breaking of records. The storm itself had nothing to parallel it in the memory of mariners. It reached hurricane speed and occasionally went beyond it. The barometric readings, I think, were low Atlantic records or close to them and surpassed only by the sudden drops peculiar to typhoons in the China Seas.[6] The duration of the storm was unusual, one whole week.

It was in the depths of winter and the wind carried snow. The call of distress came from the *Antinoe* at dawn and in a blizzard. The *Antinoe* didn't know where she was. She was at least out in the worst part of the Atlantic somewhere south of Cape Race. There was the dramatic feature of the newly invented radio compass pointing its finger in the direction of the drifting derelict. Fried picked her up at noon, lost her, then picked her up again nine hours later under conditions which left British marine authorities breathless with respect. The navigation and daring behind the search and the rediscovery could hardly be equalled since the Elizabethans. The launching in succession of each of the six lifeboats from the height of seventy feet, the freeboard of the *Roosevelt*, when the ship herself was rolling twenty-five degrees, was in itself an exploit. And then the inter-raciality of the life-crews. Look at their names – all in the same boat a homely Anglo-Saxon named Sam Fisher, wedged in between Fu[g]elsang, a Dane, and Wertanen, a Finn, a soft-vowelled Latin name for the ...* preceded and ...* followed by a couple of explosive sneezes[7] from Czechoslovakia and Russia. I might read this. The difficulty I had of working them into the metrical scheme.[8]

There was so much of the high stuff in the whole event, a funeral service at sea in a storm with the wind ripping the ritual into shreds, the hoisting of the flag half-mast on the *Roosevelt* at dawn, and a desperate though successful attempt on the part of a sailor on the *Antinoe* to run up a flag on the jack-staff to salute the *Roosevelt*'s sacrifice and then both running up the flags to their full height again to assert that the job was still on. Then the time of the exposure to which the *Antinoe*'s men were subjected – four days without food, shelter, drink, or warmth, holding on to the weather rails, then the rescue in two great instalments when most of the *Antinoe*'s crew, asleep with exhaustion, were pulled up on the *Roosevelt*'s deck by means of the cargo slings. Then the discovery later that Tose[9] of the *Antinoe* had performed a similar service for a Philadelphia crew ten years before. Finally, to crown the whole dramatic achievement, the *Roosevelt* had to end up at the port of Plymouth, England, to deliver up the castaways. The whole affair was designed in the councils of the gods to be sung. My one regret is that I didn't do it better. It should have had a Homer. For Fried had all the noble qualities of Ulysses.

3. I should like to present a few facts concerning the event upon which this poem is based. The *Roosevelt* which accomplished the rescue is owned by the United States Steamship Lines, a large ship

carrying a maximum of four hundred and thirty-six passengers and two hundred and twenty-three of crew. She is five hundred and sixteen feet long, rated at 14,000 tons, average speed twenty knots, very high freeboard – sixty-two feet to the boat-deck – a fact which was of great significance as a help and a menace in the attempt of the rescue. Her route was from New York to Queenstown and Bremen. George Fried, the captain, Robert Miller, the first officer. The *Antinoe* was a British freighter, two hundred and eighty[10] feet in length and two thousand tons, known as a three-island boat with forecastle, amidship super-s[truc]ture and poop deck; low freeboard made all the lower through a heavy load of grain. Harry Tose, the captain.

The *Roosevelt* left New York on Wednesday, [the] twentieth of January 1926,[11] ran into bad weather on the following day – the beginning of a storm which by the common judgement of Atlantic captains who were out in it was the worst known in a generation. By Saturday night it had reached its maximum, which it maintained for nearly five days, with variations never allowing the lower limit to sink much below the sixty miles an hour [mark]. Piled on top of this were squalls of snow, and in one of those blizzards at four o'clock on Sunday morning when the *Roosevelt* was somewhere south of Cape Race, the wireless operator came to Fried with a distress signal from the *Antinoe* which did not know her own position beyond a calculation of drift added to rough bearings of twenty-four hours before. It was known afterwards that the *Antinoe* at the time of her despatch was one hundred miles out of her estimated position, and the *Roosevelt* herself out though to a less[er] extent. Fried immediately started for the general direction of the ship trusting mainly to the radio compass, which at that time [being] comparatively of recent invention was installed on only a few of the crack ocean liners. Relying on such aid alone when at times in a blizzard of snow the officer on watch could not see the bow of his own ship, Fried located the *Antinoe* at noon on the Sunday. In spite of the fact that there was quite a depth of water in [the] stokehold and engine room, and that the steering gear was damaged, Captain Tose of the *Antinoe* answered the signal of the

Roosevelt as to whether he wanted to abandon his ship by stating that he had no intention of giving up his vessel until he had tried to make a few repairs to steering gear and pumps. Would the *Roosevelt* stand by in the meantime? Later, however, Tose signalled that the situation was hopeless, but as the seas were so terrific the *Roosevelt* could not launch a boat, and at nine o'clock that night in a squall the *Roosevelt* suddenly lost sight of the wreck, at the same time as she noticed the ominous failure to get wireless contact. Everybody on board believed she had gone down, but as there was the barest chance she might still be afloat the long search began and continued for nineteen hours until they located her again sixty miles further on, this time without the direction finder, a search which is and will ever remain as one of the most loyal deeds ever known to the Atlantic. And the effort of the *Roosevelt* in the next three days to rescue the twenty-five Britishers is regarded by both English and American seamen as without a parallel at least in the history of steamships.

The smashing up of the lifeboats one after the other; the abandonment of one rescue device in favour of the next; the attempt on the part of the doomed ship to acknowledge by salute the sacrifices of the *Roosevelt*; the improvising of methods to face emergencies which were not anticipated by experts in life-saving; the inter-racial character of the life-crews are the outstanding features of the incident. There was also the problem in the distribution upon the water of the *Roosevelt*'s fuel oil. Apart from the fact that the ship was using up day after day her source of power, the oil, while it lessened the break of the surf, made it almost impossible for the capsized men to swim. Many tragic experiences have emphasized this, notably, the Battle of Jutland where there were more casualties through oil than through shells.

4. ... The[12] rescue of the little British freighter, the *Antinoe* (Antinoƈ[13] in sailor pronunciation and so observed in the story) by the ss *Roosevelt* under the command of Captain George Fried. Some of you may remember that it happened thirty years ago in what was known as the storm of 1926. The barometric readings made a low

Atlantic record and the rate of the wind was hurricane speed. At dawn on Sunday morning, in a blizzard in January, the *Roosevelt* received an s.o.s. from the *Antinoe*, a British grain freighter which, with bunkers flooded and steering gear out of action, was not able to tell her own position. I was tremendously struck by one part of the message. Here are the exact signs of the *Antinoe*'s call as it came in to the cabin of the *Roosevelt* radio: three dots, three dashes, and the dots again. 'British freighter, *Antinoe*. Don't know position. Sixteen hours ago – rough latitude, north forty-six and ten, rough longitude thirty-nine, fifty-eight. Been hove-to ever since; the present rate of drift to east two knots approximate.' It was a call, a cry delivered by the key of the transmitting instrument, and it was heard by the *Roosevelt* radio. Captain Fried took the message but all he knew was that a ship was sending out a call for help and that since noon the day before she had not known her bearings. Just at this time a message had come from the *Aquitania* and the two captains conferred with each other as to which one should go to the help of the wreck. And as the Cunarder was going west against the storm, it was agreed that Fried should take on the job. On the *Roosevelt* there was installed a comparatively recent invention, the direction finder, by means of which a distant ship sending out a wireless s.o.s. might be located. The wireless chief put on his headphones and listened as he moved a wheel and kept his eye upon a pointer on a compass. As he moved the wheel, the signals from the *Antinoe* became stronger until they got to their maximum strength and then the operator saw the indicator point to a degree on the dial of the compass. He knew that the *Antinoe* was over there, in that direction, but how far he couldn't tell. Fried put the bow of the *Roosevelt* on that bearing. He knew that the hand pointed directly to the home of the signals sent out by the operator on the *Antinoe*. Like asdic and the later radar, and the earlier and simpler shriek of the whistle getting its echo from the cliffs, there was nothing that the eye could see except an instrument, here in the *Roosevelt*, just a finger pointing as if saying: 'There, out there.' The answer came back from the *Antinoe*: 'Tarpaulins ripped. Another hatch let go. Bad list. Grain swelling fast. Seams loosening now. All lifeboats gone from starboard davits. How many knots are you making? How far away do you reckon you are? Cannot wait much longer.' Fried pursued the sounds right home to the heart of the wave zone in the instrument of the *Antinoe* and at length he saw the freighter two hundred yards away ...[14] Fried pumped oil on the water, and waited for a sign of the abatement of the wind, but the storm and the blizzard seemed to be increasing indefinitely, and in the midst of a squall of snow he lost sight of the *Antinoe* and at the same time the wireless contact ceased. All on deck of the *Roosevelt* believed that the *Antinoe* had gone down in that last squall. At the same time messages kept coming in from other ships and here I imagine never was radio put to more humane employment on the sea. All during the search signals were streaming through the ship's antennae: *Solvang* in collision, bulkheads crushed; the *Curlew* aleak, and under jury rig,[15] *Carlstad* searching; *Carlotta* helping *Orebro*. The *Bremen* hastening to the *Laristan*, engine trouble, serious, twenty-two aboard. No record of the *Antinoe*. That search of Fried in that long interval of call and silence was tremendously significant in the records of human action. It was a wonderful instance of sea-shepherding, out to seek and save a life which was lost. The keys kept rapping – 'Where are you *Antinoe*?' No answer. The freighter was believed to be lost by every law known of wind and weather. Yet there was one chance out of a hundred or one out of eight hundred that she was afloat, and it was with those terribly adverse odds the *Roosevelt* kept searching.

Supposing she was afloat, what would be her probable position? There were certain facts on which the calculations could be based. Fried knew the force of the wind. His instruments could tell him that. He knew the exposed surface of his own ship on the windward side and he could make a guess at the hull of the *Antinoe*. He tried to figure out the drift and direction of the waterlogged freighter. Yet there was always the thought in the captain's mind that the *Roosevelt* might collide with the stricken ship which would mean certain destruction to both. The search with all those variables and risks continued until Fried picked her up nineteen hours after and sixty miles further down the course of the wind. A miracle of navigation. The *Antinoe* in that interval had had her navigating bridge swept away. Her stokeholds were flooded, her steam off, her lights off.

Fried called for volunteers to go in the first lifeboat and this famous rescue is noted for the internationality of the boat crews. Here is the actual list as on the shipping register: Robert Miller, the first officer, commanding. Ernest Heitman, bosun's mate, no relative. Uno Wertanen, master-at-arms, aged twenty-eight, a Finn, his mother at Helsinfors the next of kin. Sam Fisher; Franelich, an Austrian; Johannes Bauer, a naturalized American; Maurice Jacobowitz of New York State, and a Dane named Alexander Fugelsang, all making up the lifeboat complement of eight. That fine mixture of nationalities all engaged in a death struggle for the preservation of life showed the high stuff in human nature.

They managed to lower the boat but she capsized when less than fifty feet away. Six of the crew managed to get back to the ropes and ladders, and were pulled up on deck, but two were in difficulty. Heitman was crushed between the ship and the boat and was slipping away when his friend Wertanen, who was being pulled up, willingly let go his hold on his rope and went after Heitman. He managed by sheer muscle and pluck to drag Heitman back to a rope, pushed his arm through the loop, but Heitman, becoming fatigued, dropped back and Wertanen went after him a second time but couldn't recover him. This time Wertanen himself couldn't swim back with the force of the wind and tide against him, so he turned to swim *with* the wind towards the wrecked lifeboat which was drifting towards the *Antinoe*. He reached the boat and half climbed over the stern and tried to jockey the boat, using his legs as a rudder, down to the ship where the *Antinoe*'s crew were waiting to lift him on board. But the oil got in his eyes and throat and the last thing seen of him was his body drifting helplessly around the stern of the *Antinoe*. Two men were then drowned in the first effort to save the crew and that night a funeral service was held on board the *Roosevelt* with the storm still at its height ripping the ritual into shreds. This was another call and answer on the highest level where it might be thought that religious faith was being put to a test that was baffling all the efforts that science was putting forth. The men assembled in the saloon while an Anglican minister read the service. There was something terribly challenging about it all, because during the service messages were going through the ether from other ships announcing their own tragedies like an ironic chorus. There were two services, this Protestant one, and later a Catholic one. I had heard that a priest was on board who felt that the two men who were drowned belonged to his own faith. I asked an officer if he would look up the number of his cabin. We found it and together we went up the stairs, following literally the footsteps of the priest who came up at midnight to the boat-deck, moved over to a davit where he held the crucifix towards the floating bodies.

In the morning the *Roosevelt* lowered her flag half-mast in token of her dead, and someone on the *Antinoe* tried and succeeded in hoisting the Red Ensign half-mast to acknowledge the salute. Then five minutes later both flags went back to their full height as colours to their fighting stations. The job was on again. Miller, again in command, managed with wonderful skill to get over to the lee side of the *Antinoe* and took on board twelve of the twenty-five. Five lifeboats were lost in the later efforts. The sixth try was successful. The thirteen were taken aboard the boat, brought over to the *Roosevelt*, where after one hundred hours of exposure to a winter storm they were like drowsed children, some of them bruised and unconscious, [and were] pulled up in the cargo nets over the rails of the *Roosevelt*. The last to be pulled up was the *Antinoe*'s master, Captain Tose, who had worn his buttons well. I looked up his record and it was found that ten years before he had, while master of another ship, rescued a Philadelphia vessel in heavy seas. So his bread was returning to him on the waters.

The men of the *Roosevelt* told me that with the twenty-five rescued the ship pulled away and they saw the *Antinoe* settling. The job was done just in time. It was a call well answered. The call of the instruments joined with the hail of the human voice and the sacrificial blood beating at the pulses. Science in league with good will; individual courage and humanity behind the machine. It is that sort of thing, and only that sort of thing, which is the hope of this world. When the *Roosevelt* arrived at Plymouth with her brood of castaways, all England, which had heard of the rescue through wireless, was on its knees in thanksgiving, acknowledging a great deed which was but characteristic of her own grand sea tradition.

'To Angelina, An Old Nurse'   January 1931

1. 'The Nurse': This is a description of a type that has long gone out of date, the nurse of the late Victorian period whose object of worship was Florence Nightingale, but unlike the lady with the lamp she stayed at home to carry out the one passion of her life and that was to administer medicine. Whenever she came near us when we were children we involuntarily opened our mouths, even when she didn't have designs on us which was exceedingly rare. In small country villages she took the place of the doctor and the druggist. She was all the time examining our throats and feeling our pulses, and then rushing for the bottles with the tablets. If we had summer freckles on our face the home might be at once quarantined for measles or scarlet fever. Her consideration for our health would have been sublime if it hadn't been altruist. The wonder of it all is that we managed to survive the severity* of the treatment.

2. Every time that Clare[1] introduces me to an audience I feel like putting my hand in my pocket and taking out a handful of salt to sprinkle over the compliments. But they spring out of the warmth of his heart. He is my oldest friend in Toronto, and outside the circle of my family he is the one loved most by me. In fact I named our daughter after him, Claire P[ratt]; that is the highest tribute I know.[2]

He has asked me to read a poem called 'Angelina, An Old Nurse.' It is based on a type I knew in a small village in Newfoundland many years ago. We had no doctor in the village. She took his place. In fact she was doctor, apothecary, and nurse, and housekeeper all rolled into one. She was a Board of Health in herself. The only role she didn't play was that of the dentist. That role was performed by the village blacksmith who of course never filled teeth. He just extracted them whenever there was any sign of a toothache. The job would be done effectively, if roughly, provided half the jaw didn't come away with the extraction. At any rate the tooth would be out. I speak from very feeling memories. But Angelina did everything else. I have called her Angélina or Angelína according to the needs of the rhyme. Well here it is.

3. I tried to describe an old nurse known to our grandmothers – a nurse who might be first aid and final aid, a dentist, apothecary, housemaid, housekeeper, cook, and possibly a doctor all in one.

'Erosion' June 1931

1. 'Erosion' sprang out of a circumstance related to my early life in Newfoundland. My father, who was a minister, found, as the most trying of all his duties, the announcement of death to a woman whose husband or son had been lost at sea. 'To break the news' had a special Newfoundland ring about it and my father had sometimes to ask the local doctor to accompany him to the house. Once I went with the two of them and I still remember the change on the woman's face – the pallor and the furrows as the news sank in. 'Erosion' was written more than thirty years after but the memory of the face is as vivid today as it was at the time of the tragic announcement.

2. Most of my shorter poems have their background in Newfoundland and spring out of personal experiences. My father was a clergyman moving from place to place every three years, and in the course of his life covered nearly the whole of the island on the sea-coast. So, for the first twenty years of my life I was never out of sight of the sea, the harbours and bays and the coastline. We knew what storms were, wrecks and rescues and loss of life. Indeed one of my first experiences of a shipwreck happened when I was about

eight years of age. A ship had gone down with the loss of some of the crew and my father had to break the news to a woman whose husband was drowned. I went with him and I shall never forget the look on her face when she opened the door. It is one of the most vivid experiences of my early life. Twenty years[1] after I wrote a short poem of eight lines upon the impression. I began searching for an image which might combine rhythm and aptness and concentration. I called the poem 'Erosion.'

'The 6000'   December 1931

1. This poem was suggested by a hundred-mile ride in the cab of a fast locomotive of the 6000 series. The speed, power, and roar of the engine presented the analogy of a monster – a bull conceived in ancient fable with fire for breath and steam for blood.

2. This poem was suggested by a ride from Toronto to Belleville in the cab of a fast locomotive of the 6000 series. The speed, power, and roar of the engine presented the analogy of a monster – a bull conceived in ancient fable with fire for breath and steam for blood. By the time I reached my destination, I was so covered with dust and smoke that I felt as if I had been caught in the stampede of a buffalo herd. The run was taken by courtesy of Mr Frank McDowell of the Canadian National Railways.

The Depression Ends   October 1932

This poem sprang out of a single word. My friend and colleague P[elham] E[dgar] shouted out at me as I was passing his room in the college one day not very long ago to come in and look at a word which he has just read in the *A.M.*[1] Here's a word which has never been in a poem to his knowledge, the word 'prognathic.' 'I'll stump you,' he said, 'to get a poem out of it.' I wanted very much to call his bluff but I must admit the word looked intractable and forbidding. We knew that the word meant a protruding jaw but how was one to get romance out of it? I asked him what was his association with the word. He replied that it represented a prohibitory jaw, a condemnatory jaw, a jaw such as a determined lawyer or dentist or a professor[2] might possess.

I went home and said to Mrs P[ratt], 'What does the word suggest to you?' She closed her eyes and saw a Dickensian character, a dominie,[3] standing, birch in hand, over a squad of cringing schoolboys, and just ready to thrash the daylight out of them. Well I saw a gaunt, angular, jumpy woman, very acidic and sharp-tongued, very nervous and melancholic, who had been installed amongst a crowd of orphans as a governess and whose chief function in life was to see that the children never got anything they liked but only what she considered good for them, always snatching chocolates and bon-bons from them and substituting prunes and oils and pills till the children became as spectral and mournful as herself. 'Well what are you going to do with her? Are you going to make her the heroine or the villain of the poem?' 'No,' I said, 'I am not going to have anything to do with her, except that she is going to suggest the content of the poem by contrast.'

I should like to put on a banquet of such an extent and variety that all the needy children of the world might come and sit down for a whole night, and eat what they like and as much as they like without any prognathic control. That's where the word comes in.[4] Well if the sky was going to be the limit and if I had absolute power, the table might just as well be set in the skies as on the earth and the company at the table might include all hungry individuals, the young and old from the time of Adam down to the present. The banquet hall would be so large that I would take light years to go round it, the illumination for the evening would be furnished by the constellations and to give it local colour the dinner would be held this year to celebrate a new era in production, distribution, and consumption, thus marking the end, let us hope, of this horrible Depression.

'Putting Winter to Bed' October 1932

This is a little fantasy which might be read, I think, either in early spring or late fall. It couldn't very well be read in mid-summer on Yonge Street when the mercury is hitting the nineties or in February when it is hitting thirty below. Easter or Christmas is the appropriate occasion, preferably Easter.

A Reverie on a Dog October 1932

1. The *Reverie on a Dog* is a partly descriptive, partly reflective poem upon a thoroughbred Newfoundland dog. The other poem I wrote some time ago[1] dealt with a rescue achieved by a dog in a great storm off the Newfoundland coast. This one is rather a biography, actual and imaginative, of the finest specimen I knew from the time of his puppyhood unto extreme old age. I may be labouring under some degree of prejudice perhaps in placing the Newfoundland breed above all others, but those who are familiar with dogs of all orders will give the Newfoundland dog the edge for the combination of desirable canine qualities, the total number of technical points. I do not want to say that his courage is greater than, say, that of the English bulldog because the English bulldog would by himself charge a battalion of elephants without calling up the reserves, but then the bulldog's courage is one kind of stupidity. He doesn't care what it is he is charging, a wolf or a locomotive, it's all the same. The Newfoundland has all his courage, ten times his intelligence, the strength of a mastiff, and a loyalty and affection to man that is unsurpassed, I would say unequivocally,* by any brute in the whole animal creation.

The dog, strange to say, is not a native of the island that gave him his name. He is an importation springing originally from the Pyrenean sheep [dog], a huge black dog of great intelligence and crossed with a ...[2] He nearly became extinct a few years ago but attempts are being made, and made successfully, of preserving the type in Newfoundland.[3] He has the noblest head of them all; [a] square head, unusually broad* forehead, widely spaced eyes like the St Bernard,* and the jaws and teeth of the mastiff.

Mac Jack[4] took three or four running leaps into the waves and in a few seconds was out alongside of his master. He even dived for him when Mac intentionally went under. Mac swam to shore with his arm around the dog's neck. He knew there was something in the quality of the appeal which wasn't shared by the other calls – and a young dog at that.

They are not at all belligerent: they rarely fight with each other or with other types, unless they are attacked. Mac told me of one incident which had a comic side to it of a large, ugly, scurvy-looking dog that had raced down from a farm in a boiling rage apparently to get at the Newfoundland on the other side of the fence. He knew that he couldn't get in and he knew the other fellow couldn't get out, hence his marvellous display of fighting urge* and daring. He kept running up and down as if looking for a hole or a gap and once in a frenzy he unwittingly leaped over the palings. He didn't know he was over until he saw the gleaming jaws of the Newfoundlander waiting for him, and then with another leap he bounded back over the fence and scuttled across country at express speed. The two leaps in and out seemed to be part and parcel of the same jump, it was so instantaneous, a two-step movement executed inadvertently.*

Their love of children, their instinct of protection, is what makes them so beloved and admired. They will swim with them in the sea water and prevent the younger ones from going beyond their depth. They'll hold them back from deep holes or wells or big rock fissures, carry them on their backs or go for them after their school hours and accompany them home, and the stories of life-savings are so frequent that they scarcely can be said [to] possess the glamour of romance.

Well anyway this poem is not a narrative! It is rather a bit of soliloquy upon the nature and habits of a thoroughbred. He is pictured as old to the full limit of his years but possessing so many links with our common humanity ...[5]

2. This poem which I have been asked to read is called *A Reverie on a Dog*, a biography, partly imaginative but mainly actual, of the finest specimen I knew of a Newfoundland thoroughbred, from the time of his puppyhood to extreme old age. I don't think that I am exaggerating his intelligence, his affection and devotion, for every incident that I am recording will be authenticated by those who are fortunate enough to possess dogs of this breed. The poem is an attempt at a dramatic monologue and it begins with the dog old to the limit of his days lying down with this head resting upon my knees.

'The Way of Cape Race'   December 1932

1. The loss of the steamer *Florizel* off Cape Race [occurred] when the captain steered west too soon and his ship was piled up on the rocks. A few of my old class-mates were drowned in that disaster. Cape Race, as you know, is one of the most dangerous capes in the world.

2. Cape Race ranks with Cape Horn as the most disastrous point in all the seas of the world. It has well earned its infamy* of being the graveyard of the Atlantic. It has one of the most powerful radar stations anywhere and one of the most penetrating* signal lights. The reefs run for miles out into the Atlantic and in storms the breakers reach seventy feet.

'A Feline Silhouette'   1932

1. Someone asked me if I had written any short poems dealing with land experiences. I said, yes – one was about an event in Toronto. I had been bothered several nights by a number of cats in the backyard with two of them facing each other on top of the fence. They were ...* and caterwauling in the deepest hostility – I could not stand it any longer, so I went to the window and flung at them

everything within reach, slippers, shoes, *et cetera*. I got an airgun and fired some B.B. shots at them but the effect only stung them into greater enmity. I thought, why I'll open up the window and read a poem to them. I did so and the cats on the fence leaped into the air at once and never came back. As you will notice there is a slight exaggeration in the poem. They could stand shoes and shots but not poetry. Such are the virtues of poetry.

2. As the poem I have just read [*The Ice-Floes*] was rather grim in subject and perhaps in treatment, I am going to read a short one mainly for the purpose of changing the theme. It is called 'A Feline Silhouette' and is on the subject of cats. The poem is founded upon a personal experience. Some time ago I used to be disturbed at night by a surprising number of cats that visited my backyard. My sleep was broken by the most infernal chorus ever heard by human ears. I would shout at them from the window. I flung everything at them which was at hand, lumps of coal and shoes. I got an air rifle and fired at them, but the shot only served to send their choral notes further up the scale. One morning after an unusually bad night, I rang up the Humane Society and asked them how many cats there were in Toronto. 'About three hundred thousand.' 'Well,' I replied, 'at least fifty-one per cent were in my backyard last night. What can be done about it?' 'Nothing,' was the answer, 'unless you can trap them.' Well that was impossible without a mile of barbed wire. Then I knew that the only way to get my revenge was to write a poem, which I did, and I read it to them at midnight. The cats immediately left and never came back. They made up their minds to get out. The principal characters described here are a black cat and a white cat facing each other on the fence while the innumerable company were engaged in argument in the yard.

3. This sprang out of a personal experience in Toronto. Some years ago we were serenaded night after night by an uncountable number of cats in the backyard with two cats on the fence, each the leader of a pack. The noise was fearful. At midnight I would get up and fling everything at them – from the window – shoes, rubbers,

golf balls, lumps of coal, but it made no difference. I even fired at them from a popgun but that only made them madder. So I thought I would write a short poem on them, which I did, and read it to them from the window. They left immediately and never came back. Well, I thought, poetry has a use after all. The cats could stand artillery fire, but not poetry.

4. ... This is part fiction, but mainly true. Something must be left to the imagination here. It was the way I felt anyway but I have forgotten the poem which was written in the spirit of fun the next day and it is anyone's guess whether it was read from the window.

'Like Mother, Like Daughter' December 1933

It is the nature of romance to construct golden ages and push them back into the past. And the more terrible we think our own generation, the more we like to linger over bygone periods, when our ideals, as we fondly and mistaken[ly] think, were actualized. We say there was never such happiness as there was in the old days, never such love, never such marriages; then men were more heroic and the women more lovely and more eternally feminine, which is all a mistake of course. This poem compares the beautiful syrens of the past with those of the present just to show that the rules of the game are the same today as they ever were, though sometimes the language and the phraseology are different.

'The Prize Cat' February 1935

1. 'The Prize Winner'[1] is a little study in atavism. Though it pertains to a prize-tabby yet it also applies to the most cultivated of the human species, male and female. The very moment we think that we have rationalized our behaviour and downed our instincts, some little circumstance may arise to show us what a parvenu the reason is, put over against instinct.

2. The next one[2] is also on a cat but a different species of animal. It is called 'The Prize Cat' and refers to Mussolini's attack on Ethiopia just before the Second World War. I had been pondering over the illusion that, with the growth of civilization and culture, human savagery was disappearing.

3. I'm glad you omitted 'The Prize Cat' because there shouldn't be two poems on cats and the one on Mussolini was too controversial and too vague for the lower schools.

The Titanic   1935

1. The story of the *Titanic* is not primarily intended to be the record of a great disaster at sea. It is that indeed, for fifteen hundred persons were drowned when the big ship went down, but the loss of life as such would not account for the world-wide interest in the event, which is almost as keen today as it was a generation ago. It is a study in irony, probably the greatest single illustration of the ironic in marine history. So completely involved was the ship in what we call the web of Fate, that it seemed as if the order of events had been definitely contrived against a human arrangement. Her sinking was absolutely incredible. She was described as the ocean lifeboat. There was never an event outside the realm of technical drama where so many factors combined to close all the gates of escape, as if some power with intelligence and resource had organized and directed a conspiracy. Apart from such provisions as constituted her normal protection like her immense size and flotation, her powerful engines and pumps – apart from all these, there were all around her within wireless touch eight ships, some of them like the *Olympic* and the *Baltic*, the biggest on the sea, talking to her, congratulating her on her maiden voyage as she sped along, and warning her of the presence of ice. The spectacle of the world's greatest ship slowly sinking to her doom in perfectly calm water, in weather ideally suited for the lowering of lifeboats, under a clear sky, sinking ablaze with electric light, sinking to the accompaniment of joyous music, was not only tragic but grotesque.

2. ... As this poem on the *Titanic* may take too long to read in its entirety at one session, I should like to present the plan of it, giving enough explanation to fill in the gaps between the parts recited.

I do not suppose that there is in this century a single event narrowly circumscribed in place and time which has given rise to more discussion and heart-burnings than the loss of the *Titanic*. Any individual episode of the Great War, as horrible as it may be, is subdued by the general background, just as the destruction of a house would be by the conflagration of a town. Such an incident as the sinking of the *Lusitania* came as the climax of a series of provocations to determine the war-mind of the United States, and in that sense [was] tremendously significant, but at least the sinking was credible and in many quarters expected as a chance of war, but the foundering of the *Titanic*, removed as it was from the bounds of belief, made the disaster the most grotesque event in the history of the sea. The appeal of the story is akin to that which holds our minds when we read about a perfect plot, where every contingency is supposed to be safeguarded, and where the defence has repaired the vulnerable spot in the heel.

The claims put up for the *Titanic* are now a matter of public knowledge. She was the biggest ship in the world, one thousand tons larger than her sister, the *Olympic*. She would furnish the most comfort in travel and would be the steadiest boat on the sea. She was the most costly, the most luxurious[1] – saloon and lounge, cabins and staterooms being decorated in all the architectural styles.

But the outstanding presumption was that of safety. She was advertised as the unsinkable ship. Under the laws of hydrostatics she couldn't go down. Back of it all was the confidence in the construction as an engineering triumph. The mechanization of the ship was so perfect that all possibilities of trouble were believed to be anticipated. So automatic was the running and control that little was left to the human judgement. In the case of fire at sea there was no need of a brigade. Even smoke in a compartment was indicated at once by a film on the navigating bridge and in less than a minute a gas extinguisher played on the threatened area. She was the latest embodiment of marine science, fitted with three engines, two reciprocating and one turbine, watertight compartments with steel bulkheads that could be closed by the hand of a child, double-acting davits, thermometers that would indicate the presence of ice in the distance. It was inconceivable for a storm to place a wave bodily upon the promenade deck.

Moreover the ship was launched at a time when the Marconi discovery, scarcely ten years old, was still inflating the mind with its dramatic performances. Those who remember the announcement of the discovery[2] may recall the sense of conquest over nature that visited the hearts of men, the trust in science for the prevention of the grosser human calamities. Wireless had not only given a richer meaning to the phrase 'the brotherhood of the sea' but it was considered as having eliminated forever the horror of the great tolls after collisions and storms. And it wasn't long before the claims began to be vindicated with growing impressiveness as the stations were multiplied on the coasts and the apparatus installed on the ships. And the years 1910 and 1911 were the banner years of rescue, steamers answering calls through winter gales with thousands rescued, and the post of Marconi operator took on a touch of heroic drama. He was the sentry of the ocean, not less than the captain himself, the symbol of duty and loyalty and watchfulness. His position added romance to the routine[3] of a steamer. The safeguards around ocean travel were becoming foolproof. Confidence was climbing. Somewhere in the scale it would merge with delusion when vigilance relaxed and sleep came to the crow's-nest. The *Titanic* was the supreme example of self-infatuation, of an assumed omniscience, of the disregard of a lesson which everyday human beings repeat but never master and [which is] expressed in the reflection – this thing was unforeseen.

The outline of the poem then is as follows:

The construction at the Harland [and] Wolff Works in Belfast and the ambitions and hopes of the line; the idea of a mechanically perfect production; her trial spin and her approval by the Board of Trade; the birth of the iceberg and its slow voyage from the Greenland coast to its precise latitude and longitude off the Banks of Newfoundland; the departure of the ship from Southampton with the superstitious accompaniments that deeply impressed the minds of some of the passengers, as for instance, the tremendous power of her engines even when the *Titanic* was just making steerageway in leaving the dock, tore the ss *New York* from the quay smashing the seven mooring cables. The collision was just averted by the rope fenders. A little further down, the *Teutonic* strained at her ropes to follow the bigger ship. The wash was so great that the *Titanic*'s engines had to stop and leave the business to the tugs of taking care of the *Teutonic*. Then when the *Titanic* was in the middle of the harbour a huge wash was seen to rise just astern that could not be accounted for by the revolution of the screws. It wasn't known at the time as it was known later that a barge sunken in the harbour had been dragged along through the mud several hundred feet by the mere suction of the *Titanic*. But once out on the Atlantic under calm skies, with the steadiest of keels, for she was fitted with a fin keel to ensure stability, with her purring engines and her smooth acceleration, all these fables and fears were abandoned to the wagging heads on the shore.

Then the first evening on the ocean – Wednesday, with the preparation of the dinner to feed 2,300; the smooth uninterrupted interval between Wednesday and Sunday; absolute calm; Sunday morning with the first messages about ice from the *Baltic*, the *Virginian*, the *Californian*, the *Carpathia*, and other ships; the failure to slow down as the warnings increased; the dinner again on Sunday at 7:30 with the conversation of a few passengers at one of the tables; the wealth, the luxury, the social significance of the company in the saloon; a poker party in Room 179 on D deck ending just at the moment of collision with one of the players calling for soda and ice.

This part I intend to omit in the reading, not by any means on account of the fact that it has to be read in the chapel of a college[4] which has for one century been associated with the tradition of tolerance,[5] but for three other reasons, the first being that I have behind me, looking down from the stained glass windows, the faces of John Wesley and Martin Luther and I feel a little nervous under that fixity of vision. The second more important reason is that the scene of the last round is put in the form of a short play in which six people are required to talk and act, and it is beyond my capacity to take the part of the whole six. The third reason is that the language but dimly understood by myself is so highly specialized that it is only meant for a technical constituency. But may I take this opportunity in passing to thank some of my friends who are in this audience tonight for having helped me so liberally out of the wealth of their vocabulary.

This scene is followed by an account of the wireless messages between the *Titanic* and the *Californian* (the *Titanic* telling the *Californian* to keep out and not jam the traffic signals; the *Californian* only eighteen miles away, big enough, near enough to rescue the whole company, actually visible to some of the officers on the *Titanic* but deaf to the signals),[6] the collision, with Smith's instructions to the officers to have the stewards awake the passengers without alarm; the refusal on the part of the passengers to entertain thought of trouble let alone disaster; the shattering of their confidence by the rockets; the lowering of the lifeboats and the medley of confusion, discipline, misunderstanding, fear, cowardice, indifference, courage up to an exalted pitch; the heroism of the engineers, the wireless operators, and the band; the race of the *Carpathia* to the scene and the smallness[7] of the margins between rescue and catastrophe. The profoundest irony was the shortage of the lifeboats when the weather was absolutely ideal for the launching. It seemed to me that there was something profoundly arresting and insidious in this fact.[8] The stage was not set for a great battle where the might of the ship was pitted against the might of a storm with breakers challenging steel and with the issue in suspension through long debate. The *Titanic* was sinking under a set of conditions unique in marine annals – a perfectly calm night, a starry sky and friendly water, sinking in a blaze of electric light and to the accompaniment of joyous music. The ironic had joined with the macabre.

Was there ever an event outside of the realm of technical drama where so many factors combined to close all the gates of escape, as if some power with intelligence and resource had organized and directed a conspiracy? Apart from such safeguards as constituted her normal protection – like her immense size and flotation, her numerous watertight compartments, her steel bulkheads, her powerful engines and pumps – there were all around her within wireless touch eight ships, some of these, like the *Olympic* and the *Baltic*, the biggest on the sea, talking to her, congratulating her on her maiden voyage as she sped along and warning her of the presence of ice. The whys and the ifs came thick and fast after the event. Why should the belief in her invulnerability stimulated by advertisement have [caused neglect of] the ordinary lifeboat provision – one-third only of her capacity? Why should the iceberg that struck her have arrived at that precise moment in that precise locality? There was only one part of the ship which was not immune to attack. The iceberg sought that line for its thrust. Why should the *Titanic* in endeavouring to avoid head-on collision, a natural impulse, find a greater peril in the glancing blow? In the words of the Washington commissioner,[9] she turned aside the brow only to take it on the temple. Why should the wireless operator on the *Californian* just fifteen miles off have taken off the phones from his ears a minute or so before the distress signal from the stricken ship? And why were the rockets which were actually seen by the *Californian* misunderstood?[10]

3. Gentlemen: I have never forgotten the thrill that possessed my soul six years ago[11] when so many of my friends who are here tonight assembled in this room to take part in a function similar to this one. I remember saying that I had never experienced anything just like it before in my life and I never anticipated another. I thought it was too rich, too choice an experience ever to have a parallel and yet here it is in full flower again. My deepest gratitude tonight at it was six years ago is to my old and trusted and beloved friend Hugh Eayrs. Our friendship has lasted now for twelve years without a rift. The abundance of his hospitality, of which this dinner tonight is only one glorious specimen, has always been, as far as I am concerned, more a personal than an official expression.

During the last twelve years of friendship which I have had with him I have seen many sides of Hughie: I have seen him in the office discussing a proposition. I have seen him at his home at a table. I have seen him at a poker game. I have seen him on the golf course, and at the nineteenth hole. I have seen him under the shower spotless and unblemished and he is the same lad throughout.

My special task tonight is to say something about the construction and the purpose of the poem on the *Titanic*.[12] My interest in the loss of the *Titanic* was always more than a desire to record a story, a concern more with the implications of the disaster than with the factual side of it, though of course the impression has to be produced through the facts. It is a study in irony, probably the greatest single illustration of the ironic in marine history. I do not think that the public have ever been completely aware of how deeply involved the *Titanic* was in the web of fate. It was as if the order of events had been definitely contrived against a human arrangement.

The White Star Line had under declared intention set out to build the perfect ship, a ship that by the way would help to rehabilitate the finances of the International Mercantile Marine, whose stock was at the time down from one hundred par to five.[13] The keenest competition prevailed in 1912 between the White Star, the Cunard, and the Hamburg-American. The Hamburg-American was building the *Imperator*, afterwards the *Berengaria*, which was also meant to be the biggest ship in the world, but she was several months behind the *Titanic* in construction, so the White Star was winning the race against the Germans. The Cunarders had won the first place for speed in the *Mauretania*, a much smaller boat than the *Titanic*, but while there was no official statement that the *Titanic* might hope to match the *Mauretania*'s rate there were many admirers close to the line who said, 'Well, we'll just wait and see.' But certainly, the White Star would capture the Blue Ribbon for size and also for comfort and luxury and above all for safety. She was advertised as unsinkable, the first ship that might in all certainty be described as a lifeboat in herself. Her very size created that impression, more than one hundred feet high from the keel to navigating bridge and one hundred and seventy-five[14] to the top of the funnels (that's as high as a fifteen-story building), and nearly one-fifth of a mile long. She had eight steel decks and sixteen watertight compartments bulkheaded by doors operated through electro-magnets by a switch on the bridge. Supposing she did meet with an accident at sea, say collision against rock or iceberg even at full speed, the worst that could happen would be the smashing in of her bows. The flotation of the ship was so great that the middle and aft compartments, waterproof as they were, would keep the ship above water for an indefinite time. No wave, however great the storm, could reach her boat-deck. Much importance was assigned to the construction of the double bottom. It was just about a risk of one to ten thousand, say, that she would lose her navigating bearings in fog or storm, with her steering engines, her new compasses, and her patent log, but supposing that she did run aground and ripped her outer plating off, there was the inner shell which would remain intact. She was equipped with every device with which marine architecture could safeguard her, fog-bells, instruments which would record the cooling temperatures of the water as the ship came into the vicinity of ice.

And the greatest of all lifesavers was the wireless which for ten years before 1912 had demonstrated its wonderful efficiency in the rescue of life at sea. I remember the intimate contact with wireless which a number of us had in Newfoundland just at the time of the achievement. I was attending the public school at St John's where we had a remarkable teacher of science, a man named Holloway, a fine amateur photographer by the way, the man who took the photographs of those two icebergs reproduced in the book.[15] We were just getting over the thrill of the discovery of the x-ray, the Roentgen ray which he was demonstrating to us in his laboratory, when he announced to us that a greater thrill was awaiting at the House of Assembly where the class in physics went to see Marconi in person.[16] The invention of course had been out sometime before this, but it was our first experience of having a message transmitted through a three-foot concrete wall from key to key without a wire. That was, however, a prelude to what happened the following day. No one knew why Marconi was in town, or what he was doing up on Signal Hill a mile away at the mouth of the harbour. It was a dead secret only disclosed the next morning when the papers headlined the fact he had bridged the Atlantic from Signal Hill to Lizard Point in Cornwall with wireless telegraphy. I mention this because accompanying the thrill was the widespread confidence and boast that the days of great disasters at sea were soon to be ended.

And the most powerful set on the ocean had been installed on the *Titanic*, with a radius of 1,000 miles at night. They said it was inconceivable in this modern age with the ocean alive with ships that a steamer could founder before her passengers and crew were taken off by a rescuing ship. The weird thing about it is the number of times the word inconceivable might have been used and was used in relation to the *Titanic*. When the news of the disaster came to New York, Marconi, who was in the city at the time, and who was preparing to go back to Europe upon the *Titanic* on the return trip, wouldn't believe the report. 'Incredible,' he said. The belief in her unsinkability was so axiomatic that the line did not consider it necessary to have the requisite number of lifeboats. In the first place the law did not require it. There was an old regulation passed in 1894 by the Marine Board of Trade requiring that all steamers of 10,000 tons should carry lifeboat accommodation for 1,000. But 10,000 tonnage was the maximum tonnage for that day, and that regulation, through some terrible lack of foresight on the part of the board, had not been revised though ships of 20, 30, and even 40,000 tons were being built in the long interval. So the *Titanic* started off on her voyage with scarcely more than one-third lifeboat provision. That didn't disturb the authorities much because it was inconceivable that the ship would suffer a[17] major disaster. But a series of dramatic incidents happened on the day of her departure which gave rise to a crop of superstitions mainly affecting people on the shore ...[18]

It was a perfect voyage from Wednesday afternoon to Sunday morning, cloudless day and night and not a breath of wind, and the first warning of ice came from the *Caronia* at nine a.m. Then all through the day and through the evening messages were sent in by a number of ships that field ice of tremendous area and a large number of icebergs had been sighted right ahead in the path of the *Titanic*. The *Californian* which played such a part – a negative part unfortunately – in the tragedy, notified the *Titanic* several times and at nine o'clock sent its final message – 'Say, old man, we've been stuck fast in this place for over an hour, field ice for miles about,' to which the *Titanic* replied – 'Say *Californian*, shut up, keep out, you're jamming my signals with Cape Race.' The *Californian* sent no further message and the *Titanic* kept increasing her speed until it reached twenty-three knots, and at eleven forty-five the bells from the crow's-nest rang and the look-out telephoned the bridge that an iceberg was dead on the starboard bow. The helm was put hard over and the ship instead of taking the berg on the bow took it on the starboard side and took it so smoothly that there was no sense of jar, no impact, not enough to wake the sleep of passengers.[19] Even with engines reversed she went on a mile afterwards, but by the time she stopped there was an amazing list of five degrees in five minutes. Smith, who knew at once how serious that was, went to the wireless room to tell the operators to get ready to send a call but not to send it until the nature of the injury had been discovered. Now, then, two of the most ironic conjunctions took place. The ship's carpenter came back with the report that the submerged spur of the iceberg had cut the ship in the one vulnerable spot, the intersection of the double bottoms, had cut a line three-hundred-feet long from the foremast to amidships, a smooth, sharp, clear cut going through the steel as if it had been cardboard. The iceberg[20] had ended its journey which may have taken two years to reach that precise point in the parallels. If it had been ten feet away, or if it had struck below or above the turn of the bilge, the result would have been different.[21] Then Smith returned to[22] the Marconi room to issue the general call for aid. This was midnight or close to it.[23] But what happened in that little interval of fifteen minutes? Just fifteen miles away was the *Californian*. Her lights had been seen, and just about the time of the collision, the one operator, knowing that his day's work was done, unclamps the phones from his ears and goes to bed, and the frantic signals of the *Titanic* a minute or so later fall upon a dead instrument.[24] A little later the *Titanic* sent up its rockets and the *Californian* actually saw them but Captain Lord claimed that he thought they were fishermen's signals and ignored them. Lord was later dismissed from his command. Sixty miles away was the *Carpathia* which got the s.o.s. and immediately put about and headed for the *Titanic* under double watch and the maximum pressure of steam, but reached the position three hours after the *Titanic* had gone down.

The next great tragic fact was the shortage of lifeboats. Had the *Titanic* carried full capacity there was ample time in the two hours and a half to get them all lowered and pulled off to safety. The incredible circumstance of fifteen hundred persons on deck merely waiting for the foundering and not one lifeboat left just astounded the world. And it was ideal weather for the launching of the boats.

Those two hours and a half were crammed with all varieties of incident, fear, and cowardice mixed with control and sublime heroism. All the thirty-five engineers,[25] those on duty and those off, remained in the holds, not one seen on the decks [again] and not one on the roster of the saved. All the officers died but one and he was picked up in the water after the ship foundered. A group of the passengers infused their own steadiness and calm into the crowds.[26] Astor, Strauss, Butt, Guggenheim, dressed in evening clothes, smoking their cigarettes and speaking words of reassurance to hundreds. And then, most dramatic of all, the band, their bodies braced[27] against any support in the gymnasium, playing their violins without intermission until they were swept off their feet at the final plunge of the ship.

4. It is a pleasure to be here today at the invitation of the school ...[28] to speak about the *Titanic*.[29] I appreciate the warm welcome of the introduction and your own kind greetings. They made me feel at home at once. I must, however, confess to a sense of embarrassment whenever I take this book in my hand. When I was notified by the Department of Education that *The Titanic* was to be a matricula-

tion text and that it would be in such distinguished company[30] as the bold Sir Bedivere and the 'man with the long grey beard and glitterin' eye,' well, I would have blushed to the roots of my hair, if that had been a physical possibility.

There is another embarrassment. I have had a lot of correspondence and telephone conversation, asking me to explain some of the finer shading of the poker game. Well, of course, the language *is* meant for a highly specialized constituency, and I always reply to students, 'Consult your teachers or your fathers,' and when the teachers telephone me for information (which is very rarely by the way), I reply, 'Consult your students.'

Now I don't want people to get the idea that I spend most of my time dealing out cards as if I were a propagandist for poker as a healthy indoor exercise. As a matter of fact I belong to a United Church college and I'm a wretched player,[31] so I had to rely a good deal on my esteemed theological friends who helped me so liberally out of their long and rich experiences in the game.

But I generally get away with it by claiming that even if the technical vocabulary is a bit too abstruse for myself as well as for others, there remains what was for me an important dramatic point of having one of the players at the conclusion call for ice which is conveniently handed through the porthole at the exact moment of collision. The game of course is imaginary, made up, indeed,[32] but on a strong basis of probability that there would be the odd game played during the voyage with more than two thousand people aboard, and the exact timing, though also imaginary, is dramatically plausible.

In fact, the game itself has a number of functions. One is to reinforce the idea of chance and the unexpected. No one knew how the cards would turn up either in the game itself or in the fortunes of the *Titanic*. Another was to illustrate the atmosphere of gaiety and pastime in the game, a part of the general festivities on board the ship, contrasted with the terribly grim reality which was soon to follow, and still again the double significance of the call for ice.

Now I don't wish to repeat too much what is already in the notes by the Macmillan editors,[33] but I should like to emphasize the main characteristic. It is stated there that the loss of the ship was the greatest illustration of the irony of Fate in marine history, that is, the irony of circumstance where a human being makes a plan which he thinks is perfect, as in the so-called perfect crime organized by the so-called mastermind, but where there is one little loophole or weak joint in the armour which he has overlooked or forgotten, which causes the catastrophe. It is sometimes called the irony of coincidence where a number of factors enter, each one taken by itself harmless, but taken in conjunction with others, fatal, and it all comes down to man's belief in his powers to control his own destiny. It is of these circumstances that I want to speak in connection with the *Titanic*. Just when we are led into the belief that our wonderful progress in science has given us watertight security, something happens, utterly unexpected, which makes for our undoing and destruction, and people exclaim, 'Why we never thought of that; who would ever have believed it?' The impossible thing has become possible, has actually happened.

So it isn't a matter of disaster in the loss of life. That is tragic of course, but tragedy needs another factor or another emphasis to bring it over into the conception of irony ...[34]

5. There are some themes that are always turning over in their sleep. They seem to be recurrently subject to high temperatures resisting all the attempts of the old family doctors to find the curative formula. I do not suppose there is in this century a single 'local' event which has given rise to more discussion and heart-probing than the loss of the *Titanic*. Witness the length of the list in the *Periodical Index*, and the volumes – two of them during the past year – relating the reminiscences of the survivors and casting new light upon the disaster. The incident hits us at the most unexpected time. I had heard many people say that after seeing the film *Cavalcade*, the one unforgettable impression was the inscription of the name ss *Titanic* on the lifeboat when the lovers were taking their journey across the Atlantic. The name has become a modern symbol for Fate ...[35]

'Silences' March 1936

1. This bit of verse is based on the idea that speech, whether it is the speech of language or just inarticulate utterance, is meant not only to convey thought but to express emotion, and that expression in itself has a social value independent of both the thought and the emotion.[1] It is a matter of common observation that any feeling which is pent-up is apt to fret and fray the heart. I suppose that is the reason why engines, whether organic or mechanical, must have valves. We often remark to one another or to ourselves – 'Say it, say it, or write it, write it. Get it out of your system. You'll feel better.[2] Don't go nursing the grudge or the hate. Swear at him and then perhaps you won't hit him.' That may be a dangerous doctrine sometimes, but the alternative of silence or repression where you just look your thoughts instead of speaking them may be more dangerous still.

And I have in mind here the vast silence under which submarine drama is enacted, the conflict and destruction that are carried on in the sea, the most primitive of all habitations of life, without one sound being made by the parties to the struggle; millions of years of perpetual warfare waged every hour without a cry or a moan.*

I've seen men on the golf course so mad over a dub shot that they would certainly have had apoplexy if they had been dumb. I often play with such types; grand fellows they are, but you have just got to let them alone for a few moments, give them yards while they are experimenting with the King's English. If you didn't they'd simply blow up or blow you up. So our beautiful language serves other functions than simply those of the expression of thought and feeling.

2. ... To come back to the more general theme of conflict on the sea with which I have been absorbed the most of my writing life,[3] I should like to read a poem called 'Silences.' I was under the impression that all of the everlasting conflict which goes on in marine life under the sea is perfectly silent. I read an article recently which claims that sounds are produced under the sea but they are

beyond the scale of human hearing. That limitation satisfies my treatment, and I think there is something fearful and ghastly about silent annihilation as in a gas chamber of a concentration camp, for example. A silent kill has a terror in it somehow different from that of a noisy struggle. I tried to capture that idea in this bit of verse called 'Silences' with which I shall conclude.

The Fable of the Goats   1937

1. The germ of the subject is contained in one of Aesop's fables[1] which recounts in very brief form the fates of two pairs of goats. One pair meet at the opposite sides of a mountain stream across which a tree has fallen. They come to the centre and disputing the passageway they butt each other over and are drowned. The other pair meet in a narrow mountain pass and one goat conceives the idea of lying down while the other softly steps over him with the result that both lives are spared. That is all which is stated by the fable. I wondered if this brief fable could be made the basis of a rather elaborate poetic symbolism which would reflect in an ironic manner contemporary world conditions.[2] Throw the scene away back into the past but modernize the spirit and the action. Give a suggestion of a world crisis and institute the parallels specific enough to get the implications and yet dark enough to leave some margin of speculation as to the personalities involved. The geographical names are fictitious, chosen mainly for euphonic results, but suggesting central Europe. A mountain range very long and very high separates the east and west by a definite and undebatable frontier. In the whole range there is only one pass on which the east and west could meet, and so narrow that two travellers couldn't cross simultaneously. The ledge is composed of the slipperiest of all rocks – schist. It is backed by a vertical mountain wall and it fronts a precipice a half mile or so deep, called the Canyon of Saint Barnabas.

On the west side of the range there are plains and foothills, the land of Carob, occupied by a virile race of goats who have in the course of their history beaten all their foreign enemies and consolidated a nation. They represent an allegedly pure stock and are all united under one great leader called Cyrus. The east side is the land of Gott occupied by a race of goats just as virile as the other race but very mixed in strain. The leader of this race is Abimelech, who has done for his herd what Cyrus has accomplished for his.[3] Now with such a barrier between east and west it might be hoped that the two tribes could live in independent security. But there were qualities in the goat blood which made that end impossible. The goat's nature was nomadic, restless, ambitious, and, above all, driven by the ambition to climb. Any height was a challenge to that impulse.[4] Moreover he was built for belligerency, the skull for defence and the horns for attack. In addition to this he was omnivorous and insatiable. A strange odour coming from the opposite side of the range made him crazy. There were always herbs and grasses on the other side which he must at all costs secure. And besides being pugnacious and obstinate he was one of the proudest of animals. There was gravity in his countenance, in his long features, in his flowing patriarchal beard. He is most sensitive to insult and immune to argument and conciliation.

Those two breeds of goats were about equally matched, which accounts for the fact that over thousands of years, in thousands of battles, not one Carobite had ever reached the land of Gott, and not one Gottite had ever set hoof on the domain of Carob. In every personal conflict on the pass both protagonists had been precipitated into the abyss. It was one sublime, immortal stalemate. If the leader of one side didn't get across, at least he had the satisfaction of knowing that neither did the other fellow. But according to the postulate of the fable there came a time when the deadlock was broken. One goat finds a solution. He kneels down and lets his enemy pass over him. Why he goes against the corporate tradition God only knows but we have the fact in the fable. The speculations furnish the main content of this poem. Had this goat's metabolism altered through a change of diet as he advanced inward from the sea? It is not likely that new shrubs and grasses would mitigate the fighting impulses nourished on Irish moss on which his ancestors had fed for thousands of years. Had his thyroid been stimulated by the seaweed in the Adriatic giving his nature a sense of the fitness of things, or was it the sight of the vultures swinging up and down the pass waiting for the remains, giving him a hint of the futility of battle? Was it one lone phagocyte[5] that in some strange mysterious way had entered the blood stream to clean up the murderous military bacteria? I had to choose which one had to do the kneeling. Was it the western Aryan or the eastern hybrid composed chiefly of the Tartar strain? I suppose as between the two classes, say, the Anglo-Saxon or Teuton on the one side, and the Mongol or Tartar on the other, there isn't much choice when it comes to a matter of belligerency or compromise, and I couldn't surrender the problem by making a Tartar fight with a pacifist like Mahatma Gandhi for that would surrender the drama. I couldn't get things started that way. I had to make the two antagonists of the same blood to get mutuality of conflict. So I have made the slightest suggestion that in the evolutionary climb the so-called Aryan was just one up on the Tartar in the generation of a rational cell. A moral phagocyte had got the jump on the bacillus.

Then after Cyrus has knelt down, why doesn't his enemy take advantage of the prostrate condition and hurl him over into the abyss? Something likewise had entered into Abimelech's nature just as valuable as that which had come to Cyrus. A touch of chivalry which could just as well come from the east, a phase of the sacredness of hospitality characteristic, they say, of the desert.

2. In *The Fable of the Goats* I had to consult a geologist in order to construct aright the structure and strata of the mountain range on which the duel between the two goats took place. I wanted an exceedingly slippery rock and Professor Thompson gave me the names of a number of rocks, amongst which was schist, which he said would be geologically and mineralogically authentic. I selected the term for two reasons. That it was exceptionally slippery especially in rain was a primary reason. It made the foothold and the fight precarious and consequently the chances of survival practically impossible for both contestants. The other reason was

that the term, although not in itself very euphonic ... fitted conveniently into the rhyme and the metrical pattern, and following from that its very repetition helped to develop the mood of dissent, argument, and belligerency which we associate with the little ending 'ist.' Consider words from the boxing ring – fist, duellist, antagonist, pugilist; terms from the matrimonial arena – bigamist, polygamist, misogynist; terms in art which indicate division and revolt like Cubist, Vorticist, Dadaist; in Theology like Calvinist, Baptist, Methodist, which suggest non-conformity and a shade of belligerency. We associate perhaps subconsciously this ending with rebellions and causes and martyrdoms. It is a noisy little sibilant expressive of energetic action. But I needed a little bit of research to discover it.

'The Submarine'   December 1938

1. This poem contains a comparison between a submarine and a shark. There are some types of sharks (viviparous) which bring forth their young alive, perfectly formed, and possessing not only the instinct but the capacity to kill as soon as they are delivered from the body of the mother. There is something terrifying in the idea that the very process of birth starts the process of slaughter. The young ones will go right after the mullet, and the point in the analogy is that the torpedo leaves the body of its submarine mother perfectly mechanized and adjusted to the task of destruction.

2. I have been asked to take up twenty minutes of this program tonight by reading some poems. The first two are new and unpublished. The latter two are taken from a volume which I brought out last Christmas entitled *The Fable of the Goats*.

The first one is entitled 'The Submarine'[1] and it contains a comparison between a submarine and a shark. There are some types of cold-blooded fish[2] which bring forth their young alive, perfectly formed, and possessing not only the instinct but the capacity to kill as soon as they are delivered from the body of the mother; the saw-fish, the leopard ray, and certain species of sharks. There is something terrifying in the idea that the very process of birth starts the process of slaughter. The young ones will go right after the mullet or the mackerel,[3] and the point in the analogy is that the torpedo leaves the body of the submarine perfectly mechanized and adjusted to the task of destruction.

'Old Harry'   February 1939

1. The next is 'Old Harry,' a treacherous rock off the shoreline that looked like a sinister human head.

2. Old Harry is a name given to a rock, responsible for a number of shipwrecks.

'The Dying Eagle'   Winter 1939

The next is called 'The Old Eagle.' It is entitled in the collection 'The Dying Eagle' but that is an error. It might have been more properly called 'The Old Eagle Has His First Sight of an Aeroplane.'

'The Radio in the Ivory Tower'   December 1939

Imagine a person today who with the desire of the hermit has withdrawn himself from the smoke [and][1] dust of cities, the shriek of motor horns, the hum and zoom of aeroplanes, the barking of dogs and the meowing of cats. So he builds for himself; like Robinson Jeffers,[2] a castle on the Californian coast, where no human life can be seen, nothing but mountains and clouds, sunrises, sunsets, and the great expanses of the sea. He brings with him, however, a radio, and on one night in the complete silence of his environment he turns on the dial and the world from which he tried to escape has come back on him with double intensity.

Brébeuf and His Brethren   **1940**

1. Once in five years or so I summon up enough courage or
presumption to subject my friends to a verse recital.[1] On the last
two occasions my themes were catastrophes, but as my audience
managed to survive through the aid of the lifeboats, I thought I
should try the experiment again, this time to invite you for one hour
to join the roll of the martyrs.

The story of the Jesuit missionaries to Canada is not only a great
act in the national drama: it is a chapter in the history of religion: it
is a saga of the human race. It is three hundred years old; it is
contemporary, attracting more attention today than it ever did. In
respect to certain expressions of the human spirit – courage, faith,
self-effacement, endurance – that sheer holding on at solitary posts
in the darkness of an approaching catastrophe which had all the
earmarks of material failure – those twenty years of the Huron
Mission can stand with any of the blazing periods of history. It will
always remain with its own message in every age.[2] Not that the
lesson of courage needs to be enforced in weeks and months like
these when the epics are written in the skies and on the beaches,
when every hour some fighting plane falling in a trail of fire to the
ground is the result of a daring magnificent gamble.

It is not just that story which is recorded in the *Jesuit Relations*
though it possesses that element. Nor is it the kind described by
Joseph Conrad when he speaks with obvious wonder of the risks
taken by men, particularly sailors, in the ordinary routines of trade.
One can understand the pull of romance in exploration and in war,
in the prospects of new worlds and races, in the discovery of the
unknown and unfamiliar, the passion of curiosity, but he says how
amazing it is that thousands of men in thousands of ships should go
around the world, get sick and die, or suffer cold and heat, fight
storms, get wrecked and drowned for the sake of bringing home
cargoes of pepper – enduring such struggles and loss and death for
pepper.

It is true that the Jesuit missions were established in a time of
exploration and colonization, when the French, Dutch, and

English were pushing back the frontiers of the New World; that immense territories were seized in war and immense fortunes gained in trade; but the missionaries were interested in neither one nor the other. No lands, no concessions, no profits were given or asked for. Their vows excluded all considerations of personal gain. They had one interest only – the religious salvation of the Huron Indians by means of the rites and mysteries of their church. That the motive was sacrificial, materially disinterested, based upon absolute conviction and sincerity, both Catholic and Protestant historians attest, Parkman[3] witnessing to the purity and self-devotion of the springs of interest. It was enough for men like Brébeuf, Lalemant, and Jogues to know that the orders of their superiors had been obeyed, letter and spirit, and that the seal of Christ had been placed upon their labours.

The fibre of the story is seen not merely in the outstanding moments of crisis which pierce the imagination, although such moments are many when the mind assessing the slim chances of physical survival called on the iron in the blood to invoke decisions. Those were the dramatic features which, when they were related in France, assumed an aspect of the sublime and raised the moral temperature of the nation. To the members of the order they were as signals at a masthead.[4] Not merely *there* was the quality shown but in the long tug of years in the constant resistance of the temptation to renounce and relinquish the tasks. The doors were often open for escape but not one of the missionaries went out. When Brébeuf returned to France upon the English occupation of Québec, he came back to the Hurons with the French restoration. When Jogues, after his Iroquois captivity and virtual martyrdom, was ransomed by the Dutch and sent to France in December, he returned the following spring to complete the martyrdom.

One must also consider the individual natures and temperaments of the men. Sensitive, cultivated, versed in the literature, theology, and the most advanced science of their day, they [were] suddenly transported to vermin-infested lodges where the dogs ate from the same platters as the natives, where during the day the smoke in the bark cabins blinded their eyes, and during the night the drums of the medicine men, combined with the eternal fleas, destroyed their sleep.[5]

And it must be pointed out that in the course of their religious endeavours they never ignored the humane and social side of their ministrations.[6] They strove to reduce disease in the villages, to improve sanitation and hygiene, to mitigate, if they could not abolish, the torture of captured enemies. They taught new methods of cultivation of the land, founding what has been described as the first experimental farm on this continent, and their efforts frequently staved off periodical visitations of famine and death.[7]

Now as this story is much too long to read in its entirety, I am going to take certain sections and fill in the gaps with explanation.

The first is concerned with the religious background of France in the latter [part of the] sixteenth century and early seventeenth century where, under the inspiration of St Francis Xavier and Ignatius Loyola, the militant missionary order flourished, and the calls came to the priests who afterwards became the canonized Canadian martyrs.

This is followed by the account of the departure from France for Québec of Brébeuf, Massé, and Charles Lalemant; of Brébeuf's first attempt, unsuccessful, to get to the Huron country, his wintering with the Algonquins, then his voyage in company with Daillon and de Noüe up the Ottawa, through Lake Nippissing, down the French River, along the coast of Georgian Bay to the village of Toanché near the shore of the Bay of Penetanguishene; his attempt to study and master the Huron tongue, which was so difficult that de Noüe, finding himself unable to understand one Huron sentence and unable to make a Huron understand one sentence of his own, gave up the endeavour and returned to Québec. Daillon also returned under orders and Brébeuf spent three years alone assiduously studying a language which had three numbers, three genders, and a feminine conjugation, and very few words to indicate abstract ethical notions. They could not understand generic relations like master-servant, father-son – only a particular master and a particular servant. He tried to get them to penetrate the formula – 'In the name of the Father and of the Son and of the Holy Ghost' – but failing to do it, he wrote his Provincial in France for permission to change it to 'In the name of our Father and of His Son and of their Holy Ghost.' The Hurons lacked all labials. The throat and tongue, palate, and teeth were very active but, without the lip sounds, the Huron chiefs in arousing the tribes to war kept the mouth wide open in a form of commanding totalitarian oratory which gave Brébeuf much apprehension.

Here I should like to point out that in writing this poem I had the good luck to find sonorous proper names, personal and geographical, to work into the verse measures. If I may be allowed a digression for a few moments, I should like to say that my attention, like your own no doubt, has been engrossed in the last week[8] with great deeds on the Atlantic revolving around great names. It is not always that the name and the deed are happily married. Occasionally, an action may be tremendous but the principal name nondescript. And often, as we all know, a name intrinsically neutral from a phonetic standpoint may become thrilling because of its associations. I do not think that the names of Blake and Drake and even Nelson are themselves exactly Miltonic but they have been fashioned into silver trumpets through their associations with valorous action and flaming battle signals. But when last week[9] the *Jervis Bay* drew off from the convoy to engage with her four-inch guns the eleven-inch of the German cruiser, what a message and what a name accompanied her to her death. As a fresh ensign went to the masthead to replace[10] the flag which had been shot away, the message was delivered to the rest of the convoy – 'We are moving closer to the enemy.' Captain Fogarty Fegen. May the name like the action live forever.

Well, I found names of this character running about through the *Jesuit Relations*. The name Brébeuf itself was magnificent for a pivotal character. The priest referred to his name as suggesting the patience and endurance and strength of the ox. He was called by the Hurons 'Echon' – he who pulls the heavy load.[11] But look at some of the Indian names. The place where Brébeuf laboured was Ihonatiria near the Bay of Penetanguishene, and when that place was abandoned he served at Teanostaye[12] and Ossossane on the shore of the Nottawasaga. The words sing.[13] And the first adult convert to be baptized was a native called Tsiouendaentaha (I hope I have it right). When the priest baptized him he called him Peter for short,[14] presumably because being the first convert he was like Peter the rock on which the local church was built. What a pity when the father had the chance of pealing forth to the skies such a sequence of sounds as – 'Te Baptizo Tsiouendaentaha.'[15] And when the missionaries came from the north back to their home in Sainte Marie they told of their successes in cabins by the Manitoulin shores.[16] Most of the historical Indian names are euphonic. Donnacona was the name of the Indian chief Cartier took back to France. Other names are Monongahela, Tecumseh, Saratoga, Mississauga, Susquehanna. I could mention others and I am only sorry that I could not work in the most musical name in Indian speech – Ticonderoga. I remember as a boy backing away from an Indian when he told me that his name was Ticonderoga. I was simply overwhelmed by the orchestration of it. I almost shed tears the other day when I discovered that this book [*Brébeuf and His Brethren*] didn't contain the names of Ticonderoga and Fogarty Fegen, but as the names did not belong to my period I knew that I had to stop somewhere out of respect for historical and geographical accuracy.

With apologies I return. The second part[17] is the French restoration, Champlain, Massé, Brébeuf in 1633 back in Québec, the voyage of Brébeuf, Davost, and Daniel along the same rivers and lakes, the building of the Mission House at the village of Ihonatiria, the efforts of the priests to impress the minds of the Indians with the mechanical wonders brought from France.

One interesting thing I saw in the *Relations* was the prediction by Brébeuf of a total moon eclipse. I asked Professor Chant[18] to give me the date of a total eclipse in the year 1635, and whether Brébeuf would know Eastern Standard Time. He looked up the records and wrote me that it occurred on August 27, 1635, and that it would be seen in the Huron country at certain hours. I thought, what a vindication of the accuracy of Brébeuf's letters.[19] His letter written immediately after the event is dated August 27, 1635. He told the Indians that the moon would be darkened on th[at] night. All the braves came out to see it and surely enough there the shadow came like a crow's wing and passed for five hours across the face, while the Huron warriors shot their arrows at it and shouted their curses in the direction of the Iroquois country, for to them it was a portent of invasion. Who were those Frenchmen anyway who could predict such an event?

The letters describe the countless annoyances and irritations [endured] by the priests.[20] And early in their labours the priests witnessed the first torture. A band of Hurons had surprised a party of Iroquois, killed most of them and brought home to the village one of them for the festival of fire. A most dramatic feature of the story is the disclosure of one facet of the Indian mind, the sense of irony shown in the treatment of the prisoner – the sarcasm and the sense of the *double entendre* in addressing the victim.[21] My scientific friends tell me that torture is a very rare phenomenon in the brute world, that perhaps it does not exist at all. The few examples cited may possibly be explained on other grounds – that of the cat playing with a mouse or bird coming most readily to mind: but the fact that a kitten will go through the same antics with a ball of wool might throw some doubt upon its real intentions when in play with a bird. Torture is characteristically a human process implying a development in self-consciousness.[22] In one respect it is an art with a sense of design and elaboration – a feeling for effect. Its presence in the Indian nature, Huron and Iroquois alike, shows that an injustice has been done to the savage by the romanticists who would strip him of all the amenities of civilization. Amongst the Iroquois tribes torture was used to satisfy their pride of conquest. It was one thing to capture and kill an enemy. It was a greater thing to subdue the will, to break down the stoical reserve, an Indian boast in the midst of suffering. To extort a cry was a triumph. But the most appalling ironic incident was in the martyrdom of Brébeuf where the Indians baptized him with boiling water repeating the baptismal formula of the Christian church. What a mixture of aboriginal instinct with sophisticated mockery.

2. ... I have been asked to speak upon the work of the Huronian martyrs of the early seventeenth century in Canada and to read a few selections from the poem *Brébeuf and His Brethren*.[23] The subject happens to be very timely, and interest seems to [be] growing steadily every year. I might spend a few minutes referring to the excavations which have been taking place during the last ten years near the town of Midland, Ontario. People interested in those sites either for historical or religious reasons, or both, have been gratified at the progress made under the supervision of the Royal Ontario Museum and the University of Western Ontario. The provincial government is beginning to realize what national monuments those sites may become, once the task of restoration is completed. Even before the work started, that is, well before the war, people would visit the shrine at Midland from all over the continent, and in the summer of 1939 as many as 400,000 pilgrims passed through the place. At that time there was not much to see. They knew that the fort of Sainte Marie was once there, but it was covered with three centuries of sod and grass and broken stone, decayed stumps and leaf mould. They knew the *approximate* location of Fort St Ignace but the archaeologists got to work to discover the *exact* location. They began digging, and, through a chemical analysis of the soil, they hit upon the palisades. They found stake mould, as distinct from surrounding clay or sand, every few inches, and they traced out the boundaries of the fort exactly. They uncovered the bastions at the corners of the fort. The archaeologists verified the accounts of the Jesuit fathers given in the most accurate and illuminating history ever written about the beginnings of a country or a civilization – the famous *Jesuit Relations*. They unearthed the foundations of the old residence of Sainte Marie and found the floors. The Jesuit letters told of how the residence was burned just before evacuation as an attack by the Iroquois was imminent. And here were the very floors, charred indeed, but still in a fair state of preservation. The four bastions were cleared, the well was discovered from which the fathers drew their drinking water and a great number of French and Indian relics were brought to the surface. Shovels, masons' trowels, awls,

fragments of hempen cloth, a silver needle case containing a needle, a file stamped with the initials J.L. which [are] supposed to be those of Jérôme Lalemant, the superior. They found also a medal bearing the image of St Ignatius Loyola, founder of the Jesuit order, and of St Francis Xavier on the reverse side. But most spectacular of all was the discovery of the three stone fireplaces, spoken of so frequently in the *Relations* – the hearths at which the fathers warmed themselves after their long journeys through the forests and over ice and snow – the very hearths at which Father Chastelain wrote in 1646, three years before the collapse of the mission, his great work dedicated to a religious society in France. Similar dramatic findings were made at St Ignace, particularly the ashes of two stakes at which possibly Brébeuf and Lalemant were martyred.

The final objective of all those interested in historical monuments is to restore the forts and residences as they actually existed three hundred years ago. It would then be possible for pilgrims to say – 'Here is the exact spot where the fathers wrote and read, where they told the stories of the[ir] travels and their labours, their failures, their successes. Here is the spot where Brébeuf and Lalemant died asking forgiveness for their enemies.'

There is something very dramatic in the very matter of exacti-tude. Indefiniteness is always a psychological loss to a pilgrim who is visiting a shrine. It is as if someone said – 'Here in this cemetery square miles in extent is buried a great statesman, hero, saint, but we cannot point out the spot.' But if the monument is directly over the remains, the visitor, pilgrim, worshipper, believer, call him what you like, gets an emotional experience, something akin to the feeling which a parent would receive standing near the soil under which a child had been buried.

So, whether one is Protestant or Catholic, one may feel as I did when I stood with Mr Wilfrid Jury, the archaeologist,[24] within a few feet of the place where Brébeuf offered up his life. It was indeed sacred ground.

A year from next summer will be the tercentenary of the martyrdoms of Brébeuf and Lalemant, 1949, and plans are being made for the production of a pageant[25] which will run through the summer, and if the plans are sufficiently wrought out, the pageant will be produced every summer celebrating the suffering and death of those two martyrs. May I say that the music has already been written by Dr Healey Willan of the Toronto Conservatory of Music. Mr Mazzoleni will be the conductor ...[26]

3. [This is] the story of Brébeuf and his fellow martyrs of the Huron Mission of three hundred years ago. I can give only the barest outline because it is a record which covers a period of twenty years. It has been called the highest heroic episode in Canadian annals and it may be doubted if there is a period in the history of any country which can surpass it in faith, endurance, and sacrificial devotion. It reads like a myth, with so much of the supernatural in it, but we know that the story is so thoroughly documented that its authenticity is everywhere accepted. The eighty-odd volumes of the *Jesuit Relations* resemble an extensive diary, giving the day-by-day observations of eyewitnesses, recording with the most minute details the habits, customs, and beliefs of the Indians and the journeys and labours of the missionaries.

All Canadian historical school-books, of course, refer to the priests, but they restrict themselves mainly to the descriptions of the martyrdoms, particularly of Brébeuf and Gabriel Lalemant. It is this which is known to students because of its more intense and concentrated drama. I suppose there is no account of a protracted passion and death so minutely and accurately related as that of those two priests.

That obviously appeals most to the imagination: it is the fifth act of the tragedy. But the antecedent story is crammed with historical and biographical drama. It goes back into the religious revival in France during the early part of the seventeenth century under the influence of Francis Xavier and Ignatius Loyola who put themselves under vows to accept and endure the harshest terms that the missionary enterprise could impose.

Of that whole group who selected the Huron country as their scene of labour the central character is Brébeuf. In dynamic, in rock endurance, in utter sublimity of courage, in sturdy intelligence, in length of service and persistence, in the combination of all these, he stands supreme. But what I wish to emphasize is that this drama ran for thirty years and more; that heroic decisions were made practically every day and that the final act of death was scarcely more than an epilogue to what one of the priests called a life of daily martyrdoms. The chances came to them again and again in their occasional voyages to Québec and even to France to relinquish their tasks. They could get out – let us remember that. Jogues, for instance, after his period of terrible torture, was sent home when he was ransomed by the Dutch, yet he went back to the Indians the following spring to complete the martyrdom.

I was struck by the number of times the priests in the Huron country renewed their vows. It could mean only one thing – that the strain of labour, exposure, and constant irritation must have so strenuously tested the will that it needed the refuge and the fortress of prayer and pledge. And it is recorded that Jogues as a prisoner in the Mohawk camp would occasionally, when vigilance relaxed, steal into the forest, strip the bark from a birch, fix it in the form of a cross, write upon it the Holy Name, and kneel before it as he registered his vow ...[27]

4. My next illustration is drawn from the work on the Jesuit Martyrs. Here the research had to take account of several score of volumes and to bring to bear the relevant facts upon the dramatic rendering of the period. It also involved a number of visits to the shrines and the sites of the ancient missions to get some knowledge of the topography, of the flora and fauna, of the rocks and trees, the trails, the waterways, the edible roots, and the proper names, personal and geographical ...[28]

There are just two points which I have time to amplify. One is a scientific point,[29] which I already alluded to in a recent recital and I hope you will pardon me if I bring it up again for wider expansion. I saw in the *Relations* a letter written by Brébeuf in which he said he had predicted an eclipse of the moon, a total eclipse, and he remarked how struck with amazement the Hurons were when the event occurred exactly as foretold. I felt a real thrill over this letter and I went to Professor Chant to tell him of it. I asked the astronomer a number of questions. Would a Jesuit priest in Canada in the early seventeenth century be sufficiently acquainted with astronomy as to be able to tell the exact time of an eclipse? Undoubtedly. The Jesuits were among the most learned men of Europe. Would a priest, knowing the time the eclipse occurred in Paris, be able to tell the exact time by the shore of Lake Huron – Eastern Standard Time? Yes. Would Professor Chant look up the records for me and tell me if there was a total lunar eclipse on August 27, 1635? With pleasure. The following day his letter came from the observatory.[30]

The other matter was a doctrinal consideration. I was moving in the mists of theology where I had to be exceedingly careful for here were many shoals and breakers. I had written the account of a torture of a captured Iroquois by a Huron band. Brébeuf was an eyewitness and I knew that the priests were always urging clemency for the victims. Those tortures ran for hours and sometimes for days and nights and the fathers must have put up their earnest intercessions. I had two lines written:

Brébeuf's first plea was for the captive's life,
But as the night wore on, it was for death.

I submitted the whole manuscript to my friend Dr[31] John Penfold, the historian of the order at the Novitiate in Guelph. I asked him to scrutinize every page to make certain that I wasn't tangling up the theological threads. He was very good to me, making certain suggestions and corrections, and the chief one was just here. Naturally the *Relations* didn't contain that second line. I put it in for effect. He said Brébeuf would never have asked for the Iroquois' death. Such a plea would render nugatory the whole Catholic belief. No Catholic could ask for the death of anyone under any circumstances. I replied that such a plea would be in accord with my desire to humanize, as far as possible, the priest. Might I put it hypothetically, saying that his heart might wish for the termination of the process of torture as anyone might wish to see a dumb animal put out of its misery. His answer was that if I stated it as a subjective opinion that Brébeuf, away down in his sympathies, would be glad to see the victim expire so as to abbreviate the torment, there would be no ground for criticism, but to pray for death was another matter. Accordingly he passed my emendation:

Brébeuf had pleaded for the captive's life,
But as the night wore on, would not his heart
Colliding with his mind have wished for death?

The number of subjunctives and questions I have made in the story is a witness to my attempt at the reconciliation of research and verse composition.

5. I have been very much interested in Dr Wallace's[32] paper and very much delighted with it because for the last year or so I have been engaged in a wrestling bout with Brébeuf myself.[33] I used to be under the impression that a primitive tongue would be somewhat simple in its structure, until I saw how bewildered Brébeuf was at first in trying to construct a grammar. Several of the priests confessed their failure – three genders, three numbers, a feminine conjugation, the endless compounds, and their difficulty in expressing generic notions. Brébeuf pointed out that they had no relative terms like master, servant, father, son; they had to particularize them. I think it was rather amusing to find Brébeuf writing home to his general to get permission to alter the *nomine patris* formula. The Hurons could understand it only if it was stated – in the name of our Father, and of his Son, and of their Holy Ghost. And then the poetic way they drew on their mythology to express simple descriptions. A fat man was called a fallen star. Brébeuf discovered that they believed that a long time ago a star fell from heaven in the form of a fat goose.

And then what a dramatic study would be the face of a chief when he was whipping up his tribe to a war fever.[34] As the language didn't have any labials the mouth would have to be kept

almost wide open all the time of the harangue. What an illumination upon modern totalitarian oratory. Some reporter described
Mussolini as unable to make a speech without showing all his back
teeth. I go back to my own job now with a profound conviction that
poetry and dentistry are allied arts.

Dunkirk 1941

1. The lifting of the British Expeditionary Force at Dunkirk has
been called the Nine Days Wonder – from May 26th to June 3rd,
1940. The Dunkirk operation was a sublime, spontaneous expression of national faith. It did not come out of premeditation, out of
carefully guarded naval and military plans. It did not come out of a
command. It was an overnight improvisation, a contagious, democratic response to an appeal more ringing than a command.
Practically every trade, every profession, and every rank were
represented on the decks of the nine hundred boats that went
across the Channel. They took the adventure in the teeth of logic.
Here are Churchill's words: 'I expected that it would be my hard lot
to announce the greatest military disaster in our long history. I
thought that perhaps twenty or thirty thousand men might be
re-embarked. The whole root and core and brain of the British
Army seemed about to perish. Suddenly the whole scene cleared.
A miracle of deliverance achieved by valour, by perseverance, by
perfect discipline, by dauntless service, by resource, by skill, by
unconquerable fidelity, has become manifest. The Royal Air Force
engaged the main strength of the German Air Force and inflicted
upon them losses of at least four to one, and the Navy, using nearly
one thousand ships of all kinds, carried more than 335,000 men, out
of the jaws of death to their native land and to the tasks which lie
immediately ahead.'

2. Of all the great themes which have emerged out of this war,
there is nothing that so challenges the dramatic sense as the miracle
of Dunkirk. It stands first amongst its mighty rivals – the fight with

the *Graf Spee*,[1] the *Altmark* incident,[2] the immortal action of Fogarty Fegen (God rest his soul) in the *Jervis Bay*,[3] and certain individual exploits like the suicidal dive of Colin Kelly upon the Japanese battleship, *Haruna*,[4] and many others passed and still to come.[5] All of those actions might be regarded as incidents having little or no critical bearing on the outcome of the war. They were of outstanding dramatic character made for the black type of the headlines of newspapers or striking titles of plays, lines which will sing in ballads, 'Are there any British down there?' 'We are moving closer to the enemy,' said Fegen to the convoy as he took on with his four-inch guns the eleven-inch of the German battle-cruiser. What a message and what a name, Captain Fogarty Fegen, that accompanied the ship to her death. These actions were superb individual symbols of courage and chivalry and of the imperishable tradition of the sea, but Dunkirk possessed every quality which sanctifies the human spirit in the face of catastrophe. Its name will always be written in letters of fire like Thermopylae,[6] Corunna,[7] and the first Verdun.[8]

Moreover, it stands for the most critical period of the war for Great Britain, because there was an hour in May 26, 1940, when some of the leading military authorities thought that Churchill might be compelled to ask for an armistice to save the British Expeditionary Force from annihilation. It wasn't a matter of a Sedan[9] – encirclement, defeat, and the capture of hundreds of thousands of prisoners. It meant sheer physical extermination with the machine-guns and bombs all out for the world's greatest massacre in history ...[10]

May I spend a minute or two upon an attempt to understand the spirit behind heroic action. Some of the greatest passages in our literature have been built up around great personal decisions to initiate action when the odds against survival were nine to one or ninety-nine to one. It is the sling and the pebble against the spear and armour, where the impulse of the heart acts against the logic of the brain, where the ultimate value of the human soul is assessed in critical sacrificial moments. (I have just been reading with a class the great sixth scene of Shaw's *St Joan* and its overwhelming pathos lies in the contrast between the decision of the maid when she tears up the recantation paper and the consequences which she knows she must face – the contrast of the maid with her youth, simplicity, honesty and naturalness, her love of life and flowers and birds and sunshine – the contrast of these things with that judicial assembly representing the world's most terrible, most uncompromising authority, interested only in one juridical point – the disobedience of making a personal independent judgement.) There can be nothing more dramatic than a conflict which represents a last stand, a fight with the back to the wall; on the one side nothing but courage, on the other side unlimited power and a ruthless purpose; the flesh and blood and bare hands against the machine-guns, the forlorn hope with nothing left but the will against the overwhelming battalions.

Whenever tragic literature, in staging the conflicts between man and nature or fate, brings out the refinement upon his face, the exaltation through suffering, it forces us to give our interpretation of life deeper implications, to make the pattern a nobler and more comprehensive one. This constitutes the main problem for idealistic literature: to get the anomalies explained, to find a place for man in a setting that makes sense to our baffled understanding, and the more we find ourselves in the presence of sacrificial deeds, the closer we get to the heart of life and the heart of the universe.

It is an amazing but to some extent a reassuring fact that the most stirring revivals of literature have come out of periods of the deepest confusion; that when the anarchic elements were appearing to take control by their sheer mass, there is a return to sanity and light under inspired leadership. That sacrificial offerings are found on the altars on such dawns, supplying as they do the test to the reality of the change, is the supreme tragic fact of our race, but the fact must be confronted like the presence of some disease deep in the vitals. It is the deed following the motive which supplies the dynamic, whether it springs out of the unforced goodness of the heart, an instinctive thing native to the blood, as we say, or out of the pull of forces where the right finally gains the ascendancy. Some of us in Ontario remember how several years ago the cities of that province were profoundly stirred by an action which took place on the Niagara River just below the falls at the time of the breaking up of the ice. It was a race for life witnessed by thousands when a number of men were manœuvring a rope into position from the Suspension Bridge on the off-chance that it might be grasped by a young man marooned on a swirling fragment of ice one hundred and sixty feet below. The attempt failed by a small margin, but the tragedy took on high colours as several people had seen the man leap from the shore onto the ice to rescue a woman. A very short drama lasting but a few moments was enacted before the step was taken, when the mind was reckoning the slim chances of survival – where the blood was counting on its iron for the job, and the issue weighed with the risk. Both lives were lost, but as the decision to save was taken with the odds so heavily stacked against life, the sacrifice assumed an aspect of the sublime. The story was flashed to the city, raising the moral temperature of the community. It had the effect on us as if a flag had been run up to the masthead bearing the signal – 'Let no one do a mean deed today.' That's the effect I get from reading of the North American martyrs.[11]

In the lifting of Dunkirk the cards were stacked against success. The common man, the non-professional, the non-military, the non-naval, the man without the stripes and buttons, went out upon the adventure of his life. The Port of London alone sent eight hundred and eighty ships' boats. The record was given in the following words: 'These small craft lifted more than 100,000 men. No boat ceased work as long as troops were in sight on shore. As the boats were sunk, the crews went elsewhere, into other boats, and carried on ... Many of the boats had not even a compass, and no navigational instruments other than a lead pencil, and if they once lost contact with their convoy their chance of getting there in the strong currents was very slight. Many of the boats were from the Thames Estuary. They had never before left the Estuary, and only one of their crews had been further than Ramsgate,[12] but the conduct of the crews of all these boats was exemplary. One thirty-three-foot motor-launch ferried off six hundred men to transports and carried four hundred and twenty direct to England.[13]

I wish to point out certain poetic phases of this adventure of deliverance. There is something irresistible about the humour of understatement. In the anticipation of a crisis when the toss is loaded against life, when a physician raises his eyebrows after a thermometer reading, one might expect silence or sobriety of statement. But that humour might spring out of death is one of the strange facts of experience like a flower amidst the weeds around a headstone. It is the Celtic incongruity of the wake with the feasting and dancing and the unconscious jokes on the corpse. It is the triumph of Shakespearean tragi-comedy, the graveyard comedy of the clowns in *Hamlet*. We have noticed some of the British comments when the debris had been cleared away after the raids. After the Coventry raid, the proprietor of a liquor saloon put up a notice – 'Business as usual; this blasted pub is open again.' He may[14] not have seen the humorous quirk in the phrasing, but it is claimed that the Women's Christian [Temperance] Union pointed out the joke. Another proprietor put up a placard in front of his partially demolished shoestore – 'More open than usual.' It took both a sense of humour and an unruffled temperament to set up that defiant and sedate announcement. Dorothy Thompson, in a recent article, mentions one example, recording the feelings of a Cockney after a bombing. He was asked if his house was hit. 'Yes,' he replied, 'but we all escaped, all but my mother-in-law who was in a bit of an Haccident.' 'What happened to her?' 'O, she had her head blowed off.' A London bobby was urging a woman to hurry to a shelter during an air-raid. She was searching for something on the street. 'Urry up, mother, what are you lookin for?' 'O, my false teeth have been knocked out.' 'Aw, forget it, mother, what do you think 'Itler's doin – droppin sandwiches?'

Joseph Conrad so admired English history and character that even as a boy his crowning ambition was to become a British master mariner, and I think that one of the greatest passages he ever wrote was by way of illustrating understatement, this time given as a phase of the Scotch character. Captain MacWhirr,[15] a phlegmatic Scot, conservative, contemptuous of modern fandangle notions about navigation and storm strategy which would take a storm on the flank, decided to put the nose of his ship right into the heart of the typhoon. At the height of the storm when the ship righted her keel after a terrific plunge, though by every law of hydrostatics she ought to have gone to the bottom, MacWhirr's only comment was – 'I wouldn't like to lose her.' The Cockney and the Yorkshireman are the masters of understatement when the bones actually rattle in the syllables.

And Winston Churchill has given us immortal illustrations of humour in the midst of crisis which must have lifted the hearts of the Anglo-Saxons out of the abyss. He answered the bellowings of Hitler and Mussolini with the quiet remark – 'We are waiting for them and so are the fishes.' And there was his recent comment upon Rommel's stubborn defence in Libya: 'The Germans are putting up a resistance worthy of the tomb that is being prepared for them.' The contrast has been pointed out by editors between Churchill's current speeches in the United States and Canada and the bellicose hysteria of the two dictators in Europe: Churchill with his blend of the sublime and the colloquial, of personal passion and historical calm, of the most exalted appeal and the homely comic thrust, and on the other hand the falsification of fact and the neurotic misuse of rhetoric on the part of the Axis propagandists.

It is difficult to understand the spirit of insouciance and repartee and banter which makes situations charged with the explosives of death appear as ordinary casual routines of life.[16] This is claimed to be characteristically British and hard to interpret to people of other races – this strange sardonic yet jaunty acceptance of the inevitable – the spirit of Bairnsfather's Old Bill or of Mason in *Journey's End.*[17]

Dunkirk exhibited that magnificent hybrid of the sublime and the grotesque, of tragedy and comedy, of light-hearted speech and the most profound seriousness of purpose on the part of men who counted their lives not dear unto themselves that they might save the lives of others. Human nature with its abysses and its mountains, its concentration camps and its cities celestial, its sadisms and its altruisms, followed a long road before the eyes of the ape looked into the face of Christ. It was on high ground that morning when the boats went down the Thames.[18]

3. The poem on Dunkirk gives an account of the great regatta which set forth across the Channel to save the British Expedition-

ary Force: the motley composition of the boats from the palatial yachts to the luggers and barges; and the equally varied composition of the crews – retired Indian colonels, old windjammer captains, rural deans, bargees, school prefects, cordwainers, costermongers, dukes, and tanners in all the complexion[s] of the English social strata. It records the struggle of the world's greatest rescue on the sea – the lifting of the 300,000 from the beaches.

The volume [Dunkirk and Other Poems][19] contains also 'The Submarine,' 'The Radio in the Ivory Tower,' 'The Invaded Field,' 'Come Away, Death,' 'The Old Eagle,' and other poems.

'The Truant'   December 1942

1. This is a poem called 'The Truant' representing man as talking back to a totalitarian God of power divorced from human considerations of kindness, equity, and justice tempered by mercy. He is called here the great Panjandrum, a silly nonsensical term like the Lord High Executioner, knowing he can crush the human species physically by his overwhelming might. Hence the language he uses is formal, erudite, and in accordance with a Gilbert and Sullivan court etiquette, and I am afraid able to vex his cousin. The theme is a conflict between the human will and an arbitrary oppression. Some of the words used in this poem I didn't know myself until I began searching for scientific terms in the unabridged dictionaries. They may rip up the tape recorder before I am finished. My sympathies and apologies are for you if they do.

2. The theme is the revolt of the human individual against tyrannical power. Man through evolution has become a truant from the original dance of the atoms. He has developed concepts, a will of his own, a moral sense and a spirit of adventure which refuses regimentation. He has left the stage[1] and gone off on his own but is discovered by the Master of the Revels whose job it is to superintend the festival of fire. The man is brought up before the great Panjandrum of the Universe for trial. He is accused of singing

out of key and of walking out of step² and the judge or Panjandrum assigns to him a penalty – not only of death but of being sent back after death to join the original molecules of fire in their eternal revolution. The judge relates the man's ancestral past and the man replies that everything of value which the universe possesses is created by man himself and that this is a part of human nature which survives death and the material universe. The free personality is something immeasurably greater than mere bulk and power and physical motion.

'The Stoics'   Winter 1942

These are the comrades-in-arms who are riding the storms on the sea that we may have calm in our harbours; who are building their homes in the air that we may dwell on the earth under unpolluted skies; who are fighting the drought on desert sands and the snows of distant hills that we may preserve the greenness of our fields and valleys. Without them we cannot reap what we have sown. We sleep because they watch. We rest because they march. We light our hearths from their bivouac fires. The highways to our schools, to our free assembly halls, to our altars are kept open through the tread of their feet. Between our right to breathe, to think, to speak, to act upon conviction, and the dark pestilence which stalks through the world today there stand only the valour of their hearts and the edges of their crusading swords.

Behind the Log   June 1947

1. This is mainly a statement of exposition and acknowledgement. In the spring of 1945 my friend, Professor Lorne Richardson (then a commander of the Royal Canadian Navy), asked me if I should like to spend some time at sea in order to gather material and atmosphere for a poem. He said that his suggestion had met with the approval of his colleagues, and he felt sure that arrangements

could be effected. In due time the invitation was ratified by Vice-Admiral G.C. Jones and I was granted every facility to go out with destroyers and corvettes, and collect from officers and crews facts, stories, moods, technical terms, and the ever-maturing crop of nautical idioms.

I began searching for an action which would combine dramatic intensity with the eternal tedium of convoy – something in the early phase of the war when the Atlantic sinkings far outpaced the building of ships and when, after the fall of Paris, Churchill's frank and audacious admissions sobered Britain to a sense of her peril. U-boats were multiplying fast and moving ever farther westward to concentrate on Atlantic shipping. Convoys were being located and trailed across the ocean with a climbing ratio of loss, which sometimes came close to annihilation. Much has been written during and since the war upon the slimness of the margins between victory and defeat, and the failure of a given convoy to get through at this most critical phase could mean general catastrophe.

The story of those ships comprising the Royal Canadian Navy and 'the fourth arm of the fighting forces,' the merchant navy, is now a part of the history of Canada's growth as a sea power, for at the close of 1942 Canada had become responsible for more than half of the convoys moving towards Europe. Those two arms of the forces worked with the finest co-ordination, and in the spirit of mutual faith which was never betrayed, but rather reinforced, by the exercise of the democratic right to grumble – the antidote to the Fascist lockjaw.

One episode in the six-year-old drama of the waters, which possessed practically all the elements required for my special task, was the struggle of convoy s.c. 42 for survival and the Battle of Cape Farewell.[1] It is significant as being the record of the first display of 'wolf-pack' strategy directed towards Atlantic shipping, and hence the experience of this convoy became invaluable in the subsequent working out of counter-measures. The odds against survival were tremendous – twelve u-boats (it was estimated) with the possibility of German surface raiders coming in for the kill. The target was sixty-six ships crawling at eight knots and protected by an all-Canadian escort of one destroyer HMCS *Skeena,* and three corvettes, *Kenogami, Orillia,* and *Alberni,* which were later joined by *Moose Jaw* and *Chambly.* Had the faster *Skeena* been destroyed, all the heroism imaginable would not have availed against the u-boats, which had a surface speed of three or four knots more than that of the corvettes.

Another feature of the drama was the harnessing of physical science to human effort. Only two or three decades past, captains were blowing their ships' whistles to determine positions by echoes. It was always a wonder to us, as schoolboys in Newfoundland, how captains of coastal steamers and skippers of 'fore-and-afters' could find their way into port through darkness or thick fog. A succession of blasts and even of shouts, striking cliffs, and rebounding, would give them the rough basis for their calculation. Our wonder was more than a mere tribute to the practical skill of navigators. It was partly rooted in mystery over a dimly apprehended process of science working through an instrument, whether a whistle or a voice. We were constantly wavering between a sophisticated pose before a blackboard demonstration of an echo and a half-abashed acceptance of a scent or a sixth sense, supposed to be shared equally by mariners and Newfoundland dogs. And then as soon as the superstitions were hammered out of our heads by the schoolmaster's pointer, a new flock surprised us with the announcement of another scientific discovery. There are many of us who are ever standing on the thresholds of workshops, looking and listening, never completely rid of the feeling that one day a spirit will enter and planet-strike the machines.

To a layman, anti-submarine detection (asdic) looked like a miracle. It is true that its sensational performance in 1941 was in a year or two to be eclipsed by radar, as shattering to human credulity as radio and wireless were in their day, yet the physics of sound, or rather supersonics, seemed then to have reached the highest pitch of technical accomplishment. The picture, actual or imaginary, of such a mechanism in operation, especially in a life-and-death crisis, could be a source of eerie dramatic tension. The operator was the heir of a long promise. He came late in the line of the sentries and the coastal skippers with their calls and answers, but when he did come he had a range far beyond their voices, and when he challenged, the foe replied from under the sea. But still it is call and answer.[2]

Further acknowledgements are due. For his kind co-operation and for his final authority to use the files at Ottawa and to gather more recent information from a most obliging personnel, my thanks are offered to Admiral H.T.W. Grant, CBE, DSO, RCN, chief of the Naval Staff. For the use of his log and the report of proceedings, and for his personal narrative, I am deeply indebted to the commanding officer of HMCS *Skeena*, Captain James C. Hibbard, DSC and Bar, RCN, who as senior officer of the escort was in command during this sixty-hour action off Cape Farewell. For securing access to officers, ratings, and sailors generally, for checking data, for many courtesies on and off the ships, and for sharing so generously with me the wealth of his experience, I am very grateful to Commander William Sclater, author of *Haida*.[3]

The names of the ships are authentic but the personal names in the story are fictitious. The convoy conference is synthetic, pieced from the *Forms* and *General Instructions*, from accounts of masters and naval control shipping officers present at various convoy conferences, and amplified a little. Apart from a few minor transpositions and enlargements for dramatic effect for which official indulgence is requested, the record follows the incident.

2. ... I have been asked[4] to speak on my own verse in respect to theme, construction, difficulties in handling technical material, and to read extracts. Of the last I shall do but little. There was a time years ago when in my callow enthusiasm I used to read verse hours on end, and though I was often in a state of exhaustion myself, I rarely realized the condition of my audience. Therefore I shall try to keep to the short synopsis of my subject, first of pointing out the difficulties in shaping presumably intractable material, and then of illustrating the intractability if not the shaping, by quoting from a new verse construction called *Behind the Log*.

I have an interest which has almost a cruel fascination for me, as I know it must for countless others, that is, the role that physical science is playing today in the construction and destruction of life, its relation to the bare elemental fact of existence. The irony deep in the life-and-death issues of our expanding knowledge is confronting us with every discovery and invention. We are learning only too well how any formula, the product of man's mind, or any instrument, the product of his hand, can be used with equal readiness to save or to kill, and I know nothing which, as material, offers a sterner challenge to drama and poetry. There was a time when writers, the dramatists and poets, relegated that material to prose out of a strange prepossession which was bound up with theories of inspiration and poetic diction, reason and imagination, and with the belief that anything so mundane as a machine should be treated only in textbooks and manuals on experimental procedure.[5]

That revolution is taking place today. I am not qualified to say how far the visual and plastic arts have gone in this direction. All I wish to point out by way of introduction is that dynamos, lathes, drills, and turbines are humming their way into the measures of verse with the same ease and intimacy as the former reaping hook and the wheel and the plough.

Three years ago[6] I was invited to go to sea with the Royal Canadian Navy to gather material and atmosphere for a poem. I went as a layman without any expert knowledge. My connection with ships had been with fore-and-afters and coastal steamers along the shores of Newfoundland where I was born and brought up. I had really to go to school and some of my teachers were my own former students who now in their reversed role did their best to kittle up my notion upon matters pertaining to the operations of His Majesty's ships in the Royal Canadian Navy ...[7]

Through all my work I was greatly helped by a few of my non-naval scientific friends. One was my lifelong friend, Dr R.W. Boyle, director of Physical Research in the National Research Laboratories at Ottawa, who a long time ago sat side by side with me in the college at St John's, Newfoundland. Boyle, I am informed, made the greatest contribution to the science of sound, or ultra-sound, of any investigator in the First World War. I had to consult him a great deal to make certain that my technical terms and their applications were correct.

I may say just here that I have always realized the importance of a certain degree of accuracy in the relationship between poetry and its subject matter, that a writer who is attempting to put a theme to verse should be at least conscious of his theme, especially if the material is to be beaten into narrative, epic, and dramatic forms. The knowledge of the subject matter *is* related to the aesthetic value of the result. Communicated moods are dependent upon a large variety of factors as all of us know – turns of phrase, rhythms, unity of impression, a common area of experience and understanding, and the feeling on the part of the reader that a segment of life, however small the focus, has been mastered and presented. This is not to say that there isn't a huge difference in the quality of errors which might be committed. There is, and some mistakes are relatively insignificant, but a writer must always be on guard to see that there is no disturbance of the mood by a sloppy inadvertence. Sometimes in an otherwise fine artistic production an error may creep in and have the same effect on a listener as if, for example, a clergyman should perpetrate a salacious joke in the midst of an evangelical sermon. Even if the joke were unintentional, the more profane element in the congregation would detect an aesthetic flaw within the moral edifice.[8]

The necessity of research in dealing with historical subjects was brought home to me by many an experience and I discovered how the laugh could be turned against a writer even in the field of verse as it has been turned against myself.[9]

I have tried to be as careful as possible to avoid the more egregious mistakes by consulting the specialists whenever a practical scientific point had to be worked out as an illustration within a dramatic context.

One of the most difficult tasks I had was the dramatization of the convoy conference.[10] It was hard to get a realistic and complete picture during the war owing, naturally, to the strictest secrecy which shrouded the departures, speeds, sizes, and routes of the convoys. While I had given to me practically every detail of the convoy s.c. 42 after it had left its base for its rendezvous in the North Atlantic, I still hankered after some description of the masters just prior to sailing. I knew that such meetings were exceedingly lively – that very democratic masters were not at all slow in expressing their opinions of their juniors in age, like the naval control shipping[11] officers who handed them their instructions, and they had also their opinions of the English commodores and the commodores had their personal opinions of some of the masters, and all of them had ideas, not by any means homogeneous, about convoy operations. All of them jealously guarded their democratic birthright of grumbling, the antidote to the Fascist lockjaw. That is one feature which we like to claim as part of the Anglo-Saxon tradition, the long-fought-for right of free expression of opinion. As great as may be the abuses in democracy, abuses which take a long time for their removal, at least we can be measurably sure that an honest conviction expressed, let us say, by a father within the privacy of his own home will not be betrayed by the son to the minions of a police state. The right to grumble is as sacred as the right to worship. That right was certainly exercised in these conferences I refer to.[12]

I managed to get hold of a number of NCSO's and captains who told me their experiences, and out of them all I made this synthetic conference. The names of the personnel are fictitious, which gave me the advantage of occasionally accommodating the names of the speakers and interrupters to the nature of the speeches and interruptions. But the names of the ships are genuine. There was no need to invent here with such real names as *Gypsum Queen, Empire Hudson, Winterswyck, Muneric, Bretwalda, Baron Ramsay, Gullpool, Empire Panther, Macgregor, Lorient, Arosa, Hampton Lodge.*[13] Besides, the conference gave me the interlude of relief much needed as the destruction in ships and life was tremendous.

While it is true that the NCSO might be a relatively junior officer, possibly a lieutenant-commander, the commodore, who would be in charge of the internal movements of the convoy, might be a retired admiral, who with much fuming and swearing had left his quiet English estate and volunteered his services for a second world war.[14] He would sit at a table with the NCSO and would be called on to say a few words to the masters after the NCSO had finished with his instructions. I wanted a name for this commodore which would be in keeping with his age, dignity, and position and I decided on Sir Francis Horatio Trelawney-Camperdown, the last two names hyphenated.[15]

Well then, what would be the content of the speeches of the NCSO and the commodore? This would not be such a problem as the instructions would be fairly common to all conferences. I was given copies of the *Forms* and *General Instructions* and my task was to try to get the speeches revolving around the forms and manuals into blank verse, sometimes formal, sometimes conversational, as befitting the variety of orders and information. This change [from prose to verse] may have been a mistake and perhaps in a second edition (if there is a second edition) I shall use two mediums. I may say just here how much I appreciate the criticism of the literary editors who without rancour or personal prejudice strive to give an objective treatment of a work, especially while the author himself, the father in question, had turned his blind spot on the freckles and warts of his youngest born.[16] Occasionally, I encountered in the *General*[17] *Instructions* a phrase or sentence which didn't have to be tampered with. It was final in expressiveness. I have had the experience before in going over old documents relating to the sea, such as the agreements made between the masters and the crews. It seemed to me that the older the documents the more rhythmic the language. Lines would blossom out in the midst of the driest legalities.[18] And there was one phrase which started off the NCSO in his instructions – 'Being in all respects ready for sea,'[19] which is a straight pentameter with a couple of sporting trochees jostling up against the leisurely run of the iambics.[20]

As soon as the NCSO and the commodore had finished their introductory remarks, the call would come for questions to which there would be no long and maidenly silence. In the early years of the war all kinds of ships were requisitioned. Every tub was set afloat and the masters came from every allied nationality. At this particular conference Danes, Icelanders, Norwegians sat with English, Scotch, Irish, and Canadians of every ancestry trying hard to understand the accent and diction of the instructing officers. I thought here was a chance to show the bewildering composition of the audience. A Norwegian captain who knows more[21] Norwegian than English is straining to catch the drift of the officer's address, and finding that he catches only the barest fragment gets up in high excitement and expresses his protest mainly in his own tongue. As I do not know any Norse, I had to make up a few lines of English verse recording the captain's protest and bring them down to the Norse-Canadian Trading Company's office in Toronto to get the lines translated. The manager did it for me very graciously and then I intentionally mixed some English words with the Norwegian so that an audience might get the vague drift.[22]

The Norse captain cannot make himself sufficiently understood, and when the NCSO asks what he says three other masters try to interpret him, first a Cockney who didn't understand a word but says it is all perfectly plain to him. He is followed by a very nationalistic Scotchman who puts the blame for the confusion on the barbarous nature of the English language, and he is followed by a Dane, a friend of the Norwegian, who manages to make some light break through the mental fog. All this may sound exaggerated, but language constituted a genuine problem in the early hectic months on the sea.[23]

I hope those in this audience who know Norse and Danish will indulge me, so that I may feel that I have steamed safely through my pronunciations, and even in respect to the Scotch I may say[24] that the Irish has a way of breaking through that tongue, and not only there indeed but through my most perfectly guarded English pronunciations. I might as well release my little bit of hypothetical humour just here, as the horizon ahead is pretty bleak.[25]

So the convoy started. To escape the subs, the escort and convoy had been instructed to take an extremely northern route via Newfoundland and Iceland to the United Kingdom. But the U-boats had news of the convoy and trailed it to those far-off latitudes and the ensuing action is known as the Battle of Cape

Farewell. It was an action so full of drama that its only parallel is that of the chase of the Murmansk convoy by the *Scharnhorst*.[26] That battle cruiser, as you remember, was big enough to destroy the lighter cruisers and destroyers and then sink one by one the whole immense convoy. So here, if the *Skeena* had been sunk, it would have been comparatively easy for twelve submarines to sink the three corvettes whereupon the heavy slow merchantmen and freighters could be picked off for leisurely extermination.

It was just here that I was given such an example of the harnessing of physical science to human effort. I had the operator's account of what he considered the first unequivocal ping in his ears telling that the echo this time indeed came from a submerged submarine. Through his instrument he would transmit an impulse from his ship, and he would listen for an echo which told him that he had struck something which had sent the echo to the receiving instrument under the same mechanics as governed a bouncing ball. Travelling at the same rate as sound [that is, the impulse], he could get the distance of the object from the ship, but what was the object struck? His call would be – 'An echo, sir, range so and so, travelling in such a direction, exact object undetermined.' Often he would say – 'I think it is a whale,' for whales would be seen and could reflect the sound, 'or an iceberg,' for icebergs were in that vicinity,' or a school of fish.' Later, with more exact calculation, he might report – 'sub sir, definitely, range so and so, bearing so and so, closing us or going away.' That ping-ping with its note going up and down the scale was like a tragic overture. Following the highest notes would come the Action Station gongs, the four-point-sevens, the point-fives and depth charges, collisions and explosions, and the areas of the sea would be covered ...[27]

3. ... I should like to indicate a few aspects of the romance of science in its relation to life on the sea, but before doing so I should make a few acknowledgements and explanations. Nearly three years ago[28] my friend Professor Lorne Richardson (then a commander of the Royal Canadian Navy and an instructor in mathematics) came down from Ottawa and asked me if I should like to

spend some time at sea in order to gather material and atmosphere for a poem. He said that his suggestion had met with the approval of the Naval Board[29] and in due time the invitation was ratified. I went as a layman without any expert knowledge … I pointed out that limitation to my naval friends and their answer was that they were interested in having a relationship established between the navy and the civilian population, that there were masses of material that never got beyond the documents, files, and bureaus – material that should be presented to the public at large and that there was a place for the dramatic and poetic rendering of the incidents. Hence I was granted every facility to go out with destroyers and corvettes and collect from officers and crews facts, stories, moods, technical terms, and the ever-maturing crop of nautical idioms.

4. I have called this piece of work *Behind the Log*. The log of the adventure is written on just a few pages as are the logs of all the great events of the war on the sea. It is made up of brief, concentrated expressions, the very anatomy of speech. The statements are made without any emotion. The log is a report, here and there containing symbols and codes for secrecy and safety, and we might read sections of it as we might a short obituary notice in a newspaper simply recording the death of a person whom we did not know. The implications would be felt only by the family and friends. The task of the writer is to suggest those implications, to show how behind the cryptic phrase or the unemotional statement there was blood, nerve, flesh, pulse.[30] Behind the log there is always the man.

I asked the captain of the *Skeena* what he would call the most terrible moment of the sixty-hour battle. He replied that the whole sixty hours made one eternal moment because he knew that, with the loss of the little escort, the whole seventy ships would go in one complete slaughter; but if he had to pick two or three moments, one would be the instant when the *Jedmore*, one of the convoy, reported to the *Skeena* that a periscope was seen passing the bow and that two torpedoes had passed ahead. That was the first terrible [evidence of the] fact that the convoy, despite its northern remoteness, had been located. That was bad enough, to have the proof that there was one in the area, but in an hour they had all the proof they needed that the pack of perhaps a dozen subs had spotted the convoy. But the worst moment came – the real nightmare – when he knew that the subs had dived into the convoy and were attacking from within the lanes.

I read lines like these in the log. '*Muneric* torpedoed and sunk. *Kenogami*[31] ordered to pick up survivors. Rockets observed in midst of convoy. Subs inside the lines. Convoy ordered to execute emergency turn of forty-five degrees as evasive tactics. Starshell could not be fired because of the blinding effect on the bridge at the time when every moment was valuable. Destroyer intended to ram the sub inside the convoy but danger of collision with ships was extreme in the darkness.' And so on. The captain told me that he was pursuing the sub down one lane while the sub was going in the opposite direction in the lane adjoining. Here is another statement: 'A merchant ship which picked up survivors from a torpedoed ship signalled that an officer had stated that no secret papers had been destroyed. As it appeared improbable that the torpedoed ship would sink, a corvette was ordered to close the merchant ship [and] embark the officer who would destroy the papers, which was done.'[32]

For the sixty hours this race against death was being run, with death the winner in the matter of sixteen ships, and always the breath-stopping thought that the escort would be destroyed, and then the extermination of the whole fleet [accomplished], while Britain waited for the oil and food and plasma and military supplies and the fate of the freedom of the world hung on the issue. And one of the most uncannily ironic features of this particular struggle as of the war in general is that tons of plasma sent across the ocean to replenish veins should have been sunk in the North Atlantic before it could replenish the veins on European battlefields.[33] That fact itself could [be a] symbol of the most ghastly waste of function[34] imaginable, were it not for the fact that behind it all there was a great base of heroic intention and sacrificial vision, but that it should futilely be shed and not given the chance to flow along preserving ...[35]

'The Deed'   Summer 1952

This poem contains two points of view – the romantic and the realistic. The traditional type springs out of the writer's prepossession with nature as it is represented by landscape, trees and flowers and birds, dawn and sunset and the like, colours on sea and land; generally the environment in which human beings live. The realistic in the broad sense represents a setting which may be drab or forbidding or commonplace but may contain an element of the beautiful or sublime from the nature of the human action.

Towards the Last Spike   1952

1. I have been asked to occupy a half hour or so in reading a few selections from a poem called *Towards the Last Spike* which I have described as a verse panorama of the struggle to build the first Canadian transcontinental from the time of the proposed Terms of Union with British Columbia, 1870, to the hammering of the last spike in the Eagle Pass in 1885.

I am fully aware that I can add nothing to the history of that undertaking. The historians and economists know much more about the construction than I do, and the geologists know much more about the Laurentian and mountain strata; so, in accordance with my own method, whenever I needed a supply of facts, I have gone to the historians and geologists and engineers and surveyors to get material which I wanted to work into a dramatic context.[1] Five summers in the Rockies and on the coast, including six weeks climbing or clambering with the Alpine Club, supplied me with enough confidence to attempt the job, which, thank heaven, is now complete, for better or worse.[2]

The allotted half hour[3] will allow me to read only a fifth of this book, so I shall try to fill in the gaps with brief explanations.

The first part is a prologue contrasting conditions of life eighty years ago with [those of] the present, which I shall omit. This is followed by a section called 'The Gathering,' a description of the effect of oatmeal on the Scotch blood and spirit of enterprise. For this I consulted specialists, Scotchmen themselves, physiologists, and dieticians, took over their data and added a few comments of my own. It is true that there were a few Americans, mainly Dutch Americans, and Englishmen and Irishmen, but the vast proportion of key men who came out in the seventies and eighties to this land of opportunity were from the heather. So, I entitled this section 'The Gathering' with the underlying caption taken from Dr Sam Johnson and Sir Walter Scott.[4]

This is followed by three pages of a nightmare[5] experienced by Sir John A. Macdonald as he revolves around the Terms of Union with British Columbia who is represented by a beautiful lady[6] courted by a sailor, California, a gentleman who has spent a good deal of his life on the sea, but who also owns huge stretches of land to the south, and when he visits the British Columbia ports he is redolent of orange blossoms from his orchards. So it becomes a rivalry between this sailor lover and Sir John. The lady, conscious of this rivalry, can afford to keep them guessing, to secure terms more favourable to herself. Sir John has to make his marriage proposal by proxy and this long-distance courtship is a handicap for him but an advantage for the sailor, because he happens to be there. However, the proposal is made and the lady suggests the terms – begin the road in two years, end in ten. The terms are submitted to Parliament the next year, 1871, and are ratified.

Then comes the Pacific Scandal.[7] Sir John answers the attack with an historic defence of five hours. The Honourable Edward Blake rises to make a still longer address indicting the government on grounds of corruption. The government is defeated in a new election which places Mackenzie in power for a term of four years.

During the Mackenzie administration there wasn't much progress in construction, first, because there was a general feeling that the road ought to wait upon the settlements which would naturally be slow in growing, and second, because Mackenzie, known as amphibious Mackenzie, favoured the watercourses, and the linking up with the American railroads towards the west. His government is defeated in 1878. Macdonald comes back overwhelmingly and proceeds with the Canadian road. George Stephen, later Lord Mount Stephen, invites Van Horne from Illinois to become general manager of the line. Van Horne arrives in Winnipeg December 31, 1881,[8] when it is forty below, and at midnight, after scraping the frost from the window with his jack-knife, gives vent to a soliloquy upon his three projected tasks – (1) the road across the prairies, (2) the terrible Laurentian stretch north of Lake Superior, about the oldest and hardest rock in the world, and (3) the western mountains[9] – all to be completed within five years. I shall omit the first and most of the third.[10]

The north shore was second only to the mountains in difficulty and some of the engineers swore that it was even worse. I wanted a symbol to represent its age, its bulk, and its toughness. I knew that its pre-Cambrian formation had been laid down millions of years before life began on this planet. So I had to do a bit of personification. I wanted a very old form, something reptilian, so I made the Laurentian range a hybrid monster, a lizard held within the folds of the pre-Cambrian Shield. I pictured this lizard as too old for life, too old for death, but possessing passive power to resist the invasion of man.[11] I have used the feminine pronoun *she* throughout, instead of *it*, with the recognized licence that a captain takes when referring to his ship. Incidentally, a friend of mine recently took a rough trip to Labrador and on the bridge in the midst of a heavy roll he asked the captain – 'Why does one always refer to a ship as a she?' and the captain roared back – 'Well, did you ever try to steer one?' That story was passed on by my friend to my wife who passed it on to me, and when she read the account of the lizard, she exclaimed – 'Why feminine throughout?' That got us right into the mystery of pronouns. We can speak of a country as a motherland or a fatherland; all right as a noun, but when the pronoun is used to refer to the fatherland, it would sound ridiculous to say *he* in the same sentence. I remember a time when as a boy I saw the battleship *Blake* steam into the harbour of St John's, Newfoundland, and I recall the mayor's speech to the captain in which he extolled the ship and her immense size. His remark was 'The *Blake* is a huge fellow, isn't she?' Had the mayor used the masculine, we might have expected the admiral himself to appear in person. So we talk about sister provinces, not brother provinces or states. It is a form of feminine propriety which we accept but do not explain. But this was not the end of our dialogue. 'I notice,' my wife said, 'that the main qualities of your lizard are extreme age, stubbornness, a dislike of movement or activity, a suspicion of men, and a desire to be left alone. It is her nature to be very drowsy, but she is not altogether insensible to dynamite. When she is roused, she can exhibit the power and violence of an earthquake.'

This lizard appears twice with an interval of three years, but I'll make the appearances continuous just here. The financial difficulties were as great as the engineering. So were the political storms, and history gives us the picture of the Honourable Edward Blake thundering in the House of Commons against the Terms of Union with British Columbia – building a road over the sea of mountains: and Sir John answering him, and the lady of British Columbia threatening to secede because the ten years had passed before Van Horne arrived. Blake's thunder over the scandal unseated Macdonald, but his second attack failed because he sent the House to sleep with his endless rhetoric. He was fine in the first hour, say, from nine to ten in the evening, but when he continued till dawn on two nights in succession, one can hardly blame the audience for falling down between the benches with creeping paralysis. The only one who really got fun out of such rhetorical procedure was Sir John himself who watched Blake's own Liberal followers go into eloquent snores after the impact of the abstractions and statistics[12] running into half a dozen decimals.

The cost was enormous and appeals were constantly being made to Sir John for loans, and he didn't see how he could face the House with further demands. It was Stephen who had to present the case and though he was a great personal friend of Macdonald's, he felt that the prime minister was avoiding him. In 1885 the pressure became tremendous and Macdonald was facing a terrible dilemma. To refuse the appeal for more funds meant stopping the railroad construction, breaking the Terms of Union, and the failure of the whole project. To grant the appeal might also mean bankruptcy. He was caught in a whirlpool of conflicting interests. How was he to get out? He had to make a decision sometime, in spite of the fact that his nickname was Old Tomorrow – temporizing and compromising.[13] In the very centre was the Riel Rebellion of 1885 and the need for rapid construction along the north shore to get out to Winnipeg. I have tried to show that contrariety of interests and its effect on him.

To hurry along, I shall pass to a crisis which created deep gloom among the directors, even in the mind of Van Horne, when they were waiting for a message from Stephen in London. When the signal Craigellachie – Stand Firm – came by cable announcing success, Van Horne and Angus were transported to hilarious joy in the boardroom. Van Horne makes just a passing reference to their schoolboy antics in flinging chairs around. I have elaborated this somewhat, and the reference in this passage to the Grand Trunk[14] is put in because that railroad at the time was the rival to the Canadian Pacific Railway.

The honour of driving the last spike at Craigellachie in the Eagle Pass was given to Donald Smith Strathcona: you may have seen the photograph.[15] His first stroke was a fumble which bent the nail. That's historical – the first time in his life, as far as one can gather, and probably the only time, this Scotchman ever fumbled.

2. I am simply overwhelmed with this hospitality. This is not the first time that E[llsworth][16] has loaded the tables for me at the York Club. A few years ago he did me the same honour on the publication of *Brébeuf and His Brethren* with about the same number of guests and a comparable menu. And on other occasions he has proved himself the same merry-hearted host and friend.

But I don't think that I was ever at a table where there was such a distinguished company present, and I feel very deeply the honour of counting you among my personal friends. I didn't think that I would ever reach this social position of breaking bread with cardinals and prime ministers, cabinet ministers, presidents and chancellors, high executives, industrialists, publishers and editors, professors and chairmen of boards, and may I say senators for here is Cal,[17] the finest brother in the kingdom of brothers. I am not indulging in superlatives for their own sake. They are really understatements of what springs warm and genuine from my heart.

I have to face the fact tonight of *Anno Domini* when I see at this table some whom I taught at Victoria College, and who, fortunately, through the law of survival of the fittest, managed to weather the instruction – Bill Zimmerman, Wilf James, Bill Maclaughlin, and were Mike Pearson present, I could boast that he was my colleague in the early twenties, and though I didn't teach him, yet I taught his wife, Marion Moody, the first year I entered the college as a lecturer. I didn't teach Gilbert Jackson; he taught me. He introduced me to political economy, and though I have since lost all connection with the subject, even forgot the features of the science, yet I still am proud to have retained the friendship of the man.

I really don't know how to thank Leonard Brockington for his introduction. He has done so many kind things for me over the air and in person that he has rolled up a debt which I shall never be able to pay in full. May I give one instance of what he did for me in Newfoundland three years ago. I had been invited down to my homeland by the St Andrew's Society to propose the toast to Robert Burns at a semi-governmental dinner. I was told that three hundred Scotchmen would be present and I felt quite nervous in anticipation. Well, Charlie Burchell, the Canadian commissioner to Newfoundland, cabled Brock, who was in England, to make an *in absentia* introduction which could be printed in the daily press the day before the dinner. Brock answered immediately with a five-hundred-word cablegram. I have never been able to find out who paid the expenses of that cable – the St Andrew's Society or Brock himself (I suspect it was himself), but no matter who was charged up with the account, the cable was so full of spontaneity and friendship that it dispersed all the nervousness at the time of the toast and speech. God bless his kind heart.

Now, Ellsworth asked me if I would give an account of the recent poem *Towards the Last Spike* and read a few selections. But before doing that I should like to refer to a shorter poem called 'No. 6000.' Frank McDowell[18] asked me to take a ride in the cab of the engine from Toronto to Montreal, and make whatever notes I liked during the journey. I must admit that I did it with some misgiving, for I had to sign papers disclaiming any financial liability on the part of the road should any accident happen to me on the run. I signed them and I was equipped with a waterproof coat, a sou'wester, and smoked glasses. I stood it for four hours and then decided it wasn't necessary to go so far as Montreal, so I got off at Brockville. By that time my eyes were so full of dust I couldn't see the throttle. Later, in composing the poem, I transferred the scene to a transcontinental trip across the prairies.

Though that ride was made many years ago I found it fresh and helpful for the bigger task last year. I was very conscious of my limitations, so I had to get the help of all the experts to fill in the gaps in my technical knowledge. I might instance one case. The poem was published in a Dalhousie anthology for students[19] and by some error the printer had inserted 6,000 tons as the load the engine pulled. Christopher Morley[20] ... was spending a weekend at my house and when he read the poem he remarked that he thought that no engine or team of engines could pull such a load on an up-grade, so in a republished volume[21] the load was made 2,000 tons. I am not sure that it was the printer's mistake or mine own. I didn't want a reader who might be an engineer to laugh at the mistake, if it was really a mistake, so the conclusion in the revised edition read as follows: ...[22]

Talking about content, I invoked the aid of scores of my scientific friends in dealing with the first transcontinental. I asked geologists what were the hardest rocks that could be cut. Professor Douglas of Dalhousie gave me some information, but he added the final comment – 'Ned, [there are no][23] fossils in the Laurentians. Those strata were laid down long before the ocean beds cast up their shells.' Well, I happened to know that much. One of the engineers who took part in the building of the Connaught Tunnel years after said – 'When you are writing about rock don't forget that one of the toughest enemies the men had to face was mud.'[24]

Then to supplement my reading I went to the historians, the financiers, and economists who spoke about the tremendous gladiatorial debates between Blake and Sir John A.; the struggles to raise money, the sacrificial efforts of men like George Stephen who pledged everything they possessed to the last penny when the threat of bankruptcy looked imminent; the calling of Van Horne and Shaughnessy and others too many to mention in the poem as I had to concentrate on the most dramatic points, and then especially the efforts of thousands of unknown labourers who immolated themselves in stone[25] through the Laurentians and the mountains.

I knew that I was an amateur on the technical side, so I had to get a point of view which might be called poetic while preserving as well as I could the factual accuracy. I had read up the story of the union with British Columbia, the threatened secessions, so I pictured British Columbia as a lady courted both by Sir John and California under the guise of a sailor lover. I pictured the Laurentian Shield as a lizard possessing power in her sluggishness and resistance to the pioneers with their shovels and pickaxes and blast[ing] powder. I went to a physical instructor and coach to get the exact terms applied in a tug-of-war[26] as I wanted to picture Sir John having a nightmare in 1870 with the east and west pulling at opposite ends of the rope.

Then I knew that though Englishmen and Dutch Americans like Van Horne and great Irishmen like Shaughnessy were tremendous in the part they played, yet the majority of the leaders were Scotchmen. Well, how was I to deal with them? I thought here was a chance to picture the effect of oatmeal on the Scotch blood, brawn, and brain. So I went to Dr Markowitz and said – 'Tell me as a physiologist and a nutrition expert – What does oatmeal do when it plunges into the stomach of a Scotchman?' and he outlined the course of the grain and its effects. First it was a capital source of energy, and it was outstandingly economical. Hence I tried ...* this way.

Then I went to another physiologist to find out the effect of alcohol upon the nervous system of a man who has reached the depths of melancholy and pessimism.[27] How does it eliminate the pessimism? How does it put the rose colour on the spectacles? I am not naming that physiologist, but his diagnosis was confirmed by a number of experts whom I consulted. I asked a number of

Scotchmen whose answers were given unequivocally and with a calm professional assurance.

'The Haunted House'   **unpublished**

This is an attempt to show the effect of a fundamental superstition upon a professed sceptic, a man who thinks he can always explain strange phenomena by a modern psychological approach. There's always an explanation, you know, but the explanation which holds patent* in a classroom is apt to lose some of its logic in the house concerned.

 # Appendixes

Appendix A: The Fable of the Goats

'The Two Goats'

Two goats of equal enthusiasm
Met on opposite sides of a chasm
Through which roared a mountain river
So awesome it made most animals shiver.
But not the two goats, who now stood and stared
At each other, just as if each of them dared
The other to start across the plank bridge
That someone had put from edge to edge
Across the deep and narrow abyss.
Each of them thought, 'I'll cross on this,'
And so they walked out, one goat on each side
Of the shaky plank that was not very wide.
It was, indeed, so frightfully narrow
That it would have baffled a goat and a sparrow
Who both tried to cross the chasm at once.
Now neither goat was known as a dunce,
But on they came, like goats with a grudge,
And met in the middle, where neither would budge.
So there they stood and butted their heads
Till both of them fell like a couple of kids

And landed without their enthusiasm
With two big splashes deep in the chasm.

From *Fables from Aesop* by Ennis Rees, pp 128–9. Copyright © 1966 Oxford University Press, Inc. Reprinted by permission. It should be noted that it seems to be only the first part of the fable that Pratt describes as his source.

Appendix B: A Reconstruction of 'The Haunted House'

Ten miles it was from human habitation
The trappers had avoided it for many years
I went to prove it all hallucination
Or legends sprung from books and old wives' fears.

I entered, built a fire, for the night air
Was chill and there was neither star nor moon
I lit a pipe and slouched into a chair
Whistling, – I know not, some bravura tune.

What notions do attack the human head –
This superstition I shall tear to pieces
And with the fragments I shall build instead
That shapely monument – a doctoral thesis!

An hour went by – I jotted down my notes
Of all nature's sounds, a scrub wolf's lonely howl
Tree toads and bull frogs with their myriad throats
Night hawk and bittern (heron) whippoorwill and owl.

One ghost is laid I thought, as from the glow
Red shapes came out to dance upon the wall
Weird forms indeed, but any fool should know
That where light is, there must the shadows fall.

A whirring in the loft then struck my ear.
What*-bats I mused are strung along that rafter
I laughed but one moment and stopped to hear
My mockery followed by the sound* of* laughter.

Ye heavenly harps,* what might this portent mean?
My unbelief came back and said a loon
Out on the lake, though well it might have been
A screaming witch dancing a rigadoon.

I turned my head and saw the door had swung
Ajar, or rather was my vision right?
The wind perhaps did it the way the thing was hung;
I pushed it to and jammed the latch down tight.

Did someone speak and did he call my name?
All in your mind or nerves the sceptic said.
My scientific faith was dying game
Still on its feet though much discredited.

I won't deny without a stronger proof
That noise came from a squirrel and a crane
The sharp staccato dinning on the roof
Those wings that brushed against the windowpane.

A curdling silence fell within the room,
I won't believe, I shouted, [at] the door;
I rubbed my eyes, by all the bells of doom
I had it latched; it opened as before.

My blood ran cold as flows the Arctic Ocean
My rooted dogma all were put to rout,
Away went physics with its laws of motion,
I fled and by the window I went out.

To north or south? I did not know or care
Whether St Laurence or the Hudson shore;
I would rather have faced a wild cat or a bear
Than cast another side-glance at that door.

This is an unpublished poem from a holograph in a notebook from Box 2, no 14, containing other poems published in *Many Moods*. The version given here is a reconstruction based on the poet's notes for the poem and numbers pencilled in beside stanzas 5 to 13. What may be a lightly pencilled 4 stands beside a stanza that I have placed fourth, but it appears on the last page of the draft. The reader will see that what appears here as stanza 5 would follow quite logically from what appears here as stanza 3. However, as the latter stanza is unquestionably marked 5, this would leave the poem without a stanza 4. The order of the material as it appears in the notebook is as follows: on the first page, the notes and stanza 13; on the second, stanza 1, drafts of lines in stanzas 8, 9, and 10, a draft of stanza 2, stanzas 5 and 6, a draft and the present version of stanza 7; on the third page, stanzas 8 and 9, a draft and the present version of the last two lines of stanza 10, stanzas 11, 12, and 2, draft lines of stanza 3, stanza 3, and the first two lines of stanza 10; and on the fourth, drafts and the present version of stanza 4 and a draft title 'A Sceptic and a Haunted House: (A Theory Exploded by [illegible]).' I have punctuated the poem lightly to facilitate reading. In line 4 of stanza 7, the words 'that danced' are written and uncancelled above the word 'dancing.'

Appendix C: 'The Loss of the *Florizel* Off Cape Race'

Infinite Sea! encompassing all lands,
That mark the bounds of earth's sore stricken ones, –
Commit we now into thy outstretched hands,
This light, our husbands, lovers and our sons.

Grey foster-mother of our hopes and fear!
Thou givest us our raiment and our bread, –
We give to thee the brine of salter tears
Than those thou weepest o'er our faithful dead.

How changed thy face from that of yesterday;
Then didst thou smile upon our humble life,
The sun danced in thy ripples blithe and gay,
Undimmed by prescience of a coming strife.

Yet now within the thresh of iron shocks,
Swung in the vortex of a lightless fate,
Thy billows stumble helpless on the rocks,
And thou – a stark and wild inebriate.

To-morrow comes and thou art changed once more,
Thy shadowed face betrays the penitent,
And from the weary tides along the shore,
Falls the moaned utterance of a hushed lament.

...

Great mothering sea! Our years are edged with pain,
Our hearts are flowerless for their leaves are old,
The comradeship of life is rent in twain,
And lonely are the graves of earth, and cold.

This is an unpublished version of a poem that appeared in a greatly revised form as
'The Loss of the Steamship *Florizel*' in *Newfoundland Verse*. The poem was
originally entitled 'Seaward,' but this typed title was cancelled and the new one
written in by hand. It is taken from a typescript in Box 8, no 62.

Notes

GENERAL COMMENTARIES

'Highlights in My Early Life'

> Broadcast delivered on 27 January 1949 in St John's, Newfoundland; a typescript of the text, Box 9, no 69.2, and record albums of most of the address, are in the E.J. Pratt Collection of the E.J. Pratt Library, Victoria University, Toronto.

1 This phrase is cancelled in the holograph.

'Memories of Newfoundland'

> Written for *The Book of Newfoundland* (1937), II, 56-7, ed. J.R. Smallwood, and used here with the permission of Newfoundland Book Publishers (1967) Limited, St John's.

'Newfoundland Types'

> There are six typescripts in the Pratt Collection that relate to the subject of Newfoundland types, all from Box 9, no 68.3. The first, reproduced here as commentary 1, has two leaves (three pages) and is incomplete. Typescript 2 consists of one leaf of a little more than a

page, marked 3 and 4, and has 'Alberta' pencilled in in Pratt's hand-writing on the back; a carbon of this typescript is also in the collection. Typescript 3, also pp 3 and 4 of a longer address, consists of one leaf (two pages) and has both pencil and ink emendations. Typescript 4 of one page is incomplete and though similar to typescript 1 is not identical. Typescript 5, reproduced here as commentary 2, of one leaf (two pages), ends with a reading of 'To Angelina ...' and 'Silences.' Typescript 6 has one page and is marked 5, indicating it was once part of a longer address.

1 According to J.E. Charlton, in the *1963 Standard Catalogue of Canadian Coins, Tokens and Paper Money* (Racine, Wisconsin: Whitman Publishing Co. 1963), from the time Newfoundland became internally self-governing in 1855 to the time of its returning to the status of a colony in 1934 because of a serious financial crisis, the island had its own currency; but, from 1934 until its entry into Confederation in 1949, Newfoundland used British currency.

2 Typescript 4 adds, 'He wouldn't get in if he said blueberry.'

3 The words 'the Newfoundland type' are cancelled in the typescript and 'it' written above in Pratt's hand-writing.

4 In typescript 2 this sentence is preceded by one that reads: 'The Newfoundland sailors dig deep into their idioms to back up their emotions.'

5 See Charles O'N. Conroy, 'Unconscious Press Humour in Newfoundland,' *The Book of Newfoundland*, ed. J.R. Smallwood (St John's: Newfoundland Book Publishers 1937), I, 154–6.

6 The text is incomplete and breaks off here.

7 The text thus far is an ink holograph added as an introduction to what was originally p 4 of a longer address.

8 Pratt's poetry is indeed washed by the sea even when his subject is explicitly non-marine, such as in *Towards the Last Spike*. He uses an extended sailing metaphor to describe Edward Blake's reaction to Sir John A. Macdonald's manœuvring: 'That plunging played the devil with Blake's tiller, / Threatened the set of his sail. To save the course, / To save himself, in that five hours of gale, / He had to jettison his meditation ...' (lines 286-9). Expanding Blake's metaphor he describes the mountains in terms of a sea: 'With crests whiter than foam: they

poured like seas, / Fluting the green banks of the pines and spruces' (lines 959-60). Their terror and beauty 'combined as in a storm at sea –/ *"Stay on the shore and take your fill of breathing, / But come not to the decks and climb the rigging"'* (lines 993-5). And the well-groomed Sandford Fleming is described as standing 'upright as the mainmast of a brig' (line 1558).

9 These last two sentences are added in ink at the top of the page.

10 In typescript 6, which contains an embellished story of 'the *Harlaw* whistler,' Pratt contradicts this statement, saying: 'I tried my hand at him but I likewise couldn't find a publisher.' No trace of such a poem has been found among the Pratt papers, however. It should be noted that manuscript versions of many of the early poems were either lost, destroyed, or, to use Pratt's metaphor from 'On Publishing,' 'thrown overboard.'

11 The closing remarks on 'Silences' can be found as commentary 2 to that poem.

'Introduction for a Reading'

Taken from an ink holograph, Box 9, no 70.7. The reading began with the section of *The Titanic* that deals with the sinking, then went on to the lines on Brébeuf's death from *Brébeuf and His Brethren*, and concluded with a reading of 'The Deed.'

1 The remainder of the sentence is a pencilled addition to the holograph.

2 Banting was fatally injured in a plane crash in Newfoundland in the winter of 1941.

From 'A Profile of a Canadian Poet'

Taken from record six of 'A Profile of a Canadian Poet,' which was recorded by VOCM in St John's, Newfoundland. The program, which was part of the CBC series 'Wednesday Night,' was in honour of Pratt's seventy-fifth birthday. Lister Sinclair narrated and edited the program, which was broadcast 1 April 1958.

'The Relation of Source Material to Poetry'

Commentary 1 is taken from 'Source Material and Poetry,' *Canadian Author and Bookman*, 21 (March 1945), 15. The typescript, Box 9, no 70.3, used as the copy text for commentary 2, seems to have been transcribed from a tape or other recording because of the number of errors it contains that are attributable to aural mistakes; it has been corrected with reference to an earlier typescript of a similar address initialled by Pratt. It is headed 'For release after 1 p.m. June 14th / Dr E.J. Pratt at Conference Luncheon C.L.A. [Canadian Library Association].' Although no year is given, it may have been 1956, since the CLA held its annual conference from 12 to 14 June that year in Niagara Falls; however, no reference to an address made by Pratt has been found in the association *Bulletin* for the conference or in the subsequent issues that reported on it.

1 Robert Bridges, *The Testament of Beauty: A Poem in Four Books* (Oxford: The Clarendon Press 1930)
2 Paraphrased from Robert Burns, 'Epistle to J. Lapraik, an Old Scottish Bard': 'Gie me ae spark o' Nature's fire, / That's a' the learning I desire' (lines 73-5)
3 Stephen Vincent Benét, *John Brown's Body* (Garden City, NY: Doubleday, Doran and Co. 1928)
4 These lines are Newton's epitaph inscribed on his tombstone in Westminster Abbey.
5 The typescript reads 'force.' The 'glowing passage' to which Pratt refers is in *The Prelude* (1850 edition): 'Newton with his prism and silent face, / The marble index of a mind for ever / Voyaging through strange seas of Thought, alone' (Book III, 61-3); quoted from *Selected Poems and Prefaces by William Wordsworth*, ed. Jack Stillinger (Boston: Houghton Mifflin Co. 1965), 219.
6 The typescript reads 'what.'
7 The typescript reads 'the.'
8 The typescript reads 'postal,' but Pratt told this story many times and the reference was always to coastal steamers.
9 The typescript reads 'ribbons,' but a copy of another typescript containing the same passage and initialled 'E.J.P.' reads 'rhythms.'

10 The typescript reads 'and.'
11 The typescript reads 'Related to a deed it and it takes ...'
12 The typescript reads 'is.'
13 The main shaft of the Moose River Gold Mines in Nova Scotia collapsed on Easter Sunday, 12 April 1936, burying three men alive; 243 hours later, two survivors were rescued, only because a drill operator, Billy Bell, refused to abandon hope for the men.
14 See note 2 to 'Introduction for a Reading.'
15 The influence of Wordsworth on Pratt's poetic theory and practice has yet to be estimated, though it is generally known that Pratt taught Romantic poetry at Victoria College for many years. Though it is beyond the scope of this work to make such an estimate, some intimation of the profundity of the influence may be obtained by citing a fuller context for the definition of poetry that Wordsworth gave in the 'Preface to *Lyrical Ballads*': 'The Man of science seeks truth as a remote and unknown benefactor; he cherishes and loves it in his solitude; the Poet, singing a song in which all human beings join with him, rejoices in the presence of truth as our visible friend and hourly companion. Poetry is the breath and finer spirit of all knowledge; it is the impassioned expression which is in the countenance of all Science.' *Selected Poems and Prefaces by William Wordsworth*, ed. Stillinger, 455-6

'On Publishing'

The text here is a composite of two incomplete typescripts, Box 9, no 69.4. The fact that the discussion of his publishing career ends with *The Cachalot* suggests that the address may have been made in late 1925 or early 1926, after the publication of that poem in the *Canadian Forum*, vi, no 62 (Nov. 1925), and before the issuing of *Titans* in 1926. However, a somewhat similar account of his career, which ends with the publication of *The Great Feud* in *Titans*, was published in *Canadian Author and Bookman*, 28 (Winter 1952–3), 5-7, when *Towards the Last Spike* was already on the market.
1 Identity unknown

2 Pratt seems to be referring here to the section of 'Clay' entitled 'Fragments from a Field.'

3 Pelham Edgar, as head of the English Department at Victoria College, appointed Pratt to the English faculty in 1920. Edgar quotes portions of a similar address to the one reproduced here in his biographical essay on Pratt in W.P. Percival, ed., *Leading Canadian Poets* (Toronto: Ryerson Press 1948).

4 The next part of the text is from a second typescript on the same theme. This address was delivered to a Montreal branch of an unidentified association at the invitation of Mr Roderick Kennedy two years after the address recorded in typescript 1.

5 A holograph comment in Pratt's handwriting at the bottom of the page is linked to the end of this paragraph by a line. It reads: 'There was no audience for this kind of writing.'

6 The rest of the sentence is cancelled in the typescript.

7 The words 'of Mr Kennedy, that of' originally followed here, but were cancelled in the typescript.

8 Ibsen, reacting to the negative response with which his play *Ghosts* was generally met, made the comment in a letter of 3 January 1882 to Georges Brandes.

9 This paragraph and the preceding one are in parentheses; the last sentence of the preceding paragraph, 'And conversely it happens ...' is cancelled in the typescript.

10 The first of two typescripts of this address resumes here.

11 Professor Phelps was one of the first university teachers to introduce Canadian literature to his students at the University of Manitoba.

12 The typescript reads 'a London publisher, England.'

13 Selwyn and Blount were the original publishers of *The Witches' Brew*, though Macmillan picked up the poem later on.

14 Some of the individuals Pratt goes on to name appeared in the draft versions, but not in the poem as we have it today.

15 The remainder of the original sentence, 'just a short distance away from where my friend Dr Pincock was teaching at the same time,' is cancelled in the typescript.

16 The club was the Caduceus Club of which Banting was at the time chairman. This last sentence is added in Pratt's hand at the end of the typed text.

'On Macmillan'

Taken from a holograph introduction, Box 2, no 15, to the reading of an unidentified poem Pratt gave at the Macmillan annual dinner. The good will Pratt felt towards the publisher is further attested to in a letter addressed to A.J.M. Smith, dated 30 November 1942, concerning copyright and payment for the Pratt poems Smith wanted to include in his anthology *The Book of Canadian Poetry*. Pratt wrote that Macmillan had been good enough to split commissions with him for fifteen years, though they owned the poems outright according to the contracts once they had paid him his original 10 per cent royalty.

1 Hugh Eayrs was the president of Macmillan Canada when Pratt's first book with the company, *The Witches' Brew*, was published in 1926.

'My First Book'

Taken from 'My First Book,' *Canadian Author and Bookman*, 28 (Winter 1952–3), 5-7

1 See note 2 to 'On Publishing.'
2 William John Alexander, ed., *Shorter Poems* (Toronto: T. Eaton Co. 1924)
3 The article is broken at this point by the heading 'No fireworks.'

INTERVIEWS

Interview by Ronald Hambleton

This interview with E.J. Pratt, the first in the CBC radio series 'An Experience of Life,' was broadcast on 22 January 1955, on the Trans-Canada network; it was published the same year in the *C.B.C. Times* (6-12 and 20-6 March) in a two-part, slightly abridged form. Ronald Hambleton is an English-born, Canadian-educated poet, satiric novelist, biographer, anthologist, and writer of radio documentaries. A typescript of his complete interview with Pratt, in the Pratt

Collection, Box 12, is reproduced here, reprinted with the permission of Ronald Hambleton and the Canadian Broadcasting Corporation.

1 Hambleton here paraphrases Keat's 'Ode on Melancholy': 'She dwells with Beauty – Beauty that must die; / and Joy, whose hand is ever at his lips / Bidding adieu' (lines 21-3).

2 Pratt is referring to his privately published *Rachel* (1917).

3 See note 2 to 'On Publishing.'

Interview by Jed Adams

The text is a transcription of a tape in the CBC archives in Toronto. The program for which the interview was recorded was 'First Person'; originally aired in 1959, the script was written and produced by Lloyd Chester. Jed Adams (Gerald Appelle) was a CBC broadcaster.

1 Pratt read the first and last two stanzas of the poem.

2 In the version of this story Pratt told to Frank Willis for another CBC interview (tape 740329-4 [3] item 1) the hotel is identified as the Royal York.

3 According to Northrop Frye, 'Edwin John Pratt,' *Royal Society of Canada Proceedings*, 4th series, 3, no 1 (1965), 161-5, 'Pratt was born at Western Bay, Newfoundland, on February 4, 1882. (This is the correct date, although on his authority it was often given as 1883).'

4 The Rev. Richard Pinch Bowles was chancellor of Victoria College from 1913 to 1930.

COMMENTARIES ON SPECIFIC POEMS

'Carlo'

Taken from *Verses of the Sea* (Toronto: Macmillan of Canada 1930), 79-80

1 The word 'part' seems a strange choice here so one wonders whether a typist did not at some point mistake a poorly written 'coast' for 'part.'

'In Absentia'

Taken from a notebook draft, Box 9, no 63, of what appears to be a letter in response to an inquiry about the poem. However, the draft includes neither salutation nor closing.
1 The words 'life-span of seventy years (in fact the whole universe)' are written in above the line.
2 This paragraph identifies the now rather obscure images of the fifth stanza: 'Fled was the class-room's puny space – / His eyes saw but a whirling disk; / His old and language-weathered face / Shone like a glowing asterisk!'
3 Hence, 'ill-starred' in the poem.
4 Hence, 'blank' in the poem.

The Ice-Floes

Commentary 1 is taken from *Verses of the Sea* (Toronto: Macmillan of Canada 1930), 73-5. Commentary 2 is taken from a typescript, Box 9, no 68.5; the typescript, which is labelled in Pratt's hand 'Ice-Floes,' continues with a description of his contact with Marconi, a story he told many times (see, for example, commentary 3 on *The Titanic*).
1 Father Dwyer taught at Assumption College in Windsor.
2 This sentence is from another version of this section of the address in Box 9, no 68.5.
3 The text from this point follows, with only minor editorial changes, that of the introductory note from *Verses of the Sea* reproduced as commentary 1 above.
4 This sentence is cancelled in the typescript. The comments on the blow-holes are reproduced as a note to line 35 of the poem in *Verses of the Sea*.
5 See the commentary on 'The Toll of the Bells.'

'The Ground Swell'

Taken from *Verses of the Sea* (Toronto: Macmillan of Canada 1930), 78-9

'The History of John Jones'

This poem was the first in a reading delivered in New York City on one of many trips Pratt made there; the reading included 'The Shark,' 'Old Harry,' 'On the Shore,' 'A Feline Silhouette,' 'The Prize Cat,' and 'The Child and the Wren.' For this reading he divided his poems into two groups: '... one dealing with the sea, mainly with a Newfoundland background, and the other with the land, but most of them based on personal memories or on the reports of people whom I knew, with here and there a touch of exaggeration for the sake of climax.' This appears to have been a common practice in the arrangement of Pratt's readings. The text of the description is taken from Box 7, no 60. Commentary 2 is from pencil notebook notes, Box 9, no 64, used as a supplement for a broadcast by the CBC; see headnote to 'The Child and the Wren.'

'The Shark'

Taken from typed notes for an American reading, Box 7, no 60; see headnote to 'A Feline Silhouette' for the context.
1 'The Shark' closes with anything but anti-climax, giving this description of the creature: 'Part vulture, part wolf, / Part neither – for his blood was cold.'

'The Toll of the Bells'

Taken from the typescript of an address, Box 9, no 69.2, entitled 'Highlight Associations in My Early Life,' which was delivered as a broadcast over the CBC in St John's, Newfoundland, 27 January 1949. This address is reproduced as 'Highlights in My Early Life,' the first commentary in this book.

'The Fog'

Taken from pencil notebook notes for an unidentified reading, Box 7, no 60; for the complete context, see headnote to 'Erosion.'

'Come Not the Seasons Here'

Taken from holograph notebook notes on the poem, Box 9, no 63. This description is crossed out in the notebook plan of an unidentified reading that was to have included 'Newfoundland,' 'Erosion,' 'The Way of Cape Race,' 'On the Shore,' 'Old Harry,' 'The Shark,' 'The Dying Eagle,' 'Come Not the Seasons Here,' and 'To an Enemy.' However, 'Come Not the Seasons Here' may not have been read at all, as what I take to be the final tally of the time it would take to read the poems does not include Pratt's estimated time for this poem.

'On the Shore'

Taken from a typed introduction to the poem, Box 7, no 60; see headnote to 'A Feline Silhouette' for the context.

The Cachalot

Commentary 1 is taken from *Verses of the Sea* (Toronto: Macmillan of Canada 1930), 80-2; commentary 2 is a note to line 22 of the poem in *ibid.*, 83-6. Commentaries 3 and 4 are taken from pencil holograph notebook notes on the poem, Box 1, no 4. Commentary 5 is taken from a partial typescript (pp 3 and 4) of an address entitled 'The Relation between Science and Poetry,' Box 9, no 70.3.

1 This word is cancelled in the holograph.

2 Although only the word 'years' is cancelled in the holograph, presumably Pratt meant to delete the entire phrase 'for three years.'

3 Although only the word 'cuttlefish' is cancelled in the holograph, presumably Pratt meant to delete the phrase 'or cuttlefish.'

4 This description is immediately followed by commentary 4 below, which may well have preceded it as an introduction to this reading, a reading I have been unable to pin down as to place and date of presentation.

5 Sir Humphrey Gilbert, whom his biographer, William Gilbert Gosling, describes as 'England's First Empire Builder,' was granted the first letters patent permitting the planting of an English colony in Newfoundland in 1578. However, it was not until 4 August 1583 that he entered the harbour at St John's, taking official possession the next day. Claire Pratt, in *The Silent Ancestors: The Forebears of E.J. Pratt* (Toronto: McClelland and Stewart 1971), 141, states that the Knights, E.J. Pratt's mother's family, had been in Newfoundland 'for nearly two centuries' by 1876, so Pratt seems to be stretching his Newfoundland lineage by over a century here.

6 The last two words are cancelled in the typescript.

7 A clause taken from another address on literary mistakes, Box 9, no 70.3, reads here: 'and that a baby whale at birth could weigh several tons.'

8 The mock-heroic exaggeration occurs in the poet's description of the cachalot's inner dimensions and workings (lines 67-79). The liver and pancreas are presented thus: '... so large / The lymph-flow of his active liver, / One might believe a fair-sized barge / Could navigate along the river; / And the islands of his pancreas / Were so tremendous that between 'em / A punt would sink ...' (lines 71-7).

9 It was a banquet of the Caduceus Club; see note 11 to *The Great Feud*.

10 This whole sentence is cancelled in the typescript.

'The Sea-Cathedral'

Commentary 1 is taken from *Verses of the Sea* (Toronto: Macmillan of Canada 1930), 95. Commentary 2 is from pencil notebook notes on the poem, Box 7, no 60. Though the note appears in the notebook under the heading 'The Iceberg,' Pratt never published a poem by that title, and the similarities of this note to commentary 1 here make clear that Pratt was in fact introducing this poem. See headnote to 'A Feline Silhouette' for the context.

The Great Feud

Commentary 1 is taken from pencil notebook descriptions of the poem, Box 1, no 4, and Box 1, no 5. Commentary 2 is taken from a carbon copy of a typescript, Box 1, no 6, for an address and reading of the poem made, as a holograph comment on a copy of the typescript indicates, to the University Women's Club in 1953.

1 The final draft from the notebook in Box 1, no 5, is deficient here and is thus supplemented by referring to the draft in the notebook of Box 1, no 4.

2 The final draft ends abruptly here and thus the rest of the commentary comes from the earlier draft referred to in note 1 above.

3 The word may in fact be 'area.'

4 A good many words are illegible here, though the last few may read 'extinct as a psychological mirror.'

5 The word 'allegory' is crossed out in the typescript and the word 'fantasy' is written in.

6 A version of the address 'The Relation between Science and Poetry,' Box 9, no 70.3, which includes a section on *The Great Feud*, adds here: 'a later evolutionary product.'

7 A holograph comment at the bottom of the first page of the typescript seems to make the most sense when read as a footnote to this comment; it reads: 'I believe spinach was and [is] used as a source of surprising nutrition resulting in bulging muscles.' However, a caret would seem to indicate that the comment is meant to follow the last sentence of this paragraph.

8 Pratt wrote in '262 – cone,' indicating the section that he was to read, but the lineation does not correspond with the poem as we have it today. He probably read the italicized section (from line 292: 'All ye

that dwell afar or nigh') plus the stanza ending with line 470: 'Echoes, like laughter from the cone.' The 'line' to which he refers in the next sentence is probably 'Give ear and know ye that the time / Has come when he that slumbereth / Shall pay the penalty of death' (lines 311-13).

9 The next five words are from a draft of this address in a notebook entitled 'Essays,' Box 9, no 63.

10 Pratt is referring, of course, to his wife, Viola.

11 The draft in Box 9, no 63, includes this anecdote here: 'It was tapioca all over again – an unintentional error. I had published *The Cachalot* before this and had read it to the Caduceus Club of which Sir Fred[erick] Banting was chairman. The cachalot was drawn to scale except for two or three minor points. I believe I did enlarge the liver somewhat and [had] given him an enormous pancreas which caused Banting to remark at the end of the address that if he could find a mammal with a pancreas as big as the one I described he could manufacture enough insulin to supply the whole world. But I didn't mean that, as the enlargement was intended in the interest of fun: Everyone knew it was. But with the dinosaur it was different and I was saved by the knowledge that the eggs were extant on the earth. So here was the explanation.'

12 Pratt seems to be confusing two critics here. In the address 'On Publishing' he talks of the poem's receiving critical attention from a writer on the *Edinburgh Scotsman* and from a critic in Aberdeen.

13 This was B.K. Sandwell, managing editor of *Saturday Night*.

'Cherries'

Taken from holograph notebook notes on the poem, Box 9, no 65; see headnote to 'To Angelina, An Old Nurse' for the context.

'The Lee Shore'

Commentary 1 is taken from *Verses of the Sea* (Toronto: Macmillan of Canada 1930), 95. Commentary 2 is from holograph notebook notes on the poem, Box 7, no 60; see headnote to 'A Feline Silhouette' for the context. Compare Herman Melville's description of the lee shore in the chapter by that name (23) of *Moby-Dick*, a book Pratt much admired, as his notes on Melville in his notebooks reveal. Melville writes of the lee shore: 'But in that gale, the port, the land, is that ship's direst jeopardy; she must fly all hospitality ... With all her might she crowds all sail off shore ... for refuge's sake forlornly rushing into peril; her only friend her bitterest foe!' Quoted from the edition edited by Charles Feidelson, Jr (Indianapolis: Bobbs Merrill 1964), 148

The Iron Door: An Ode

Taken from pencil holograph notes on the poem, Box 1, no 5. Though there is nothing specific to indicate this, the description of the poem may have been prepared for a recital given at Hart House Theatre at the University of Toronto on Wednesday, 11 October 1929.

1 Pratt cancelled the extra adjective 'darkness.'
2 The words 'in front of the door' are cancelled in the holograph and 'at the side' is written in by hand.
3 The words 'or hope' are cancelled in the holograph.
4 The references to characters made in this paragraph are out of order as far as their appearance in the poem goes. The boy appears first; the master mariner, referred to earlier in the commentary, second; Pratt's mother third; and the young man who sacrifices his life in vain follows. The woman who batters upon the door is preceded by searchers after beauty and truth, the latter two not being mentioned in the commentary.
5 Several words that perhaps read 'of the problem' are cancelled here.

'Sea-Gulls'

The text is taken from holograph notes, Box 7, no 60, for an unidentified reading; see headnote to 'Erosion' for the context. In the last line Pratt refers to the sea-gulls as 'those wild orchids of the sea.'

'The Child and the Wren'

Commentary 1 is taken from holograph notebook notes on the poem, Box 7, no 60; see headnote to 'The History of John Jones' for the context. Commentary 2 is taken from holograph notebook notes, Box 9, no 64, probably for a CBC broadcast intended for lower school children. The reading included 'Erosion,' 'The Shark,' 'Sea-Gulls,' 'The Child and the Wren,' 'The History of John Jones,' and 'A Feline Silhouette.'

1 The little girl was most likely his daughter Claire, as the poem was originally dedicated to her when it was published in *Canadian Poetry for Children*, ed. J.W. Garvin (Toronto: T. Nelson 1930), 163-4.

The Roosevelt and the Antinoe

In addition to the introductory note published in *Verses of the Sea* (Toronto: Macmillan of Canada 1930), 95-6, reproduced as commentary 1 here, there are three typescripts in the Pratt Collection relating to this poem. Typescript 1, Box 2, no 11, which is the source for commentary 3, has only one page and has the title 'Roosevelt and Antinoe' in Pratt's hand. Typescript 2, Box 2, no 11, from which commentary 4 is taken, is a fragment of two leaves, one typed on both sides and one with only half a page of type; it bears the title 'The Roosevelt and the Antinoe' written in Pratt's hand (a carbon of this half page is also in the collection). Typescript 3 is also a fragment consisting of a single leaf with the title 'Call and Answer' written in Pratt's hand. Commentary 2 is taken from pencil holograph notebook notes on the poem, Box 9, no 65; the draft and final version of this description are on successive pages of the notebook and both were consulted for the sake of accuracy, but where the two differ the final version is quoted here.

1 An additional short paragraph that follows the one reproduced above identifies the lines reprinted in *Verses of the Sea* as an excerpt and explains its context within the poem.

2 The occasion was a testimonial dinner given for Pratt by his friend and publisher at Macmillan, Hugh Eayrs, to celebrate the publication of the poem. A program for the evening is among the W.A. Deacon papers in the Thomas Fisher Rare Book Library. The cover reads: 'A complimentary Dinner / to / Professor E.J. Pratt, m.a., Ph.D., / upon the occasion of the launching of "The Roosevelt and the Antinoe" / at the Library, St Martin's House / Chairman / Mr Hugh Eayrs / February 28th, 1930 At seven-thirty o'clock.'

3 Dr Clarence Hincks, who was for a long time an international leader in the field of mental health, was an intimate friend of Pratt's; his daughter, Mildred Claire, got her second name from Dr Hincks.

4 The *Florida* was an Italian freighter whose thirty-two-man crew was tracked down and rescued by Fried, then captain of the *America*, on 23 January 1929, under conditions only slightly less dramatic than those of the *Antinoe* rescue: the captain of the *Florida* found it necessary to keep his engines turning over in order that his rudderless and badly listing ship not sink in the stormy seas, so that the ship was constantly changing position; and, as the radio contact between the two ships was lost for some time, the task of merely finding her was great. It was, however, hours rather than days (as it had been in the *Antinoe*'s case) before she was found; the *America* was not the only ship able to help her (as the *Roosevelt* had been in the earlier rescue); and the *America* lost a lifeboat but no men.

5 Above the first part of this sentence Pratt added a comment that appears to read: 'which I consulted even now on Saturday night.'

6 There are references to Joseph Conrad's *Typhoon* in Pratt's lecture notes, and a comparison of Pratt's poem and Conrad's short novel could be an interesting study.

7 The holograph originally read 'explosive coughs and sneezes' but apparently thinking that coughs could hardly be explosive Pratt cancelled the word 'coughs.' Presumably he meant to delete the following 'and' as well.

8 This fragmentary comment suggests Pratt intended to enlarge extempore on this topic.

9 Tose was the captain of the *Antinoe*.

10 This number is typed over 'two hundred and ninety-nine.'

11 The typescript reads 1026.

12 The first word is capitalized in pencil in the typescript as the leaf was originally part of a longer address, probably made in 1949, since the reference to the storm of *thirty* years ago originally read *twenty-three*.

13 I think Pratt means to indicate that the 'e' is not pronounced. He needs to make this point because in classical Greek pronunciation the final 'e' would have been articulated. The twentieth-century sailors, however, would not likely have had this knowledge and would, therefore, have pronounced 'Antinoe' to rhyme with 'radio,' 'ago,' 'snow,' etc., as Pratt does in his poem.

14 These dots are in the typescript.

15 A nautical expression meaning under a makeshift rig.

'To Angelina, An Old Nurse'

Commentary 1 is taken from notebook notes for an unidentified reading, Box 9, no 65, which also included 'The Haunted House,' 'Putting Winter to Bed,' 'The Way of Cape Race,' and 'Cherries.' Commentary 2 is from pencil notebook notes for a reading of the poem, Box 9, no 63. Commentary 3 is from a typescript of an address entitled 'Newfoundland Types,' Box 9, no 68.3.

1 Pratt is referring to his friend, Dr Clarence Hincks; see note 3 to *The Roosevelt and the Antinoe*.

2 This sentence is cancelled in the holograph.

'Erosion'

Commentary 1 is taken from the draft of a letter on notebook paper, Box 7, no 60, with the abbreviated closing, 'Very afec. / Ned'; no salutation appears, so it is impossible to tell to whom the letter was written. Commentary 2 is taken from pencil introductory notebook notes for an unidentified reading, Box 7, no 60, which included

'Erosion,' 'Sea-Gulls,' 'The Fog,' 'The Way of Cape Race,' and 'A Feline Silhouette.'
1 Commentary 1's dating of thirty years is more likely correct, since Pratt would have been eight in 1890 and 'Erosion' was not published until 1932.

'The 6000'

Commentary 1 is taken from *Ten Selected Poems* (Toronto: Macmillan of Canada 1947), 143. Commentary 2 is from an ink holograph description of the poem in Box 27, Edith and Lorne Pierce Collection, Queen's University Archives, Douglas Library, Queen's University, Kingston.

The Depression Ends

Taken from pencil notebook notes, Box 7, no 51, possibly prepared for a reading of his poetry at an open lecture series at which Pratt was invited to read by Dr Henry Fraser Munro. Mrs Pratt provides the information that while teaching summer school at Dalhousie Dr Pratt came to be close friends with Munro, who was appointed super-intendent of education for the province of Nova Scotia in 1926. The reading referred to above included *The Ice-Floes*, 'The History of John Jones,' 'Sea-Gulls,' 'Erosion,' 'Cherries,' 'The Way of Cape Race,' 'The Prize Cat,' 'Old Age,' 'Onward,' 'A Puzzle Picture,' *The Depression Ends*, 'Putting Winter to Bed,' and part of *The Roosevelt and the Antinoe*. A brief introduction and this list of poems appears beneath the description of *The Depression Ends*. On the facing page are given some additional notes regarding other of his colleagues' reactions to his asking them what the word 'prognathic' meant (reactions 'varying all the way from silence to blasphemy') as well as some of those colleagues' specific responses. However, as these do not seem to have influenced the poem, they have not been included here.
1 I have been unable to identify positively what Professor Edgar was reading, but it may have been the *Atlantic Monthly*.

2 This third suggestion replaced the earlier 'or even a registrar.'
3 A schoolmaster or clergyman.
4 The word appears in the poem at line 146 to describe a 'dietetic aunt-in-law, / With hook-nose and prognathic jaw,' who will not be allowed to influence the banquet.

'Putting Winter to Bed'

Taken from pencil notebook notes on the poem, Box 9, no 65; see headnote to 'To Angelina, An Old Nurse.'

A Reverie on a Dog

Commentary 1 is from a pencil holograph in a notebook, Box 2, no 14; the description seems to have been intended for an unidentified poetry reading. Commentary 2 is from a pencil holograph in a notebook, Box 2, no 15, of an address made to an unidentified association at the invitation of a Miss C. In a pattern typical of his readings, Pratt promises to talk first about dogs, and then says that 'at the end I may have some observations to make about some wild cats that I have known just to introduce a little variety and vivacity into the subject.' Presumably the poem to be read to establish the contrast was 'A Feline Silhouette.' It may have been 'The Prize Cat,' though I suspect this latter may not yet have been written at the time of the reading, as Pratt asks in the address if he 'might inflict upon the association a *new* [my emphasis] poem [he] had perpetrated upon a Newfoundland dog'; to judge from periodical publication dates, this poem was written by early 1932, whereas 'The Prize Cat' probably dates from late 1934.
1 Pratt refers here to 'Carlo.'
2 There is a space in the holograph here, presumably indicating that Pratt needed to check up on this point. There is in fact controversy over the exact origin of the Newfoundland: one theory holds that the breed resulted from a cross between the Pyrenean sheepdog and the English water spaniel; the other maintains it derived directly from the

Tibetan mastiff that shares a common ancestor with the Pyrenean sheepdog in the Malossian breed.

3 At this point the holograph is no longer completely in sentence form. The name Macpherson appears here in the text and it undoubtedly refers to the Hon. Harold Macpherson, author of 'The Newfoundland Dog' in *The Book of Newfoundland*, ed. Joseph Smallwood (St John's: Newfoundland Book Publishers 1937), I, 133-40, a book to which Pratt was also a contributor. There is evidence in the commentary that Pratt read this article, because of his reference to a dog charging a train. The memory is, however, confused, for Macpherson relates the tale of a dog owned by the Rev. G.G. Howse and this dog, which was a Newfoundland, does blindly injure himself, whereas Pratt contends that no Newfoundland would exhibit such stupidity.

4 This story, which is not set off as a separate paragraph in the holograph, seems to begin *in media res* and ends with a rather abrupt shift of thought, suggesting the tale would be fleshed out in the telling. In his article 'The Newfoundland Dog' (see note 3 above), Harold Macpherson reveals that his brother, Dr Cluny Macpherson, had a dog named Jack, who, when set upon by a bulldog, held him in a snowdrift to subdue him. This incident shows up in Pratt's poem. However, the story of the mock rescue is assigned by Harold Macpherson (p 140) to a dog named Billy: 'I cannot do justice to the exploits of "Billy," who, when a ten-months pup, was taken with a bathing party for his first time to the salt water. He could not be coaxed into the surf; but when his master swam some distance out, held up his hand, shouted and sank, only then the puppy, thinking him in distress, with a howl plunged in and swam to his assistance.'

5 The line and a half that follow here may be part of a story Pratt wanted to tell about a rescue by a dog; they appear to read: 'Telephone couldn't get him out of the office. Come home lad. He made the two miles in 5 minutes.'

'The Way of Cape Race'

Commentary 1 is from pencil notebook notes for an unidentified reading, Box 7, no 60 (see headnote to 'Erosion'). The description obviously also provides information relevant to the poem 'The Loss of the Steamship Florizel,' which was published in *Newfoundland Verse*; an early unpublished version of this poem, suggesting the personal relationship Pratt had with the disaster, is given as Appendix C. Commentary 2 is from pencil notebook notes for an unidentified reading, Box 9, no 65; see headnote to 'To Angelina, An Old Nurse.'

'A Feline Silhouette'

Commentary 1 is taken from pencil notebook notes for an unidentified reading, Box 7, no 60; for the complete context, see the headnote to 'Erosion.' This entry is actually for '*The* Feline Silhouette.' Commentary 2 is taken from the typed introductory notes, Box 7, no 60, to a Confederation Week (1-7 April 1949) reading at the United Church of Dr Ernest Marshall Howse, a close personal friend of Pratt's. Pratt said in his introductory remarks: 'In fact, his father was converted under the ministry of my father, a Methodist clergyman who travelled all over Newfoundland in his various circuits. The Reverend Charles Howse, the father of this Doctor Howse, used to refer to my father as his spiritual father. I leave it to your United Church upbringing and training to unravel those theological threads.' Commentary 3 is taken from pencil notebook notes, Box 7, no 60, to an American poetry reading which may have begun with 'Like Mother, Like Daughter' (see note to that poem) and included 'The Shark,' 'Old Harry,' 'On the Shore,' 'A Feline Silhouette,' 'Silences,' 'The Lee Shore,' 'The Iceberg' (that is, 'The Sea-Cathedral' – see headnote to the poem), and 'The Prize-Winner.' The draft of the introductory notes is to be found in the notebook in Box 9, no 64, and it is here that it is made evident that they were drawn up for an American poetry reading. Originally Pratt seems also to have planned to read 'Cherries,' 'a description of a display of temper between a boy and a girl,' but the final typescript makes no reference to this poem. Commentary 4 is a supplementary pencil notebook note, Box 9, no 64, intended for a CBC broadcast (see headnote to 'The Child and the Wren').

'Like Mother, Like Daughter'

Taken from holograph notebook notes on the poem, Box 7, no 60. The poem may have been the first in a reading given by Pratt: this description appears at the top of a mutilated notebook page without a title, but it seems to me (Sandra Djwa, to whom I showed the titleless description, first made the identification) to apply to 'Like Mother, Like Daughter'; see headnote to 'A Feline Silhouette' for the context.

'The Prize Cat'

Commentary 1 is taken from typed notes on the poem, Box 7, no 60; see headnote to 'A Feline Silhouette' for the context. Commentary 2 is from pencil notebook notes in *ibid.*; see headnote to 'The History of John Jones' for the context. Commentary 3 is from the pencil draft of a letter, Box 9, no 64, to a man identified only as Mel who was helping to put together a reading of Pratt's poetry for school children. He had suggested that 'The Prize Cat' be omitted from the list Pratt had submitted to him, though his reasons for the recommendation are not stated.
1 The poem was first published under this title when it appeared in *Queen's Quarterly*, XLII, 1 (Feb. 1935), 109.
2 He had just read 'A Feline Silhouette.'

The Titanic

In addition to the introductory note in *Ten Selected Poems* (Toronto: Macmillan of Canada 1947), 133, reproduced here as commentary 1, there are seven typescripts and seven (possibly eight) holograph commentaries in the Pratt Collection that relate directly to *The Titanic*. Typescript 1, Box 3, no 18, is a single page of an address delivered to the Victoria University Alumni. The opening paragraph, in which Pratt acknowledges the presence of 'His Honour and Mrs Bruce' and thanks the latter for his kind introduction, is heavily cancelled, suggesting that the address was also used on a later occasion. The typescript is incomplete, but a pencil draft of this address in Box 3, no 16 (on two loose leaves) furnishes a complete script and is referred to here as holograph 1. An earlier draft of this address in Box 3, no 17 is referred to as holograph 2. Typescript 2, Box 3, no 18, consists of one leaf of two pages and is also incomplete. It was for an address given at a testimonial dinner for Pratt put on by his Macmillan publisher and friend Hugh Eayrs. A program for the evening is in the Pelham Edgar Collection of the Victoria University Library and the front cover provides the information that the 'Salute' was held 'upon the publication of *The Titanic* at the Library, St Martin's House' on 15 November 1935, at 7:30 o'clock with Hugh Eayrs acting as chairman. The script of the address is completed by reference to two pencil drafts in the black notebook in Box 3, no 17 (holographs 3 and 4) and to a similar address (typescript 3) delivered at Corpus Christi, Texas, an address that survives only in fragmentary form. Typescript 4, Box 10, no 70.8, is also incomplete and is similar in text to typescript 3. Typescript 5, Box 3, no 18, which is also incomplete, is a single page of an address delivered at Lawrence Park Collegiate Institute in Toronto. Typescript 6, Box 3, no 18, provides the text for an unidentified address and consists of two leaves of one page each. Typescript 7, Box 3, no 18, is a fragment of an unidentified address and consists of one leaf of one page (a carbon of this address is also in the same box). Holograph 5, Box 3, no 17, is actually part of a draft of the address of typescript 1, but as this text was completely omitted from the final version the holograph is listed separately here. Holograph 6, Box 6, no 44, provides a partial text of an address given 'at the invitation of my friend Mr Milne' and concentrates on irony as distinct from tragedy, making specific reference (without using the technical term) to *hubris* as a force operating in *The Titanic*: 'but there is something akin to the ancient or classical idea of human presumption set over against the Gods or a presiding Fate.' A note to lines 47-52 published in *Ten Selected Poems* (p 134) actually uses the term: 'Wireless had created a presumption of security and confidence (*hubris*) – the outstanding sin of pride which in the Greek myths would attempt the most daring ventures such as the slaying of the cattle on the Isle of Helios by the crew of Ulysses, or the theft of fire from Zeus.' Holograph 7, Box 3, no

17, is a draft of the introductory note published in *Ten Selected Poems* and reproduced as commentary 1. In Box 2, no 8, there is a pencil holograph that makes reference to a poem 'based upon the loss of the *Titanic*,' but whether the poem is Pratt's is at least questionable since the brief commentary is in the midst of descriptions of other poets and their works. It may well have been an introduction to Thomas Hardy's 'The Convergence of the Twain,' and the sole interest of the brief paragraph is the documentary evidence it gives that Pratt knew Hardy's poem, for he wrote: 'The event gripped the imagination of Thomas Hardy who saw in it an illustration of the manner in which Fate achieves the frustration of human plans.'

Commentary 2 is taken from holographs 1 and 3 and typescript 2, Box 3, nos 16, 17, and 18. Commentary 3 is from holographs 3 and 4 and typescript 2, Box 3, nos 17 and 18. Commentary 4 is from typescript 5, Box 3, no 18, and commentary 5 from holograph 5, Box 3, no 17.

1 Holograph 3 goes on to say, 'a museum of periods as Joseph Conrad described her.'
2 The last three words are from a draft of the Macmillan address, holograph 4.
3 The rest of the text is taken from a pencil draft of the address in Box 3, no 16, holograph 1.
4 Victoria College Chapel was the location of the reading.
5 Pratt's tolerance would have overtones of Methodist 'temperance' to his listeners, especially coming after references to soda and ice.
6 The section in parentheses is drawn from holograph 2.
7 Holograph 2 reads here: 'the irony of the smallness.'
8 This sentence is taken from holograph 2.
9 Pratt is referring to the statement of the man in charge of the United States Senate Committee's investigation into the disaster, Senator William Alden Smith. Geoffrey Marcus, in *The Maiden Voyage* (New York: Viking Press [Penguin] 1969), 218, quotes Smith's comment from his address upon the presentation of the committee's report to the Senate as follows: '... the officer of the watch, distracted by the sudden appearance of extreme danger and in his effort to avert disaster, sharply turned aside the prow, the least dangerous point of contact, exposing the temple to the blow ...'
10 This address in variant forms was likely given on several occasions.

When first written (holograph 2), Pratt had not finished the poem and so completed the address with these comments: 'I haven't the construction and the launching yet completed. So I'll pass over that and start with the passage of the iceberg. I have tried not to steal Dr Roberts's thunder here and the description is brief and that's followed immediately [by] the account of the ship leaving Southampton with the comments upon her inauspicious departure.' In that reading he probably also omitted the section on the poker game, as a pencil comment in the draft of the poem that follows would indicate: 'I'll pass over the poker game until I get some of the technical jargon professionally verified. I'm consulting Dr Edgar on that point.' This earlier address may well have been made to the Writer's Club in Montreal in early April 1935, an occasion to which Pratt refers in a letter to W.A. Deacon (8 April 1935) stating that he read 'unfinished portions of *The Titanic* last Saturday to the Writer's Club.' Deacon Collection, MS. Coll. 160, Thomas Fisher Rare Book Library, University of Toronto

11 On 28 February 1930, Eayrs had given Pratt a similar dinner to mark the publication of *The Roosevelt and the Antinoe*.

12 This introductory portion of the address does not appear in the final typescript of the address, but is part of holograph 4. An alternate introduction that lists some of those present at the function and is revealing as to aspects of Pratt's character and values, reads as follows: 'The three greatest things a man can wish for in this world are first, his friends, second, his health, third, his work. Thank God for the first two. The third is such a variable.'

13 The paragraph to this point is in parentheses and cancelled in the typescript.

14 Holograph 1 reads 170, but Walter Lord, in his chapter 'Facts about the *Titanic*' in *A Night to Remember* (New York: Holt, Rinehart and Winston 1971), gives the height from keel to funnel-top as 175 feet.

15 Pratt is referring to the 1935 edition of *The Titanic*.

16 The effect of Pratt's meeting with Marconi can be ascertained by a description he gave of it in his address on *The Titanic* given at Corpus Christi: 'When we saw Marconi we backed away from him as if he were some manifestation of Deity. There he was all right, a tall, handsome,

spar[e], ascetic-looking man with fine aquiline features. He shook hands with a few of us, and I felt that after the shake I didn't want to touch anything for a week. In fact, it was with the greatest difficulty that my mother could get me to wash my hands. It looked like sacrilege. I felt electricity in the fingers. I thought that if I touched anything I'd get a spark.' Taken from Box 10, no 70.8. A variant description of the meeting was published in Pratt's 'Memories of Newfoundland,' *The Book of Newfoundland*, ed. J.R. Smallwood (St John's: Newfoundland Book Publishers 1937), II, 56-7, reproduced as the second commentary in the first section of this book.

17 This word is from holograph 4; the copy text reads 'the.'

18 This sentence is drawn from a draft of the address (holograph 4) but may well have been inserted in the actual presentation of the address as there is a holograph addition to the typescript that reads 'The departure of the ship,' and is followed by an arrow leading to the right edge of the page, though there is nothing written on the reverse.

19 Typescript 3 more correctly reads: 'the sleep of most of the passengers.' I have followed this typescript for punctuation of this sentence, as the Macmillan typescript (2) is inadequate at this point.

20 Typescript 3 enlarges on the description of the iceberg at this point, reading: 'The iceberg, say two or three years before, had been a huge fragment of a Greenland glacier. It had broken off from the Greenland Cap and floated out into the Baffin Strait or the Davis Strait, got caught by the current of the Labrador and started its southern journey. (I had seen some of those monsters from the decks of Newfoundland ships in the northern waters, and the size is incredible.) And on the journey of let us say 2,000 miles the outside layers would be stripped off through summer heat and storm and erosion, until by the time it reached the transatlantic shipping lanes, only the inner core would remain but that core would be as dense and hard as flint.'

21 Typescript 3 adds: 'Both time and space, the second and foot, conjoined for the assault.'

22 The rest of the address is taken from holograph 4.

23 The last four words are from typescript 6.

24 Typescript 3 (and after the first two sentences, holograph 3) adds here: 'No blame was attached to this operator. He was alone and his job was

over for the day. Still the *Titanic* had another chance. The third officer of the *Californian*, Groves, noticing something queer about the *Titanic*'s behaviour, whose lights were seen in the distance, and feeling uneasy, went to the Marconi room, woke up Evans the operator and asked – "What ships have you got Sparks?" Evans sleepily replied, "O, only the *Titanic*, a dull day." Groves then went over to the instrument. He knew Morse and something about the set. He put on the phones and tried to make contact, but the apparatus needed more skill than Groves could give it. A little later he went outside and looked in the direction of the *Titanic* and was amazed to see rockets. So he went to the captain's cabin, knocked on the door, woke him up and said – "The T[itanic] sir is sending up rockets," to which Captain Lord replied – "Are they white rockets?" "Yes sir, white rockets" (which are distress rockets). Lord said – "O, they are probably fishermen's signals," and went to sleep ...'

25 In typescript 3 Pratt specifically identifies the number of engineers and assistants who were 'not seen on the decks again' as thirty-seven.

26 In typescript 7 Pratt enlarges on one incident 'which stands out among the incidents of that sinking ... and that was the behaviour of a woman, Mrs Ida Strauss.' Referring to her sacrificing her place in a lifeboat to remain with her husband, he says: 'Such actions are made for poetry.'

27 This word is from typescript 6, the copy text being deficient here.

28 The words 'school through Miss Reddick' are crossed out here and 'Mr Rodney' (Mr Rodway?) written in faintly above. Miss Reddick was a teacher of English at Lawrence Park Collegiate, but there is no record of anyone with a name like Rodney at the school.

29 It is impossible to tell here whether Pratt is referring to the ship or the poem (though I suspect it is the latter); the word 'Titanic' was neither underlined nor in quotation marks in the original.

30 The rest of the clause referring to characters in other poems is cancelled in the typescript. The 'bold Sir Bedivere' appears in Tennyson's *Morte d'Arthur* and the 'man with the long grey beard and glitterin' eye' is the title character of Coleridge's *The Rime of the Ancient Mariner*.

31 The words 'and I'm a wretched player' are cancelled in the typescript.

32 Sandra Djwa has called my attention to Pratt's bringing together the

glancing reference to a card game in Lawrence Beesley's *The Loss of the Titanic* (New York: Nautilus' Library 1912) and Thomas Hardy's card game in *The Return of the Native* (1878).

33 In *Ten Selected Poems*; see commentary 1.

34 The incomplete paragraph is cancelled in the typescript.

35 The rest of the holograph in essence follows the material of typescripts 1 and 2. The excerpt reprinted here follows the first four sentences of Pratt's 'The Convergence of the Twain,' *Canadian Comment*, 4 (Oct. 1935), 9.

'Silences'

Commentary 1 is taken from typed notes for an American reading, Box 7, no 60; see headnote to 'A Feline Silhouette' for the context. Commentary 2 is from a typescript of an address called 'Newfoundland Types,' Box 9, no 68.3, an address that in some cases seems to have included a more general poetry reading. Some of the types Pratt discusses include the originals of such characters as John Jones and such universal competents as Angelina. See 'Newfoundland Types' in the first section of this book for other portions of this address.

1 The word 'feeling' is written above 'emotion.'

2 The following note comes at this point in the holograph: 'It applies to the serious side of life and it applies to sport – can explain rooting, cheering, nagging.'

3 The paragraph to this point is cancelled in the holograph.

The Fable of the Goats

There are two typescripts and one holograph in the Pratt Collection relating to this poem. Typescript 1, Box 3, no 21 (from which commentary 1 is taken), entitled 'Dr Pratt's Explanation of *The Fable of the Goats*,' consists of two leaves with one and one-half pages of type; there are also two copies of this typescript. The second typescript (commentary 2) is a version of 'The Relation of Science and Poetry,' Box 9, no 70.3. The holograph is in a notebook in Box 3, no 21.

1 For a version of this fable, see Appendix A.
2 In holograph 1 Pratt refers to this fable as the one 'which above all others has an eternal application and might today as never before be taken to heart by the world.'
3 In notes that follow the holograph draft there are these two fragmentary lines that may suggest how Pratt saw this accomplishment: 'consolidated a nation / accomplished for his created a vast totalitarian state.'
4 The holograph adds here: 'A goat's natural stance is at a look-out on the top of a hill or a roof.'
5 A phagocyte is a leucocyte (a small, colourless cell in the blood, lymph, or tissue that destroys disease-causing organisms) that ingests and destroys other cells, micro-organisms, or other foreign matter in the blood and tissues.

'The Submarine'

Commentary 1 is from *Ten Selected Poems* (Toronto: Macmillan of Canada 1947), 144. Commentary 2 is from a pencil holograph in a notebook, Box 4, no 30, for an unidentified reading.

1 'The Submarine' was first published in the *Canadian Forum*, 18, no 215 (Dec. 1938), 274-5, so the reading must have taken place before that date.
2 The holograph reads 'fish cold blooded.'
3 The sentence to this point appears as a note underneath this paragraph, but I have inserted it here after consulting the similar note in *Ten Selected Poems*, 144.

'Old Harry'

Commentary 1 is taken from a typed introduction to the poem, Box 7, no 60; see headnote to 'A Feline Silhouette' for the context. Commentary 2 is taken from a tape of a reading given in March 1956 in the Victoria University Library, which included 'The 6000,' a fragment of

The Titanic (line 1015 to the end), 'Erosion,' 'Old Harry,' 'The Shark,' 'The Drag Irons,' 'From Stone to Steel,' 'Cherries,' 'The Truant,' the passion and death of Brébeuf and Lalemant from *Brébeuf and His Brethren*, 'The Prize Cat,' 'The Highway,' 'On the Shore,' 'The Empty Room,' 'Seen on the Road,' and 'Sea-Gulls.' The CBC radio archives also have a copy of this tape (750617-2(1) band 4).

'The Dying Eagle'

Taken from the pencil notebook notes, Box 6, no 44, made for a radio broadcast that included the section of *Brébeuf and His Brethren* that describes the 'passion and death of Brébeuf and Lalemant at St Ignace in the Huron territory on March 16, 1649'; 'In Absentia,' which might be entitled 'The Professor shuts the door of a classroom, goes off fishing and gets hold of a big one'; 'The History of John Jones,' 'The Shark,' '[A Woman] On the Shore,' 'Sea-Gulls,' and 'The Way of Cape Race.' Pratt's seriousness about the change of title is further indicated by his remarks to A.J.M. Smith in a letter dated 16 January 1943: 'I am enclosing "The Old Eagle." It is *old* not *dying*, though "dying" would not be inappropriate.' Microfilm, A.J.M. Smith Collection, MS. Coll. 15, Thomas Fisher Rare Book Library, University of Toronto

'The Radio in the Ivory Tower'

Taken from pencil notebook notes on the poem, Box 4, no 30. This description, and that of 'The Submarine' which precedes it, are both struck through.
1 The holograph reads 'of.'
2 As Pratt reminds us in lecture notes on the twentieth-century American poet Robinson Jeffers, Box 10, no 38: 'Jeffers lives in a stone tower at Carmel on the Californian coast. He has placed man against the vast backgrounds of sea and mountains and galaxies. The only things worthwhile in the universe are the age-old insentient things ...'

Brébeuf and His Brethren

There are six typescripts and two holographs of commentary related to this poem in the Pratt Collection. Typescript 1, Box 3, no 25, reproduced in its entirety as commentary 1, consists of four leaves typed on one side and was meant for an evening recital of parts of the poem; there are three additional copies of this script, two in file no 25 and one in no 24. Typescript 1A, Box 3, no 25, is the same address minus the last two sentences. Typescript 2, Box 3, no 24 (used for commentary 2), has two leaves with three pages of typing and some holograph emendations; it was the text of an address to a Newman Club (under the auspices of the Basilian Fathers, who published one edition of *Brébeuf*). Typescript 3, Box 3, no 24 (commentary 3), consists of one leaf with two pages and was for an unidentified reading. Typescript 4, Box 3, no 24 (commentary 4), is a single page, originally p 8 of a much longer address entitled 'The Relation between Science and Poetry' for which the researches for *Brébeuf* were used as an illustration; the address appears to have been read at a conference as there is in it a reference to an earlier paper delivered by a Dr Kerr. Typescript 5, Box 3, no 24, is also a single page and is obviously incomplete; it follows typescript 1 for a good part of its text. Typescript 6, Box 10, no 46.9, is part of an address on Shakespeare and the relation of life and literature that contains a fairly lengthy digression on *Brébeuf*. Additionally there are two holograph commentaries: holograph 1, Box 3, no 24, may be a draft of typescript 1 and holograph 2, Box 3, no 22, appears to be a draft of typescript 6. Commentary 5 is taken from typescript 6 and holograph 2.

1 Perhaps this was the York Club reading to which Pratt refers in typescript 5 relating to *Towards the Last Spike*.

2 Pratt uses these last two sentences (with only a few variants) in his preface to William Sherwood Fox's *St Ignace: Canadian Altar of Martyrdom* (Toronto: McClelland and Stewart 1949).

3 Pratt used the works of Francis Parkman in composing the poem. In a letter to Pelham Edgar, written from Halifax on 2 August 1945, in response to a query on sources from his friend, Pratt wrote: 'Parkman's two volumes on the Jesuits. I used P. for the bird's eye view and went to the *Relations* for exact details.' Edgar Collection, no 12.16

4 Typescript 2 reads 'blasts from a trumpet' here, a simile more closely related to the imagery used in the poem itself.

5 Pratt expands on these early but continuing trials in his poem at lines 143-59 and returns to them at lines 603-5.

6 Pratt is careful to include the record of such activities in his poem, a fact Vincent Sharman seems to ignore in claiming that the Jesuits taught only 'abstractions that bring nothing to a vast majority of Indians' 'Illusion and Atonement: E.J. Pratt and Christianity,' *E.J. Pratt*, ed. David Pitt (Toronto: Ryerson Press 1969), 115

7 Typescript 2, which begins with a description of the excavations at the Huron missions, adds two extra sentences here that were later cancelled by an ink 'X.' It reads: 'In this respect the excavations revealed many interesting finds. One pit was found containing the seeds of several vegetables, particularly squashes, and the shell of a hen's egg which has been brought to the Royal Ontario Museum.'

8 See note 9 below.

9 The *Jervis Bay*, which was escorting convoy HX84 (37 ships) from Halifax to Great Britain, engaged the *Admiral Scheer* on 5 November 1940.

10 The typescript reads 'displace,' but it seems likely Pratt meant 'replace.'

11 This sentence comes from typescript 3.

12 Though typescript 3 reads 'Toanché' here, typescript 1 is correct, for Brébeuf served at Toanché before his time at Ihonatiria.

13 This sentence is a holograph addition to typescript 2.

14 Typescript 2 reads here: 'one reason because it was easier to pronounce, the other because, being the first convert …'

15 Holograph 1 reads: 'such a sequence of melodic sounds as "We baptize thee Tsïoüĕndáĕntáha."'

16 Typescript 3 adds here: 'I was wonderfully interested in Brébeuf's attempt to master the Huron language. Champlain, his personal friend, said that Brébeuf learned more of the Huron language in two years than the average Frenchman would in a score of years. He compiled a grammar of the speech, studied the sounds as they came from the lips of the native orators, their powers of persuasion and incitement. He noticed that the speech had no labials. The lips did not close. The sounds were made with the mouth open, giving full play to

the vowels. What the lips failed to do, the tongue, the teeth, palate, larynx and throat and lungs accomplished. This habit of speech was a great technical help to me ...'

17 Those lines that comprised the second part of the reading vary from one typescript or holograph to another.

18 Professor C.A. Chant of the University of Toronto's David Dunlop Observatory in Richmond Hill.

19 In a version of 'The Relation between Science and Poetry' Pratt adds: 'There is a clean cut and refreshing authenticity about the letters and records of those priests which make them an artistic joy to read and to work up in narrative or dramatic form' (Box 9, no 70.3, a holograph addition to the typescript). Pratt then goes on to say: 'But I also noticed with pleasure that the letter [from Professor Chant] did not say anything about the weather on that night. Was the sky cloudy? Did it rain? Was there mist? I had decided that if the letter had reported rain, here would be one place where dramatically I had a right to intervene. I would make the change to a perfect and cloudless night in defiance of meteorology as one can't bring off an eclipse in a drizzle. The dramatic end must take prior place when the factual point was historically of little significance.'

20 The last three words are from holograph 1.

21 The holograph version adds '20-22 Put in new stuff,' perhaps referring to amplification of an earlier address, that amplification being the last two sentences of this address, which do not appear in typescript 1A.

22 This observation finds its way into the poem at lines 676ff.

23 An arrow indicates that a holograph note intended to replace the typed introductory paragraph (which is cancelled) was meant to be inserted here. The writing, which is extremely crabbed, in some places cancelled but legible, and in others totally illegible, appears to read: 'It is a pleasure to do this because I have found in the Basilian [all cancelled] family a band of blood brothers whom I respect and love and I come down with the benediction of Father McCorkell of Toronto, a much-loved friend and academic colleague of the University of Toronto. He sends his blessing to you. And if there is a finer group of men in the [cancelled and then illegible] ... of the world I have yet to find them.'

24 From the University of Western Ontario.
25 As Pratt's letters to Pelham Edgar show, this project for the 'Oratorio' met with many frustrations because of the war. A hopeful note on the back of a draft of 'Still Life,' Box 4, no 31, tells us: '*B[rébeuf] and His Brethren* is being broadcast as a radio symphony by the C.B.C. over the national network on Sunday, September 26, [1943] from 10:15 to 11:00 p.m.' (see also note 19 to the Introduction).
26 Dr Willan and Pratt were very good friends. Ettore Mazzoleni was appointed principal of the Royal Conservatory of Music in 1946 and served as an associate conductor of the Toronto Symphony from 1943 to 1948; he also served a term as president of the Canadian Arts and Letters Club of which Pratt was a member. This entire last paragraph is cancelled in the typescript; the rest of the text is almost identical with parts of typescript 1.
27 The rest of the script consists of the discussion of torture and the sonorous names connected with the Huron mission, a discussion found in typescripts 1 and 2.
28 Pratt goes on to make reference to a paper given by a Dr Kerr in which he insisted, to Pratt's delight, 'upon the value of names.'
29 The rest of this sentence is cancelled in the typescript.
30 The letter, which is now among the Pratt papers, Box 3, no 24, is dated 5 June and reads: 'Memo for Professor Pratt // According to my note the date you gave me was *1636 August 27*. Dr Heard and Miss Northcott have made a careful search through Oppolzer's *Canon der Finsternisse*, and there is no eclipse on this date. But there was a total lunar eclipse on *1635 August 27* (Gregorian). The details of the eclipse are: Total phase began – 9:02 p.m. (E.S.T.) Total phase duration – 1 h. 34 m. [Then in Pratt's hand appears this comment – 'Total duration of eclipse in all phases 5 hrs.'] Eclipse visible in Canada. Sun sets at Goderich on August 27 at about 7:14 p.m. E.S.T. This is the only eclipse (of sun or moon) which can be connected with this date. // C.A. Chant.'
31 This is a holograph emendation from the original typescript's 'Father.'
32 The revised limited edition of *Brébeuf and His Brethren* (Toronto: Macmillan and Co. 1940) was illustrated with a drawing of the site of Fort Ste Marie by Harry D. Wallace, but a Dr Paul Wallace donated a copy of the book to the Victoria University Library, and perhaps it is to

this Dr Wallace that the comment refers. Dr Paul Wallace is the author of *The White Roots of Peace* (Philadelphia: University of Pennsylvania Press 1946), a book on the Iroquois confederacy, as well as other works on North American Indians, a fact that leads me to believe Pratt is most likely referring to him.

33 Since the typescript of the address on Shakespeare and the relation of life and literature, Box 10, no 46.9, is torn at the top and only partially legible, the first sentence is taken from a holograph draft of this section in Box 3, no 22.

34 See *Brébeuf and His Brethren*, lines 244ff., for the way in which Pratt wove this observation into the fabric of his poem.

Dunkirk

Commentary 1 is taken from *Ten Selected Poems* (Toronto: Macmillan of Canada 1947), 136–7, except for the sentence 'They took the adventure in the teeth of logic,' which is taken from a typescript, Box 4, no 28. This typescript is reproduced, except for overlapping passages, as commentary 2. Commentary 3 is taken from a holograph in a notebook, Box 4, no 26; this was perhaps a draft of an introduction for the projected volume or simply a description for a friend.

1 On 25 December 1939 three British ships, the light cruisers *Ajax* and *Achilles* and the heavy *Exeter*, defying the three-to-one advantage in armament and firepower, harried the German battleship *Graf Spee* until it was forced into the neutral harbour of Montevideo, Uruguay, and ultimately to sink itself to avoid capture.

2 On 11 November 1940 the crew of the British destroyer *Cossack* invaded the neutral territorial waters of Norway in order to rescue 326 British seamen kept in verminous prison quarters aboard the *Altmark*. Disguised as a German merchantman, the *Altmark* served as an armed tender (supply ship) to the *Graf Spee*; at the time of her seizure she had on board all the survivors from the seven British ships sunk by the *Graf Spee*.

3 See note 9 to the commentaries on *Brébeuf and His Brethren*.

4 The *Haruna* was sunk on 24 July 1945.

5 The section on Kelly and the remainder of the sentence are cancelled in the typescript.

6 In 480 BC a small body of Spartans and Thespians delayed the entire Persian army of Xerxes at this small mountain pass in eastern Greece until the main body of Spartans could be drawn up and the Athenians could mobilize their navy.

7 On 26 July 1588 the Spanish Armada sailed from La Corunna against England. The following year a British expedition led by Sir Francis Drake and Sir John Norris burnt the ships in the harbour and sacked the lower part of the port in retaliation.

8 Verdun was the scene of a six-month-long bloody battle, from February through August 1916, during the Great War. The outnumbered French under General Pétain held the fortress against the Germans until they abandoned the assault, having suffered almost as many casualties (330,000) as the French (350,000). The entire first paragraph, except for the first sentence, is cancelled in the typescript.

9 Sedan was the principal battle of the Franco-Prussian War of 1870. The vastly superior German forces easily defeated the French, forcing their main army to surrender and taking among the thousands of French prisoners the Emperor, Napoleon III.

10 The typescript at this point follows the text of the note from *Ten Selected Poems*, reproduced as commentary 1 above, before going on to discuss 'the spirit behind heroic action.'

11 This sentence is a holograph addition to the typescript.

12 A seaport in Kent, southeastern England.

13 This and the previous three paragraphs are all lightly cancelled.

14 The rest of this paragraph, which is at the top of p 3 of the typescript, is lightly cancelled.

15 The central character of Joseph Conrad's *Typhoon*.

16 It is the atmosphere and tone of 'casual understatement' that Pratt attempts to capture in the dialogue of 'Heard on the Colliers,' section 4 of *Dunkirk*.

17 Pratt refers here to Bruce Bairnsfather's character in *From Mud to Mufti, with Old Bill on all Fronts* and to Robert Sherriff's character in the play *Journey's End*.

18 The typescript has been emended by Pratt in several places and many

paragraphs have been lightly cancelled, perhaps indicating a different reading of the address which called for briefer remarks of a less scholarly nature. At the bottom of the last page this holograph passage is cancelled: 'All of us are aware of the importance of a context to give significance to a given word or phrase or a passage. There is something in the question – who said it? – to determine the value of the thing said. How dramatic are McArthur's words after his escape from the Japanese lines – "I have come through! I shall return." Taken by itself the statement may possess no emotional character. Spoken by such a man, with such a character, after such an exploit, and how overwhelmingly dramatic becomes that simple short-word sentence.'

19 This volume never materialized and *Dunkirk* was issued separately as a pamphlet in the fall of 1941. As late as 8 August of that year the plan was still for the larger volume, as we find Pratt writing to Pelham Edgar: 'This last week I have worked furiously at *Dunkirk* which is just about finished. The Macmillans want it as a fall book though it is too late for the fall list. However Huckvale [Robert Huckvale became general manager of Macmillan in 1940] and Upjohn [Frank Upjohn was a senior editor at Macmillan] said they will turn on special steam if I can get it in their hands by the first of October, which I can do. It is shaping out into four or five hundred lines mainly descriptive of the Regatta – composition of ships and crews and the great lifting operation.

'The volume will have – *Dunkirk* as a leader, followed by the shorter poems turned out during the last three years.' Letter to Pelham Edgar, 7 August 1941, Edgar Collection, no 12.16. The shorter poems Pratt mentions in the description of the volume above were published two years later in *Still Life* (1943). A comment in a letter Pratt wrote to A.J.M. Smith on 8 October 1941 explains why the larger *Dunkirk* volume never appeared: 'The price of manufacture is rising so rapidly that they [Macmillan] have decided not to bring out my edition of *Dunkirk and Other Poems*. They said it would cost $200. which is absurd – that is, to do it properly with adequate binding. Accordingly, they are producing just the *Dunkirk* in soft cover next week.' Microfilm, A.J.M. Smith Collection, MS. Coll. 15, Thomas Fisher Rare Book Library, University of Toronto

'The Truant'

Commentary 1 is taken from a holograph in pen on a small piece of paper, Box 4, no 34. This description was apparently prepared for a reading given in the Victoria College library in March 1956. As a tape of this reading is in the Pratt Collection, I have supplemented the holograph with reference to that tape. See headnote to 'Old Harry' for the context. Commentary 2 is from a pencil holograph description of the poem, Box 4, no 33, that follows some early drafts.

1 Pratt seems to have thought of the poem in dramatic or semi-dramatic terms. In a draft in a notebook in Box 4, no 33, the words 'Off-Stage' are written and cancelled twice before the first line of the poem. Then in the draft in Box 4, no 30, the words 'Still on the Rungs' (uncancelled) precede the opening line, and 'Off-Stage' appears at the top of the second page of the draft, also uncancelled.

2 At one early stage of composition (see draft in notebook of Box 4, no 30) Pratt seems to have been considering 'Out of Step' as the title for this poem, suggesting that it was to be a rewriting of the earlier twelve-line poem of that name published in *Many Moods*.

'The Stoics'

Taken from a pencil holograph in a notebook, Box 4, no 30. Though the title does not appear above this description, this paragraph follows several drafts of the poem, and is followed by later drafts.

Behind the Log

Commentary 1 is taken from the 'Foreword' to *Behind the Log* (Toronto: Macmillan of Canada 1947), xi-xiv. In addition to this foreword, there are six incomplete typescripts of commentary related to *Behind the Log* in the Pratt Collection. Typescript 1, Box 5, no 42 – consisting of two leaves, the first of which is typed only on one side, the second on both

– is used as the central copy text of commentary 2, but it is supplemented where possible in the body of the commentary by additional material from other typescripts; where this would interfere with meaning or easy reading, such additional material has been relegated to the footnotes. The second typescript, Box 5, no 42 – excerpts from which make up commentaries 3 and 4 – has three leaves and four pages of typing; all that remains appears to be pp 1, 4, 5, and 8 of an address called 'Ironies and Echoes' (a pencil draft of part of this address can be found in Box 5, no 37). The third, Box 5, no 42, is marked in Pratt's hand, 'Behind the Log in part'; it is a single leaf typed on both sides, with pp 4 and 5 marked in pencil on the top left-hand corners. The fourth, Box 10, no 46.4, is a single leaf typed on one side with '1' pencilled at the top; it is part of an address to an unidentified group of writers. The fifth, Box 5, no 42, is a single leaf with two-thirds of a page of typing; it appears to have been stapled to pp 4 and 5 of typescript 1 at one time and to be the end of an address. The sixth, Box 5, no 42, is a single leaf, typed on both sides, labelled pp 2 and 3; it follows typescript 1 fairly closely, though with some expansion.

1 The words 'and the Battle of Cape Farewell' are drawn from a partial typescript (pp 2 and 3) of the address 'The Relation between Science and Poetry,' Box 9, no 70.3. The Battle of Cape Farewell took place, as Pratt puts it in the poem, 'With the back-curtain of the Greenland ice-cap' / Time – '41 autumnal equinox' (lines 57-8).

2 This sentence is drawn from a typescript in Box 10, no 46.4. The present paragraph is identical in both sources – typescript and published foreword – except for the opening words, which in the typescript read 'To a novice like myself asdic ...' and the words following 'physics,' which in the typescript read 'of ultra sound seemed ...' A typescript in Box 2, no 12, pursues the theme: 'This theme of call and answer, call and silence, ironies and echoes, had in my lifetime a number of marvellous illustrations that laid hold on me but there are two that stand out particularly ...' Pratt goes on to detail the futile call of the *Titanic* to the *Californian* for help and the incident of the *Roosevelt* and the *Antinoe* as his two examples.

3 Sclater's *Haida* (Toronto: Oxford University Press 1947) was, like Pratt's *Behind the Log*, illustrated by Grant Macdonald.

4 These words are pencilled in to replace the original 'The President has asked me.' The original opening of the speech made reference to the honour Pratt felt at being asked to address 'this association especially during this evening session,' but the speech was obviously emended for later use. The original audience cannot be determined.

5 A holograph comment at this point in the typescript, 'Read written,' suggests Pratt may have made some supplemental notes, but these do not appear in the typescript.

6 Since in the 'Foreword' Pratt indicates that the invitation from Lorne Richardson came in the spring of 1945, this address must have been made in 1948, close enough to the publication date of the poem (late 1947) to allow Pratt to call *Behind the Log* a 'new verse construction' as he does in the opening paragraph of this address.

7 This sentence comes from typescript 6. The commentary from this point follows paragraphs two and four of the 'Foreword.'

8 This latter sentence is added in Pratt's hand at the bottom of p 2 of the typescript, with an arrow indicating that the sentence is meant to appear here in the address.

9 The last clause of this sentence is a holograph addition to the typescript. Originally Pratt then went on to relate a story of the inadvertent but painful mistake of a professor of history who had composed a poem meant to praise a colleague that instead, because of his mistake, insulted the eulogized man; as this section of the typescript is cancelled, and as the story as well as the preamble appears in 'The Relation of Source Material to Poetry' printed in this work, I have omitted it here.

10 Typescript 2 adds the information that it was Professor Richardson who suggested the inclusion of the conference for completeness' sake, but it was Pratt who saw the dramatic advantage of the relief it would provide.

11 The typescript reads 'service,' a mis-expansion of the abbreviation NCSO that Pratt also uses in subtitling the third section of the poem.

12 The last three sentences are from typescript 3.

13 The last two sentences are cancelled in the typescript.

14 At this point typescript 5 reads: 'So I decided on a synthetic name which might reflect the traditions of the British Navy, namely, Sir

Francis Horatio Trelawney-Camperdown, the last two names quite appropriately hyphenated. With the help of some of my naval friends I made up the speeches of the NCSO and the commodore and put them in blank verse. Then I tried to articulate some of the opinions expressed and unexpressed which I called internal rumblings.'

15 At this point typescript 3 reads: 'I managed to work Drake and Nelson in there, and "Shall Trelawney die?" and a famous English sea victory and the hyphen speaks for itself.' Typescript 2 adds: 'He might sport a monocle. (Incidentally when I asked an officer in the naval administration at Ottawa to look up the actual name of this individual I found it was Mackinnon (Mackenzie, confidential), but another convoy might conceivably have had a Trelawney-Camperdown even if he didn't have the baptismal names of Drake and Nelson.) (I might say for off the record, that my first choice was Sir Francis Horatio Trelawney-Clutterbuck which Pelham Edgar liked very much until he suddenly woke up to the fact that this was the real name of the British Trade High Commissioner at Ottawa. There was some consternation at this, so the name was changed to Camperdown, the name of an English victory, and hyphenated readily and euphonically with Trelawney.)'

16 The last two sentences are taken from a holograph note to typescript 3.

17 The typescript reads 'Formal,' which seems to be a conflation of the words in the phrase 'Forms and General Instructions' Pratt uses above (p 136).

18 A holograph note at the bottom of the third page with an arrow to this position in the text, reading 'You will be making seaward on the ebb,' is obviously one of those lines of 'found' poetry Pratt incorporated into the poem, here as line 146.

19 See Behind the Log, line 148

20 Typescript 3 at this point adds this holograph note: 'I have always had an aversion to over-romanticizing the simplicity of a great deed.'

21 Typescript 1 breaks off here, so the rest of the text is based on typescript 3, which, while not identical throughout, does follow substantial portions of typescript 1 word for word and thus most probably provides an accurate picture of what Pratt went on to say in the remainder of the first typescript.

22 See Behind the Log, lines 300–5

23 In typescript 2 this bracketed addition appears: 'In the first draft of the Dane's speech I made an error of fact. After he had finished with his cousin the Norwegian, the Dane is making a complaint of his own. The anti-torpedo nets were notoriously hard to handle, getting them out, getting them in, and there was a crop of superstitions about them. The crews hated them: they were such a nuisance I made the Dane the spokesman for this trouble and Captain Brand informed me that the nets were not in use in 1941, so I had to change to paravanes which suited my purpose just as well if I lingered a little over the pronunciation. So I got through with my Dane ...'

24 Typescript 2 at this point acknowledges a debt to a colleague from University College, Professor R.S. Knox, 'for reading this part aloud to me.'

25 Pratt presumably read lines 325-32 here. This whole paragraph is in parentheses, however, and then cancelled in this typescript, but several others indicate a reading of these lines at approximately this point.

26 On 25 December 1943 the *Scharnhorst* left the Altenfjord to attack the Arctic Convoy JW55B. The convoy, which had left the United Kingdom on 20 December, was detected on the 22nd. Three Canadian ships, the *Iroquois*, the *Haida*, and the *Huron*, were among the convoy escort that finally sunk the *Scharnhorst* on 26 December.

27 The numbers here refer to the calibre of the armaments and ammunition of the convoy escort. Typescript 3 breaks off here, and none of the other typescripts is sufficiently similar at this point to suggest with any accuracy how it might have continued. Perhaps Pratt simply went on to read from the poem, lines 675ff. being the section possibly read.

28 This address was likely given in late 1947; see note 6 above.

29 In a version of 'The Relation between Science and Poetry' Pratt mentions specifically here the Hon. Angus Macdonald; later he also thanks Dr [Gilbert] Tucker, Captain Brand, and Captain Hibbard for technical information.

30 Or, as Pratt puts it in the poem, to 'smell mortality behind the log' (line 53).

31 In the poem Pratt narrates that it was the *Orillia* that was ordered to pick up survivors (see lines 640ff.).

32 A modified version of this entry forms lines 663-71 of the poem.

33 Pratt incorporated this irony in lines 1121-6 of the poem.

34 The phrase 'waste of function' is written well above the sentence before, but as the word 'waste' is cancelled in the sentence and then the phrase written above, it would seem that Pratt intended to have it inserted here. Another line that similarly appears above this section and may be meant to be inserted after 'That fact itself' reads, 'that blood should be offered to save life and that is so sad it is an element of religious faith.'

35 The holograph runs off the page here and becomes illegible. The last three sentences of the text are all in holograph at the bottom of p 8 of the copy typescript, entitled 'Ironies and Echoes.' However, a similar passage in an address on 'Calls and Answers' allows us to conjecture how this passage went on in essence: 'One of the most insistent calls during the war was for plasma. An uncannily ironic feature of the struggle was that tons of plasma should have been delivered from Canadian and American ports and sunk in mid-Atlantic before it could replenish the veins on European battlefields. That it should be so shed and not given the chance to flow along life-giving channels is the most ghastly waste of function that the mind can conceive. If the sacrifice of life could be attended by the saving of another, the process could find its place in the Christian faith, but otherwise the process could stand for a symbol of the ironic in its ultimate rigour. Eve[r] since his life began, man has been calling for blood in all that polarity of mood from vengeance to redemption, from the curse to the prayer. The range of his need has ever outpaced the spread of his knowledge. And as long as there is an aggressor left in the world who will try to impose his will by force upon the free spirit of man, whether it is done by direct outside attack or by inside treachery, as long as this threat lasts, the beacons will blaze on the headlands and the s.o.s.'s will crackle through the ether' (taken from a typescript in Box 10, no 46.4).

'The Deed'

Taken from a signed typescript of the poem, Box 7, no 52; the description itself is in Pratt's hand at the top.

Towards the Last Spike

There are five typescripts in the Pratt Collection that relate directly to this poem and all are in Box 6, no 49. Typescript 1 has two leaves (three pages) and was for an unidentified reading. Typescript 2, from which commentary 1 is taken, has been torn, leaving only half a page; it is a carbon copy of the commentary text used for a reading delivered before the publication of the poem. Typescript 3 has two leaves (two and one-quarter pages) and provides an account of the poem meant to preface an unidentified reading. Typescript 4 has one leaf (one page) and is an account of the poem, also for an unidentified reading (there is also a carbon of this address in the collection). Typescript 5, from which commentary 2 is taken, has one leaf (two pages) and was for an address delivered at a York Club dinner in Toronto.

1 Typescript 2 adds at this point: 'So it is not a formal history which I have attempted though it is historically based. It is half a record and half a fantasy.'

2 Typescript 3 adds this information: 'I was interested in the subject because of the magnitude of the pioneering job, and because of the scepticism of many statesmen and engineers as to the possibility of its achievement. Canada had barely four million of population, whereas the United States had forty million when the Americans built the Union Pacific, and, when the Canadian Pacific was finished, the American authorities conceded that the United States had nothing in its history to parallel the road in daring and skill and energy.'

3 Since the typescript originally continued 'this evening' (which was later cancelled and emended by hand to read 'this afternoon') the address was probably delivered on more than one occasion; this likelihood is strengthened by the fact that later in the sentence the original typescript reading of 'ms.' is emended to 'book.'

4 Typescript 2 adds at this point: 'This part doesn't belong to the realm of make-believe except possibly that which refers to the effect of oatmeal upon the blood.' The caption referred to above reads: '("Oats – a grain which in England is generally given to horses, but in Scotland supports the people." Dr Samuel Johnson. "True, but where will you find such horses, where such men?" – Lord Elibank's reply as recorded by Sir Walter Scott.)'

5 Pratt is referring here to the original book-form publication; in *The Collected Poems* (1958), the nightmare runs from line 102 until it is 'delivered of its colt' at line 135.

6 In typescript 4 Pratt writes of British Columbia as a 'beautiful lady with whom Sir John has a poker game across a telepathic table of 2,000 miles or more in length.' Originally the section now called 'The Long-Distance Proposal' was called 'Across a Telepathic Table,' as an examination of an early draft of the poem in Box 6, no 46, shows.

7 Typescript 3 adds at this point: '[of] 1872 when a member named Huntingdon accuses the Government of having accepted a gift (from Sir Hugh Allan) of $160,000 for election expenses.' Typescript 4 adds: 'Well, of course, that is told in the history texts, so I had to put the charges in the form of a menu which is offered to the House of Commons by the Honourable Edward Blake, leader of the Opposition. He presents the dishes which are not very savoury. The main dish is an egg, now an omelette, which through age has become very high.'

8 Typescript 3 adds: 'and initiates a period of railroad construction never equalled, so they say, for drive and accomplishment in the peacetime operations of the world.'

9 The poem is divided into three sub-sections labelled simply by number.

10 The second section presents the Laurentian reptile and the third opens with the metaphor of the sea of mountains.

11 Typescript 3 prefaces this sentence with: 'To safeguard myself against inaccuracy ...'

12 The rest of this sentence is cancelled in this typescript, but not in typescript 3.

13 The last clause of this sentence is cancelled in this typescript, but not in typescript 3.

14 Van Horne is pictured in his boyish exuberance as stuffing 'a Grand Trunk folder down his [Angus's] breeches' (line 1519).

15 It is of course impossible to say where Pratt first saw the photograph himself, but it is interesting to note that the *Canadian Forum* of May 1927 (VII, no 80), printed the picture on p 249 (as part of the Canadian Pacific's Diamond Jubilee advertising series) along with a text from *The Life of Lord Strathcona and Mount Royal*, and that Pratt's poem 'The Sea-Cathedral' was also published in that issue on p 237. Other

advertisements in the series included portraits of and biographical notes on Lord Mount Stephen (Feb. VII, no 77, p 151), the Fathers of Confederation (March, VII, no 78, p 185), William Van Horne (April, VII, no 79, p 215), Thomas Shaughnessy (June, VII, no 81, p 289), and a reprint of Pauline Johnson's poem 'Prairie Greyhounds' from *Flint and Feather* (July, VII, no 82, p 321).

16 Dr Claude Bissell reports that Ellsworth Flavelle, son of the millionaire businessman Sir Joseph Wesley Flavelle, was a poker buddy of Pratt's.

17 Pratt refers here to his brother Calvert Coates Pratt, who was appointed to the Canadian Senate in 1949 when Newfoundland joined Confederation.

18 Franklin Davey McDowell, in addition to being Public Relations Representative for the Central Region, Canadian National Railways, also won the Governor General's Award for fiction in 1939 for *The Champlain Trail*, a novel about Huronia, and was vice-president of the Canadian Authors' Association, 1944–5.

19 C.L. Bennett and Lorne Pierce, ed., *The Canada Book of Prose and Verse*, Book 4 (Toronto: Ryerson and Macmillan 1935), 544-7

20 The American novelist, poet, and essayist (1890–1957).

21 It is hard to say which volume Pratt is referring to since the 'mistake' is repeated in *Many Moods* and all editions of the *Collected Poems*.

22 Unfortunately the typescript does not give the revised reading, but in a reading recorded by the CBC (tape 750617-2[1] band 4, date unknown), Pratt substitutes 'two thousand tons of caravan' for the original 'six thousand ...'

23 The typescript is faulty here, reading: 'Ned, do no not fossils ...'

24 Pratt did not forget, writing: 'those northern bogs / Like quicksands could go down to the earth's core. / Compared with them, quagmires of ancient legend / Were backyard puddles for old ducks' (lines 1374-7).

25 Pratt commemorates their sacrifice in the section of the poem entitled 'Ring, Ring the Bells.' Here Pratt pictures sorrow as 'tapping its fingers on a coolie's door' (line 1144), though when F.R. Scott in 'All the Spikes But the Last' asks, 'Where are the coolies in your poem, Ned?' (line 1), this more socially aware poet is calling attention to Pratt's failure to come to terms with the Canadian railway magnates' and the Canadian government's exploitation of the Chinese labourers.

26 The special register or jargon was used in lines 109-33 of the poem.

27 Pratt made good use of the information gleaned in this way in the last half of the second section of 'Hollow Echoes from the Treasury Vault' (lines 1466ff.) where he speaks of 'Something miraculous' changing the air: 'A chemistry that knew how to extract / The iron from the will' (lines 1466-8).

'The Haunted House'

Taken from pencil notebook notes on the poem, Box 9, no 65; see headnote to 'To Angelina, An Old Nurse' for the context. 'The Haunted House' was never published in Pratt's lifetime, but a text reconstructed from drafts in a notebook, Box 2, no 14, is included here as Appendix B.

Index

Aberdeen, Scotland 34, 174n12
Abraham Lincoln 48
Adams, Jed (Gerald Appelle) 47–54, 168n
Aesop 109, 155–6
Alexander, Prof. William John 38, 167n2
Argentia, Nfld. 14
Arts and Letters Club 195n26
astronomy 124
Atlantic Monthly 88(?), 180n1

Bairnsfather, Bruce 131, 197n17
Banting, Sir Frederick 18, 28, 36, 67, 163n, 166n16, 174n11
Barrymore, John 31, 49
Basilian Fathers 192n, 194n23
Battle Harbour, Nfld. 55
Bedivere, Sir (*Morte d'Arthur*) 106 188n
Bell Island, Nfld. 51
Belleville, Ont. 88
Benét, Stephen Vincent 20, 164n3; *John Brown's Body* 20, 164n3
Binyon, Laurence 15–16

Birney, Earle 53
Blackwood's 77
Blake, William 35
Bobcaygeon, Ont. 34, 40
Bonne Bay, Nfld. 55
Book of Newfoundland, The 14, 161n 162n5, 181n3, 187n16
Bottom (*Twelfth Night*) 35
Bowles, Rev. Richard Pinch 52, 168n4
Boyle, Dr R.W. 25, 137–8
Brébeuf, Jean de 46–7, 115–25 *passim*
Bridges, Robert 19, 164n1; *The Testament of Beauty* 19, 164n1
Brigus, Nfld. 3
Brockington, Leonard 150
Brockville, Ont. 151
Bullen, Frank 64; *The Cruise of the Cachalot* 64
Burchell, Charlie 150
Burns, Robert 10–11, 20, 150, 164n2
Byron, George Gordon, Lord 22, 35

call and answer 25, 28; addresses on 176n, 204n35; as theme 200n2; at sea 8, 82, 84, 85, 97, 136; call and no answer 83
Calvin, John 35
Calvinism 42, 112
Canadian Author and Bookman 36, 164n, 165n
Canadian Broadcasting Corporation 15, 163n, 167n, 168n, 195n
Canadian Forum 206–7n15
Cape Farewell, Battle of 134, 136, 141–2, 200n1
Cape Race, Nfld. 78, 80, 92, 104
Cavalcade (film) 107
Chant, Prof. C.A. 118–19, 124, 194n18–19, 195n30
chemistry 22–3
Christian 8, 18, 119, 204n35
Churchill, Sir Winston 26, 126, 127, 131, 134
Clarke, Prof. George Herbert 15
Coleridge, Samuel Taylor 24, 188n30; The Rime of the Ancient Mariner 188n30
communication 5, 26, 37, 77; in poetry 18, 32, 54; communicated mood 19, 21
Conquistador, The 21
Conrad, Joseph 114, 130, 177n6, 185n1, 197n15; Typhoon 177n6, 197n15
'Convergence of the Twain, The' 189n32
Corpus Christi, Texas 184n, 186n16

courage 114; at sea 85, 99; Brébeuf's 123; of Newfoundlanders 8; of Nfld. dog (cf. English bulldog) 90; wartime 127
Cruise of the Cachalot, The 64
Cupids, Nfld. 3

Dalhousie University 151, 179n
Deacon, William Arthur 186n10
deeds 27, 75, 86, 128, 202n20; beauty of 5; in war 4, 117; loyal 81; mean 4, 8, 27, 129; Nfld. as place of great 4; relation of facts to 27; sacrificial 8, 17–18, 128; sublime 9
determinism 43, 44
doom 41–3, 81, 95; Calvinists' insistence on 42; Pratt as harbinger of 41; shadow of 43
Douglas, Prof. 151
drama 78, 111, 122, 142; as genre 53, 137; heroic 8, 97; ironic 43; national 114; of Jesuits 122–3; of the waters 134–5; sacrificial 8, 129; submarine 108; technical 95, 99; tragic 27; dramatist 23, 32, 137
dramatic 3, 121, 138; decisions 4; events 7, 26, 59; individuals 14, 198n18; McArthur's words 198n18; material for poetry 20, 35, 66, 134, 194n19; monologue 92; dramatic poetry 19, 21, 37, 194n19; purpose in relation to poetry 20; qualities in Behind the

Log story 134, 136; in Brébeuf story 115, 119, 121, 125, 194n19; in Dunkirk story 126–7; in exactitude 121; in *Roosevelt* and *Antinoe* story 78, 79; in *Titanic* story 103, 105, 106; in *Towards the Last Spike* story 152; of last stand 128; of technical advances 78, 97, 135; rendering 123, 143; 'Truant' as dramatic poem 199n1

Dryden, John 22, 53

Dwyer, Father 59, 169

Eayrs, Hugh 36, 39, 76, 100–1, 167n1, 177n2, 184, 186n11

Edgar, Prof. Pelham 30, 38, 88, 166n3, 180n1, 186n10, 192n3, 195n25, 198n19, 202n15

Edinburgh Scotsman 34, 72, 174n12

Eliot, T.S. 53

epic, poetry 19, 21, 138; Pratt as epic poet 47; qualities of Capt. Fried 79; in war 114

Ethie (ship) 55

Everlasting Mercy, The 51

evolution: animal 68–9, 71, 173n6, human 132; evolutionary: climb 111, product 173n6, theme 68

'Experience of Life, An' 41–7, 167n

fable 88, 98; Aesop's 109, 110, 155–6, 190n2

fabulous 63

faith 114, 122; *Brébeuf*, about 47; good faith of Macmillan 36;

in material vs in Christ 47; Pratt's parents' 8, 43; true faith of Nfld. 6

fantasy 69, 90, 205n1

fate 109, 128, 144; connection with irony 43, 95, 101, 107; with tragedy 47; Hardy 185n; human presumption vs fate 184n; Pratt's temptation to believe in 42–3, 45; *Titanic* as modern symbol for 107; fatalist 44

Fegen, Capt. Fogarty 117, 118, 127

'First Person' (CBC series) 47–54, 168n

Flavelle, Ellsworth 149, 150, 207n16

Florizel (ship) 59, 92, 158–9

Fortune, Nfld. 3, 16

Forward Movement of the Missionary Enterprise 51

From Mud to Mufti, with Old Bill on all Fronts 131, 197n17

Frye, Northrop 168n3

Galileo 24

geology 68, 111, 145, 151

Gilbert, Sir Humphrey 66, 172n5

Gilchrist, Prof. 22

Grand Bank, Nfld. 16

Grand Banks 61, 97

Grant, Admiral H.T.W. 136

Gray, John 39

Greenland (ship) 3, 8, 60

Greenland 57, 97

grotesque 69, 95, 96, 131

Gulliver, Lemuel 35

Haida (book) 136, 200n3

Hambleton, Ronald 41–7, 167n, 168n

Hamlet 130

Hardy, Thomas 43, 44, 185n, 189n32; 'The Convergence of the Twain' 185n; *The Return of the Native* 189n32

Harlaw (ship) 16–17, 163n10

Haydon, Benjamin Robert 24

heroic 8, 15, 49, 94, 121, 135; drama of Marconi operator 8, 97; effort at sea 74; in Nfld. 4; story of Jesuit martyrs 122, 123, of *Titanic* 49, 99, 105, of *Roosevelt* and *Antinoe* 76; spirit of heroic action 127–9; mock-heroic 67, 172n8

Hibbard, Capt. James C. 136, 203n29

Hincks, Clare 76, 86, 177n3, 178n1

history 23, 69, 122; behind *Towards the Last Spike* 145, 148, cf. American rail history 205n2; in relation to poetry 21; invented in *Fable of the Goats* 110; natural 19; of Canada as seapower 134; of Jesuit mission 114; of Nfld. 59, 66; of religion 114; of sea 96, 101; of speech 26; of steamships 81; in relation to war 4, 127, vs drama 194n19; historians 22–3, 115, 145, 151; historical: accuracy 118, background to *Brébeuf* 122, calm of Churchill 131, events behind poem 20, interest of sites of martyrdom 120, monuments 121, names 118, poem 20, 29, 66,

prose 18, 21, record behind *Towards The Last Spike* 149, research necessary in dealing with historical subjects 22, 138; unhistorical 20

Hitler, Adolf 131

Holloway, R.E. 7, 102

Holyrood, Nfld. 14

Howse, Rev. Charles 182n

Howse, Dr Ernest Marshall 182n

Huckvale, Robert 198n19

humour: incongruous sources 130; in convoy conferences 141; in midst of crisis 131; of understatement 130–1; quick wit of Newfoundlanders 13; types of 19; unconscious 10, 13, 14, 22–3

Ibsen, Henrik 33, 166n8

idealistic literature 128

irony 24; and fate 43, 107; connected with *Titanic* 45–6, 95, 99, 101, 107, 184n; Huron sense of 119; in life-and-death issues 137; in Rev. John Pratt's work 44; prophetic 73; ironic: chorus 85, enigma of Nature 8, in relation to *Titanic* 95, 99, 101, 104, incident in Brébeuf's martyrdom 119, look of crest of death in *The Iron Door* 74, of world conditions 43, 109, part of convoy experience 144, 204n35, of *Great Feud* 71

Jackson, Gilbert 150

James, Wilf(red) 150

Jeffers, Robinson 113, 191n2
Jervis Bay (ship) 117, 127, 193n9
Jesuit Relations 114, 117, 118, 120,
    121, 122, 123, 124, 192n3
John Brown's Body 20, 164n3
Johnson, Dr Samuel 146, 205n4
Jones, Vice-Admiral G.C. 134
Journey's End 131, 197n17
Jury, Wilfrid 121

Keats, John 24, 41, 168n1
Kepler, Johann 24
Knight, Capt. William 3, 51
Knox, John 35
Knox, Prof. R.S. 203n24

Labrador 42, 55, 57, 147
Lalemant, Gabriel 46–7, 115, 121,
    122
Lamb, Charles 24
language 94, 108; common 71;
    democratic freedom of speech vs
    fascist lockjaw 134, 139; Devon
    10; dialects 71; difficulties assoc-
    iated with Huron 116–17, 125,
    193–4n16, with language of con-
    voy conferences 141; facility of
    language in early Pratt poems
    38; history of speech 26; inade-
    quacies of 37; Irish 10; log as
    anatomy of speech 143; Nfld. 4,
    6, 10, 11–13, 162n4; of Methodist
    preaching 13; of Panjandrum
    132; of sea 162–3n8; political
    rhetoric 148, 151; specialized
    99, 106, 134, 138, 140, 143; totali-
    tarian oratory 117, 126, 131

Lawrence Park Collegiate Institute,
    Toronto 184n, 188n28
Literary Digest 77
Lizard Point, Cornwall 7, 103
London Bookman 38
London Mercury 38
Luther, Martin 98
lyric 19, 21; lyrical 37

McCorkell, Father 194n23
Macdonald, Sir Gordon (governor
    of Nfld.) 11
Macdonald, Grant 200n3
McDowell, Franklin Davey 88, 150
Mackenzie, Alexander 146
Maclaughlin, Bill 150
McLeish, Archibald 21; *The Con-
    quistador* 21
Macmillan (Publishing House) 36,
    39, 40, 107, 166n13, 167n, 177n2,
    198n19
Macpherson, Dr Cluny 91, 181n4
Macpherson, Hon. Harold 181n3,
    n4
MacWhirr, Capt. (*Typhoon*) 131–2
Manchester Guardian 38
Marconi, Guglielmo 7, 45, 102–3,
    169n, 186–7n16
Markowitz, Dr 152
Masefield, John 15–16; *The Ever-
    lasting Mercy* 15
Mazzoleni, Ettore 122, 195n26
Melville, Herman 175n; *Moby-Dick*
    175n
Methodism 42, 50, 51, 71, 112
Methodist College, St John's 7, 137
Milton, John 35; *Paradise Lost* 29

Moby-Dick 175n
Montreal Star 31
Moody, Marion 150
Moose River Mine Rescue 28,
  165n13
Moreton's Harbour, Nfld. 35
Morgan-Powell, Samuel 31
Morley, Christopher 151, 207n19
Morte d'Arthur 188n30
Munroe, Dr Henry Fraser 179n
Musgrave Harbour, Nfld. 18, 28
Mussolini, Benito 95, 126, 131

narrative 19, 21, 37, 138; Pratt's
  poetry 41, 43; *A Reverie on a Dog*
  not a narrative poem 91; working Jesuit letters into narrative
  form 194n19
natural: history 19, impulse 100,
  instincts 68, order of things 70,
  solidarity 69; naturalness of St
  Joan 128
nature 7, 23, 70, 71, 76, 104, 145;
  animal 71, 91, 110, 111; as inanimate existence 5; as subject of
  Romantic literature 5; conquest
  over 7, 97; fire of 20; human 27,
  84, 131, Indian 119, of human
  action 145, Jesuits 115; laws of
  24; of fate 128; sights of 67, 75;
  Nature 67, 69
New York 15, 16, 76, 77, 80, 103,
  170n
Newton, Sir Isaac 24, 35, 164n4–5

Paracelsus 35
Paradise Lost 29

Parkman, Francis 115, 192n3
Pearson, Lester B. (Mike) 150; *see
  also* Moody, Marion (wife)
Penfold, Dr John 124
Pepys, Samuel 35
Periodical Index 107
Phelps, Prof. Arthur 34, 40,
  166n11
Phelps, Lal 40
philosophy 30, 31, 44
physics 7, 22, 23, 102, 135
physiologist 146, 152
Pierce, Lorne 31, 38, 39
Pincock, Dr 166n15
Poetry (Chicago) 52–3
Pope, Alexander 22, 24, 33
Portugal Cove, Nfld. 50
Pratt, Senator Calvert Coates 149,
  207n17
Pratt, Claire 49, 86, 172n5, 176n1,
  177n3
Pratt, E.J.: *Behind the Log* 133–44,
  199–204; *Brébeuf and His Brethren*
  (poem) 47, 114–26, 163n, 191n,
  192–6, (book) 118, 195n32; *The
  Cachalot* 36, 40, 61–7, 77, 165n,
  171–2, 174n11; 'Carlo' 55–6,
  168, 180n1; 'Cherries' 73, 174,
  178n, 179n, 182n, 191n; 'The
  Child and the Wren' 75, 170n,
  176; 'Clay' 30–3 *passim*, 35, 38,
  44, 166n2; *The Collected Poems of
  E.J. Pratt* (1958) 52, 207n20;
  'Come Away, Death' 132; 'Come
  Not the Seasons Here' 61, 171,
  171n; 'The Deed' 145, 163n, 204;
  The Depression Ends 88–9,

179–80, 179n; 'The Drag Irons'
191n; *Dunkirk* (poem) 126–32,
196–8, (book) 198n19, 'Dunkirk
and other Poems' (planned book)
132, 198n19; 'The Dying Eagle'
[The Old Eagle] 113, 132, 171n,
191n; 'The Empty Room' 191n;
'Erosion' 87–8, 171n, 178–9,
179n, 191n; *The Fable of the Goats*
109–12, 189–90; *The Fable of the
Goats and Other Poems* 112; 'A
Feline Silhouette' 92–4, 170n,
171n, 179n, 180n, 182, 183n2;
'The Fog' 61, 171, 179n; 'From
Stone to Steel' 191n; *The Great
Feud* 40, 68–73, 165n, 173–4;
'The Ground Swell' 59, 169;
'The Haunted House' 153, 156–
8, 178n, 208; 'Highlights in My
Early Life' 3–5, 161; 'The High-
way' 191n; 'The History of John
Jones' 16, 60, 170, 179n, 191n;
The Ice-Floes 38, 56–9, 93, 169,
179n; 'In Absentia' 56, 169,
191n; 'Introduction for a Read-
ing' 17–18, 163; 'The Invaded
Field' 132; *The Iron Door: An Ode*
74–5, 175; 'The Lee Shore' 73–4,
174–5, 182n; 'Like Mother, Like
Daughter' 94, 182n, 183; 'The
Loss of the *Florizel* Off Cape
Race' 158–9; 'The Loss of the
Steamship *Florizel*' 159n, 182n;
'Magic in Everything' 49; *Many
Moods* 158n, 207n20; 'Memories
of Newfoundland' 6–9, 161; 'My
First Book' 36–40, 167n; 'New-

foundland' 171n; 'Newfoundland Types' 9–17, 161–3, 189n;
Newfoundland Verse 31–2, 33, 38,
39, 159n; 'Old Age' 179n; 'Old
Harry' 113, 170n, 171n, 182n,
190–1; 'On Macmillan' 36, 167n;
'On Publishing' 28–36, 163n10,
165–6, 174n12; 'On the Shore'
61, 170n, 171, 171n, 182n, 191n;
'Onward' 179n; 'Out of Step'
199n2; 'The Prize Cat' ['The Prize
Winner'] 75, 94–5, 170n, 179n,
180n, 182n; 'Putting Winter to
Bed' 90, 178n, 179n, 180; 'A Puzzle Picture' 179n; *Rachel* 43,
168n2; 'The Radio in the Ivory
Tower' 113, 132, 191; 'The Relation of Source Material to Poetry'
18–28, 164–5; *A Reverie on a
Dog* 90–2, 180–1; *The Roosevelt
and the Antinoe* 49, 76–86, 176–8,
179n; 'The Sea-Cathedral' 67–8,
172–3, 182n; 'Sea-Gulls' 75,
175, 179n, 191n; 'Seaward'
159n; 'Seen on the Road' 191n;
'The Shark' 60, 170, 170n1,
171n, 191n; 'Silences' 17, 108–9,
162n, 163n11, 182n, 189; 'The
6000' 88, 150, 179, 190n; *Still Life
and Other Verse* 198n19; 'The
Stoics' 133, 199; 'Studies in Pauline Eschatology' 34; 'The Submarine' 112–13, 132, 190, 191n;
Ten Selected Poems 179n, 183n,
184n, 185n, 189n33, 190n, 196n;
The Titanic 45–7, 48–9, 95–107,
163n, 183–9, 191n; *Titans* 40,

165n; 'To Angelina, An Old
Nurse' 17, 86–7, 162n, 178; 'To
an Enemy' 171n; 'The Toll of the
Bells' 60–1, 170; *Towards the
Last Spike* 39, 145–53, 162n8,
165n, 192n1, 205–8; 'The Truant'
132–3, 191n, 199; *Verses of the
Sea* 168n, 169n, 169n4, 170n,
171n, 173n, 175n, 176n, 177n1;
'The Way of Cape Race' 92,
171n, 178n, 179n, 181–2, 191n;
The Witches' Brew 33–5, 40, 52,
166n13, 167n1; and Healey Willan, *Brébeuf and His Brethren: Oratorio* 122, 195n25
Pratt, Fanny Pitts Knight 4, 42, 43,
66, 172n5, 175n4
Pratt, James (Jim) 3–4
Pratt, Rev. John: as clergyman 4, 5,
8, 12, 42, 44, 50, 51, 87; as father
2, 3, 4, 13, 42, 87, 88
Pratt, Viola 31, 72, 89, 174n10; as
wife 16, 30, 34, 40, 147, 148,
174n10
Pratt, William 3
'Profile of a Canadian Poet, A' 18,
163
psychology 30, 31, 32, 33, 121, 153

Queen's Hotel, Toronto 50
Queen's University, Kingston
15

realism 40; realistic 138, 145;
realists 24
rescue: Nfld. 4, 9, 18, 87, 90, 97, 99,
102; on the sea 8, 22, 76–86 *passim*, 103, 132; sacrificial 8, 129
research, in relation to poem 20, to
Pratt poem 35, 40, 112, 125;
necessity of in dealing with historical subject 22, 38; research
laboratories 25
Return of the Native, The 189n32
Richardson, Prof. Lorne 133, 142
Rime of the Ancient Mariner, The
188n30
Roberts, Sir Charles G.D. 186n10
Robinson, Edwin Arlington 20
romance 35, 89, 91, 97; as genre
94; in exploration and war 114;
of science 142; of whale fishery
65; romantic 20, 27, 145; roman-
ticist 119; unromantic 35, 63
Romantics 24, 26; Romantic: fallacy 23, literature 5, 165n15
Royal Ontario Museum 120, 193n7
Ryerson Press 31, 38, 39

sacrifice: deeds of 17, 28, 79, 81,
129; in relation to Christianity
204n35; natural subject for
thought and expression of Newfoundlanders 4; and poetry
188n26; sacrificial: action 4, 8,
128, blood 85, devotion 122,
link with heroism 127, nature of
Jesuit mission 115, offerings
128–9
St Andrew's Society 10, 150
St Joan 127–8
St John's, Nfld. 3, 6, 8, 9, 10, 14,

45, 57, 59, 60, 102, 137, 147, 163n, 171

Sandburg, Carl 48, 53; *Abraham Lincoln* 48

Sandwell, B.K. 73, 174n13

science 25–6, 35, 39, 85, 97, 107, 135; humanization of 135; 142, 165n15; Jesuits versed in 115; of political economy 150; of sound 137; physical 137; Pratt's teacher 7, 102; relation to poetry 21, 23, 26, 28, 35; romance of 142; trust in 7, 97; *see also* astronomy, chemistry, geology, physics, zoology; scientific 23, 25, blunder 71, discovery 135, facts in poems 66, 123, Pratt's scientific friends 21, 119, 137, 151, material 23, 35, observation 71, matter-of-factness 71, point to be made in poetry 138, prose 18, 21, terms 132; scientist 17, 24, 25, 27, 28, 45, 72

Scientific American 77

Sclater, Commander William: *Haida* 136, 200n3

Scott, F.R. 207n24

Scott, Sir Walter 52–3, 146, 205n4

Selwyn and Blount (Publishing House) 34, 40

Shaw, George Bernard 127; *St Joan* 127–8

Shelley, Percy Bysshe 24

Shorter Poems 38

Signal Hill, Nfld. 7, 45, 103

Sinclair, Lister 163n

Smith, A.J.M. 167n, 191n, 198n19

Snow White 70

spirit: human 35, 114, 127, 204n35, Nfld. 5, of insouciance, repartée, and banter 131, of mutual faith between Navy and Merchant Marine 134; spiritual: approach to deeds 5, gulf 25, heritage 47, Nfld. heritage 9, union 28

sublime 86, 110, 145; blend of with colloquial 131, with grotesque 131; courage 123; deeds 9, 145; heroism 105; qualities in Jesuit mission 115, 123; sacrifice 129

Tennyson, Alfred, Lord 188n30; *Morte d'Arthur* 188n30

Testament of Beauty, The 19, 164n1

Thompson, Dorothy 130

Thompson, Prof. 111

Titanic (ship) 45–7, 48, 49, 95–107 *passim*

Tom Brown's School Days 15

Toronto 6, 39, 50, 51, 73, 76, 78, 86, 88, 92–3, 150

totalitarianism 126, 132

tragedy 18; and sacrifice 129; as genre 27, 38, 122; at sea 61, 85, *Titanic* 48, 104; blended with comedy 130–1; inevitability of 43; of Jesuit mission 122; of *Titanic* vs *Brébeuf* 46–7; relation of God to 43, 46; relation to fate 47, to irony 107, 184n; tragic 44, 81, 87, 107, 142, connected with *Titanic* 95, 105, experience 8,

81, literature 128, Pratt as tragic poet of sea 44, situation at sea 41, unintentional error 21, war 81, 142
Typhoon 177n6, 197n15

University of Toronto 30, 31, 44, 50, 175n, 175n23
University of Western Ontario 120, 195n24
Upjohn, Frank 198n19

Victoria College (University), University of Toronto 51, 52, 54, 88, 98, 106, 165n, 168n4, 183n, 185n4, 190n, 199n

Wallace, Dr (Paul?) 125, 195–6n32
Webster, John 38
'Wednesday Night' (CBC series) 163n
Wesley, John 35, 98
Willan, Dr Healey 122, 195n26
Wordsworth, William 24, 28, 164n5, 165n15

Yeats, W.B. 54
York Club 149, 192n1, 205n

Zimmerman, Bill 150
zoology 72

This book
was designed by
WILLIAM RUETER
and was printed by
University of
Toronto
Press